T0356768

MEDIKO

The Life and Legacy of DR. RAPHAEL THOMAS, Medical Missionary to the Philippines

Jim Ruff, D. Min.

WESTBOW PRESS®
A DIVISION OF THOMAS NELSON & ZONDERVAN

PREFACE

The beauty of the Philippines and her people; the dedication of a mediko, a doctor, to his people; recovery from tragic loss; adventures in a strange land; the values of strategic planning; the need for compassionate leadership; or the impact of both humility and determination in one heart: any of these would qualify as themes in the story of Dr. Raphael Thomas. Yet the greatest theme of his story is this: what would happen if a man who loved God, and desired to be used by Him for the greatest good, were given the opportunity to pursue the healing of souls and the healing of bodies among people he would learn to love and would long to prepare to deliver the same spiritual and physical healing to others?

This book has been a labor of love for many years. Portions of it were written as projects while working on a Doctor of Ministry degree. Other portions were squeezed in between other ministry responsibilities. The final work on the book has been done over the last three years. The excitement of beginning to dip my feet in the ocean of correspondence left by Dr. Thomas has only grown as I have waded more deeply into all that he wrote, and all that was written about him.

I never met Dr. Thomas, but in conversation with Dr. Harold Commons in his last years, I felt the years falling away and the person of Raphael Thomas began to form in my mind through the wise and witty explanations Dr. Commons gave me about this man he described as "like a father" to him.

It is my hope that Raphael Thomas, his times, his humor, his heart, and the amazing people connected to him will begin to form in the reader's mind; that the evangelistic zeal and fervor for missions that flowed through the veins of this man of God in the early twentieth century will, through the transfusion of this biography, bring greater strength, energy, and faith to twenty-first century followers of the Lord Jesus Christ.

ACKNOWLEDGEMENTS

An honest summary of those who influenced my life, and the writing of this book would be quite long, but I must mention a few, especially to answer the question of why a missionary to Japan wrote the biography of a missionary to the Philippines. Thanks to Apolonario (Paul) and Vi Apoong and Leo Calica, special friends in seminary and in the Philippines. To Dr. Jim Parker, my mentor, co-pastor, and avid supporter of Paul Apoong's ministries in Dagupan (Now together with Paul in glory). I had the privilege of seeing Paul's churches and schools while I was visiting the Philippines in the early 2000's. That trip was made with my friend and colleague, Kent Craig, Executive Administrator for East Asia with the Association of Baptists for World Evangelism (ABWE), and missionary to the Philippines. During that trip we went to Iloilo where I visited Doane Baptist Bible College and the graves of members of Dr. Thomas' family you are about to meet. My thanks also to Dr. Ken and Alice Cole, from whom I learned much about the Philippines and Thailand during visits and ministry opportunities in both countries, and who consented to an interview. Thanks are also due to Dr. Russell Ebersole, missionary to the Philippines, who was Far Eastern Administrator during our first term in Japan, but who had already been a long-time friend and inspiration. I cannot fail to add Dr. Wayne Haston, my colleague in training, whose excellent leadership as leader of the Training Division of ABWE provided me a second opportunity to visit and teach in the Philippines. Other members of the training team also helped me along the way.

I received help from Pastors, teachers, and administrators in the Philippines who (sometimes anonymously) sent materials to me, and who served as readers of the manuscript in response to my requests for their help in determining how the book will be received in the Philippines. Among them I must mention Miss Lalaine Ismael, Rev. Eddie Rayos, Pastor Walter Ibanes, Miss Joanne Grace Rayos Aniñon, and Pastor Ton who, with Phil and Barb Klumpp, provided some helpful documents years ago. Craig and Elaine Kennedy, ABWE missionaries to the Philippines, also provided encouragement and a valuable reference source: Elaine's *Baptist Centennial History of the Philippines* (1900-1999).

The American Baptist Historical Society provided incalculable help in providing documents during my several visits to their Valley Forge, Pennsylvania archive. In addition, the dedicated staff of the ABHS, which is now in Atlanta, Georgia, were helpful to me in providing proper formatting information for my many citations and in granting permission to quote their archived materials. This would be a good place to mention that many of the letters I received as copies or microfilm from the ABHS were also found in the raft of documents in the archives of ABWE that had been carefully preserved by Dr. Thomas, and they are so marked in the endnotes.

I would also like to thank Ms. Diana Yount of Andover Newton Theological School, for her help in finding and copying several documents I requested early in my research. Thanks to Jim Latzko for making me aware of the Maxwell letters, and to Pastor Ruhlman and Sarah Mathews of Tabernacle Baptist Church for providing copies of some of them to me. I want to thank colleagues at ABWE, who encouraged me and helped with materials. Mark Henry, Jeff Raymond, Bill Commons, Jean Brown and David Woodard deserve special mention for their friendship, encouragement and support. I appreciate the patient guidance and expert work of the staff of WestBow Press.

I must also mention professors at Baptist Bible Seminary, Clarks Summit, Pennsylvania, especially Dr. Mike Stallard and Dr. Jim King for their critical eyes during the early years of my research. I am thankful for the opportunities I had to serve as the part-time librarian /archivist /historian at ABWE during my fourteen years at the International Headquarters and Training Center. I want to thank my adult children, Yvonne, Joel, and Tim, and their husband and wives, for their patience with my looking for time to finish the book. Finally, I want to thank my wife of over 53 years, Jan, for her constant encouragement and support, and for her gently asking "Are you almost done?"

MAPS

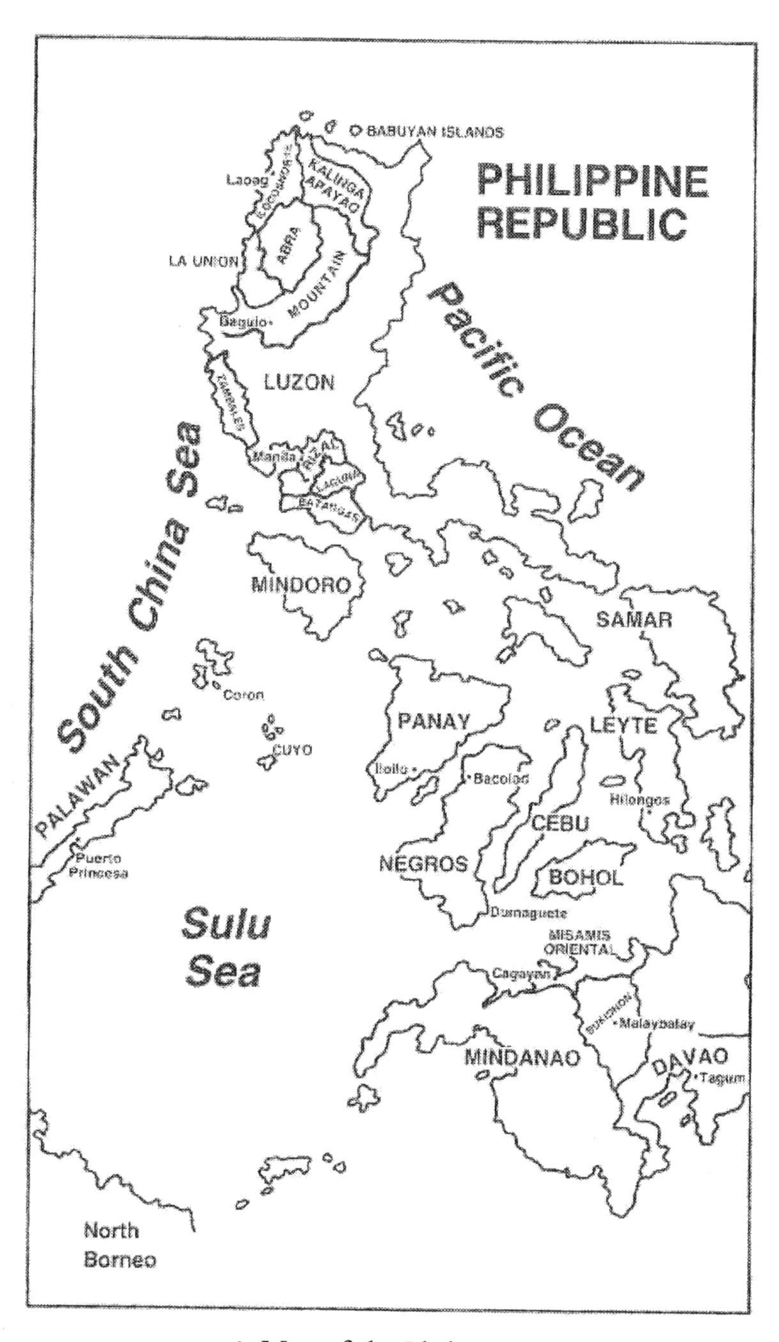

1. Map of the Philippines

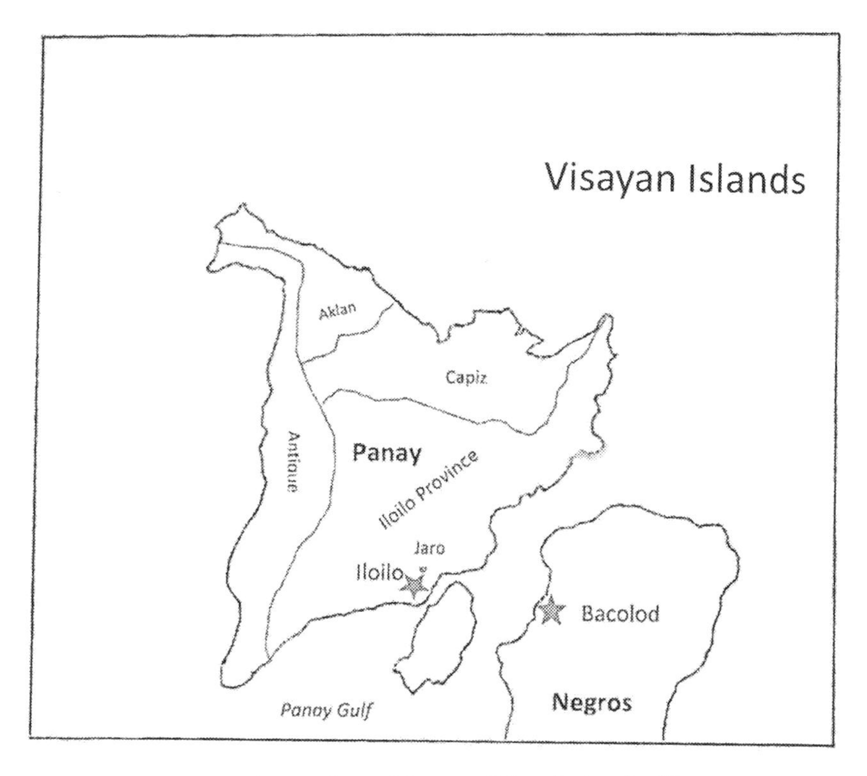

2. Panay and Northern Negros Islands in the Visayans

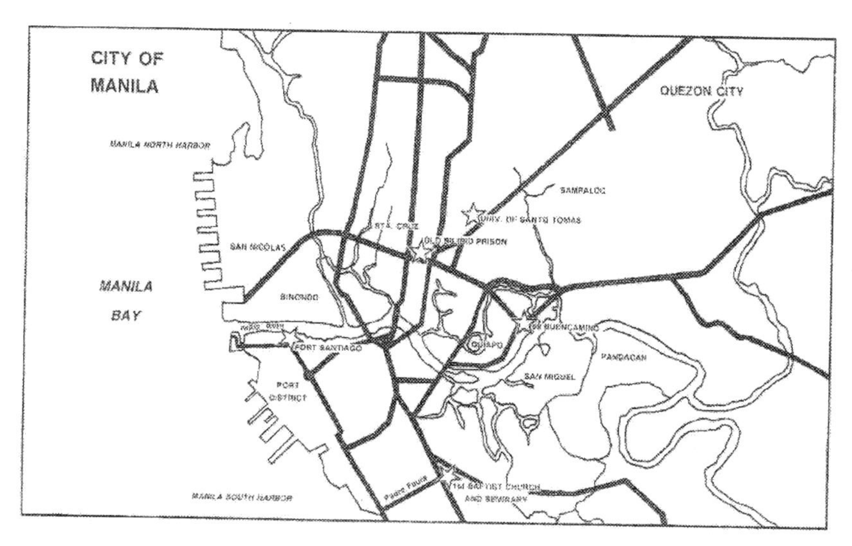

3. City of Manila

INTRODUCTION

How does a person become a missionary? What are the passions, the spiritual realities, the hopes, and the desires that cause an individual to surrender to the rigors, dangers, struggles, and challenges of the life of service of the missionary? How is a heart of love, compassion, and determination focused on a certain people group, whether in one's own country, or one far away? Perhaps the best way to answer these questions is to focus on the life of one such individual, and this book seeks those answers in the life of Raphael C. Thomas.

Dr. Raphael C. Thomas was a man standing astride two centuries. His life was lived through a period of great spiritual and religious ferment, industrial and technological advance, world-wide conflict, and incredible opportunity. He grew up in a pastor's home yet went to the best of schools. He was a man who knew the Lord and His Word and chose to use his medicine not for fame and wealth in the world, but for a means to serve people and lead them to the Lord. He served the people of the Philippines with two mission boards: in one case as an appointed missionary, and in the other as a founder. He lost family members in the Philippines, but gained the hearts of the people, and a reputation as a man of principle and a man of God.

Through the study of the life, thought, and times of Raphael Thomas, glimpses of the convictions and motivations, the principles and policies that he gained and applied throughout his life and ministry can profitably be seen, evaluated, and compared to those that underlie the ministries of missionaries today. The greatest profit will come by viewing God's development of the man and his principles as a missionary to realize what he can teach us today.

During the twentieth century, there were many debates about the function(s) of missions and missionaries, the need for missionaries in developed countries, and even the occasional complicity of missionaries in colonial activities of world powers. Since such debates continue to this day, even in evangelical circles, it will be helpful to understand what was meant by "missionary work" in the days of Raph's surrender to service as a missionary. In a conference of missionaries in Japan in 1900, B. W. Waters summarized this understanding well: "...our ultimate object is to establish in this land an indigenous, independent, self-supporting church. The primary aim of missions is to preach the gospel in all lands, the ultimate aim is to plant the church in all lands." [1]

This accords well with Raph's own 1953 statement, which will be presented in greater detail in Chapter 28:

> From the outset it has been, as I remember it, and I think that the other "old timers" would agree with me, to make EVANGELISM the foundation of all our efforts. By this I mean mass evangelism, preceded and followed up by personal, house visitation, and field evangelism; and church membership the objective. The second most important objective, of course, was the establishment of more SOUND BAPTIST CHURCHES, which eventually were to become INDIGENOUS, self supporting; self governing and self perpetuating. The next, and exceedingly important objective, was to raise up a WELL EDUCATED MINISTRY.

In that he intended all this ministry to be accomplished in conjunction with meeting the needs of the people through medicine, it is apparent that a thoroughly holistic model was in the minds of these missionaries, that is, ministering to the physical, mental, and spiritual needs of the people of the Philippines.

CHAPTER 1

The Formative Years

HERITAGE

The lines are fallen unto me in pleasant places;
yea, I have a goodly heritage.
—Psalm 16:6

Attorney-at-law Jesse B. Thomas, supporting his precious wife Abigail, walked slowly away from the graveside of his tiny son, Welles, overwhelmed with pain at the loss of their child. As he held the tiny hand of his daughter Adi, the anguish was increased when that precocious little one spoke. "Papa, I want a pair of scissors," she said. He asked her why. She replied, "Because I wish you to cut off a lock of my hair, as I am going to lie in the snow with Birdie." A few days later, she like her brother, died of scarlet fever.[2]

Jesse and Abigail lost two more children. Their son Jesse Burgess Thomas died at about the age of six; and Charles Huntington Thomas died at age eleven. Anyone who has not lost a child as an infant can barely begin to understand the emotional and psychological strain of the loss of so many beloved children in their youth.

But it was the shock of the loss of his children to scarlet fever that caused this successful lawyer to change his choice of careers. He had long felt that God wanted him to preach, and through this tragedy God confirmed that call.

Jesse (1832–1915) had married Abigail Anne Eastman (1832–1919) in 1855. The reason for Jesse's decision to become a lawyer is not difficult to understand. His father, and his great-uncle, whose names he shared, were famous lawyers. Since the presence of many men named Jesse Burgess Thomas may be confusing, see Appendix 1.

Jesse's father, often called Jesse Burgess Thomas Jr. (1806–1850), was a confidant of Abraham Lincoln in Illinois. Abe Lincoln tried over thirty cases before him. He was born in Lebanon, Ohio, and was a member of Illinois state House of Representatives (1834–35), the Illinois state attorney general (1835–36), a circuit judge in Illinois (1837–39), and a justice of the Illinois state Supreme Court (1843–45 and 1847–48).

Judge Thomas's uncle Jesse (1777–1853), who became the first Illinois state senator, was the author of the Missouri Compromise that included in part a provision that slavery was to be allowed only south of the thirty-sixth parallel.[3] He was a member of the Indiana Territorial House of Representatives (1805–1808) and later a delegate to the US Congress from the Indiana Territory (1808-09). He served as a federal judge (1809-18) and, after serving as a delegate to the Illinois state constitutional convention in 1818, became the U. S. senator from Illinois (1818–1829). He sadly ended his life by committing suicide in Mt. Vernon, Ohio on May 3, 1853.[4]

Yet, despite this heritage, and his exceptional ability as a lawyer, Jesse realized that he should leave law, seek additional education, and become a pastor. During the years of this transition, Jesse and Anne had four more children. Jessie Elma, Madora Carlota, and Leo Boone Thomas all lived into the twentieth century. Their last child, Raphael Clark Thomas was born in Chicago on October 3, 1873. Coincidentally, the year of future missionary Raphael's birth was the year in which David Livingstone, the famous missionary and explorer in Africa, died.

Jesse's pastorates were in San Francisco, Chicago, and Brooklyn. In 1874, Jesse became pastor of First Baptist Church of Brooklyn. As a result, the Reverend Jesse B. Thomas became a part of the social scene in New York City. He lived at 167 State Street, which still stands today, located in a long row of townhouses.

CHAPTER 1

While they will seem amusing to a twenty-first-century reader, the customs of the day to be remembered by those who were prominent citizens, including Jesse Thomas, were many and part of their schooling and socialization. Just to prevent any of those customs from being forgotten by the residents and those involved, the best newspapers published articles like the following:

> CALLS - The Social Phase of New Year's Day.
> 30 December 1882
>
> > New Year's Day in the social aspect promises to be more generally observed than usual of late years, providing the weather is propitious. The caterers have had more orders for the arrangement of tables, and the florists have been busier with decoration for the reception parlor than they have been in some years past. Most every lady who opens her house to callers on the 1st of January will receive in full dress attire, and to many of the houses gas will be burned all day for the purpose of showing off the toilets to the best advantage and of giving the scene more striking effect. In the evening, at the houses where a number of young people receive, parties will be given. Gentlemen who pride themselves on etiquette will not begin calling until noon, and then they will not be foolish as to don their full dress suits, but wear either Prince Albert coats or neat cutaways. Pen-tailed coats are made for evening and their use out of place only furnishes amusement for the giddy girls of fashion. . . . The names of some of Brooklyn's prominent citizens and fair ladies who will receive callers on Monday are given below:
>
> MAYOR LOW will receive calls at his office, City Hall, from 10 A.M. to 12 M.
> SHERIFF STEGMAN, assisted by UNDER SHERIFF HODGEKINSON, will receive friends at Raymond Street Jail between the hours of 10 A.M. and 2 P.M. . . .
> Rev. Dr. R. S. STORRS at No. 80 Pierrepont street.

> Rev. Henry WARD BEECHER at No. 124 Hicks street.
> Mr. BEECHER
> will announce the fact in Plymouth Church to-morrow.
> *Rev. JESSE B. THOMAS, D.C., at 167 State street.*
> Rev. Dr. TALMAGE at No. 1 South Oxford street, corner of DeKalb avenue ...[5]

Pastor Jesse was eventually asked to teach church history at Newton Theological Institute, a Baptist graduate seminary located in Newton Centre, Massachusetts. It was located on an eighteenth-century country estate of twenty-three acres.[6] His writings concerning Baptist church history, baptism, and theology are still of interest today.[7]

THE EARLY LIFE OF "RAPH" THOMAS

Such was the world into which young Raphael, nicknamed "Raph" (pronounced like "graph" without the *g*), was introduced.

Having grown up in a Christian home, Raph was also exposed to the gospel early. He recalled that his experience at conversion was "one of joy rather than of an especially deep sense of sin," but he could recall "no especial moment" he could name as the exact starting point of his new experience. At the age of eleven, when he joined Pierrepont Street Baptist Church in Brooklyn, New York, he had "fairly well defined and clear" views as to "what the Christian life required and involved."[8]

Raph attended private secondary schools including the Brooklyn Polytechnic Institute and the Boston Latin School. At Newton High School he played on almost every athletic team, claiming that he shined "with the girls as they fell heavily for the brass buttons and tinseled epaulettes when I was Major of the High School Battalion."[9] Though he claimed to hate algebra, he excelled in public speaking and became class orator at Newton.

Raph graduated from Newton High School in 1892. This was twelve years after the first conference held under the direction of Dwight L. Moody at his Northfield home, and seven years before Moody's death. In a long letter written late in his life to a young missionary couple, Raph emphasized that he had visited Northfield several times when Moody was alive.[10] It is probable that he went in the company of his father. Since he would have been twelve at the time, it is even possible that Raph was present at the Northfield Conference in 1885, when A. T. Pierson spoke on missions and challenged those present to prayerfully strive toward the accomplishment of the great commission worldwide by the year 1900. Moody presided over a committee, including Pierson, J. E. Studd, and A. J. Gordon, that produced "An Appeal to Disciples Everywhere" to join them in that gigantic endeavor. Though ultimately unsuccessful, that appeal did capture the hearts of many, including that of Raphael Thomas.

These visits were crucial in the development of the life and thought of Raphael as a young man. He later wrote that it was "at Northfield, in Moody's time" when he "paced up and down on a hillside near where Moody now lies buried and heard the call to do more than just practice medicine or earn a salary." Raph wished to spend his life "where it would pay the *highest dividends*."[11]

CHAPTER 2

Higher Education and Higher Influences

When wisdom entereth into thine heart, and
knowledge is pleasant unto thy soul.
—Proverbs 2:10

HARVARD COLLEGE

The next phase of Raph's preparation for life and ministry was at Harvard College. The Harvard in which he matriculated in 1892 was quite different than it had been in the mid-eighteenth century. That earlier Harvard operated under educational traditions from the seventeenth century, though its Unitarian professors carried on little of the evangelistic fervor of the seventeenth-century school. While the backlash of the Evangelical-Calvinist countermovement began to isolate and shrink the power of Harvard College, a spirit of reform was building that would once again catapult the college into the forefront of enlightened institutions of higher learning.[12] The presidency of Charles W. Eliot provided the motive force. At Eliot's 1869 inauguration, he spoke of a spirit of freedom in education, of choice, and of change. Among the changes, good or bad, that were firmly in place by the time of Raph's entrance into Harvard were the elective system of class selection, self-government by the students, and the abolishment (in 1888) of compulsory chapel attendance.[13]

Sir Edwin Arnold, during his travels in the United States and Asia, visited "the chief educational centre of the United States" in 1889. In the fascinating account of his journey, *Seas and Lands*, Arnold commented on the history, setting, and areas of study at Harvard. Perhaps of greater interest to today's student is a table he assembled of annual costs to students at the College:[14]

	Least	Economical	Moderate	Very Liberal
Tuition	$150	$150	$150	$150
Books and Stationery	28	35	45	61
Clothing	70	120	150	300
Room	22	30	100	175
Furniture (annual average)	10	15	25	50
Board	133	152	152	304
Fuel and Light	11	15	30	45
Washing	15	20	40	50
Societies and subscription to sports (annual average)	...	...	35	50
Servant	...	...	35	50
Sundries	45	55	85	150
Total	$484	$592	$812	$1,360

Since Raph actively participated in sports, Arnold's quotation of the "regulations of the Gymnasium" are also of interest:

> Upon entering the University, each student is entitled to an examination by the director, in which his physical proportions are measured, his strength tested, his heart and lungs examined, and information is solicited concerning his general health and inherited tendencies. From the data thus procured, a special order of appropriate exercises is made out for each student, with specifications for the movements and apparatus which he may best use. After working on this [prescription] for three or six months, the student is entitled to another examination, by which

> the results of his work are ascertained, and the director enabled to make a further prescription for his individual case.[15]

In an article on "Harvard University in 1890," Charles Eliot Norton described the students enrolled in 1890, just two years before Raph entered Harvard, as follows:

> In the present year, 1890, there are 2079 enrolled at Harvard, of whom 1271 are in the undergraduate department. They come from forty States and Territories of the Union, and a few from foreign countries. They represent every grade in society, from poor to rich; every variety of creed—Orthodox, Liberal, Roman Catholic, Agnostic, Jew; every shade of political opinion; and they meet and mingle on terms of even more complete equality than those which commonly exist in society.[16]

Though he claimed to have "barely skimmed through" his examinations for Harvard University, and not to have been "an intellectual prodigy," Raph did extremely well there as a student. He won the coveted Boylston prize for public speaking and graduated Cum Laude from the college![17] As for the rest of his busy college experience, in his own words, he was

> on the tennis team at Harvard with Dwight Davis and Holcombe Ward, the National Doubles champions at the time. I was Vice President of the Wendell Phillips Debating Club, President of the College Y.M.C.A. and later Intercollegiate Secretary of the Boston Y.M.C.A., and in other ways a "regular fellow" with plenty of healthful social relationships.[18]

INFLUENCES OF MISSIONARY MOVEMENTS AND THE YOUNG MEN'S CHRISTIAN ASSOCIATION

It was in his first year or two at Harvard that Raph first seriously "entertained a desire" to become a foreign missionary. This same period was alive with interest and opportunities in evangelism and missions. Arthur T. Pierson and others were writing articles and books concerning the possibility of reaching the world for Christ before the beginning of the new century; and conferences dedicated to evangelism, the Christian life, and missionary themes were legion. Particularly important to this examination of the influences in Raphael's life and thought was the development during his lifetime of the Student Volunteer Movement for Foreign Missions.

It was in 1884 that five Princeton men drew up and signed what became in 1886 the official declaration of the North American Student Volunteer Movement. In that same year, C. T. Studd and Stanley Smith informed their classmates at Cambridge University that they intended to go to China as missionaries.[19] Robert Wilder, one of the founders of the movement, wrote of that year:

> Thus simultaneously on both sides of the Atlantic the Spirit of God kindled missionary fires which are burning now in most of the universities and colleges of these two lands, and which we trust will continue to burn until the Light of the World break upon the non-Christian nations.[20]

Dwight L. Moody lent a hand in the development of this great volunteer movement, despite some early reservations about it.[21] In 1886, Moody invited delegates from each college's Young Men's Christian Association (YMCA) to send delegates to Mt. Hermon for a month of Bible study and study of methods for outreach to college students. Mr. Moody and several teachers worked with 250 students from 90 associations, many of them already committed to serve the Lord in missions. From that year Mr. Moody wisely called to his side leaders from both the YMCA. and the Student Volunteer Movement to challenge those who attended Northfield, the Chicago Institute, and other meetings to commit their lives to world evangelism. He also raised great sums of money for missions.[22]

John R. Mott, one of the early leaders of the movement described its purposes in the following way:

> The primary and paramount function of the Movement is that of recruiting. It seeks to enroll a sufficient number of well-qualified volunteers to meet the requirements of

> the mission boards of North America. Its well-understood purpose also involves the cultivation of the whole range of missionary interest and activity among all classes of students and the leading of the students who are not to become missionaries to recognize, accept and prepare themselves to discharge their responsibility to maintain the missionary enterprise by their advocacy, by their gifts and by their prayers.[23]

Mott further emphasized that to better realize these purposes, the movement sought to maintain a close relationship with mission boards, Student YMCA, and Young Women's Christian Association movements, and other student religious societies.

Raph had served as a Student Volunteer President of the College YMCA while at Harvard. The college YMCA preceded Brooks House as the center of 'religious life' at Harvard. He was approached about becoming the new Secretary for Religious Work at Harvard, but the finances could not be arranged. Thomas did agree to become Intercollegiate Secretary for the Boston YMCA in 1897, remaining in that position through 1898.[24] The Young Men's Christian Association of Greater Boston was the first chapter formed in North America. Influenced by the London YMCA, Captain Thomas V. Sullivan (1800–1859) saw the YMCA as a way to provide a "home away from home" for sailors. It provided an atmosphere for evangelical religion to thrive, for spiritual and moral influences to prevail, and for young men to improve themselves through education and service. Early in 1896, Henry T. Fowler described the impact of the YMCA on collegians in the pages of Harper's New Monthly Magazine.[25] In Fowler's words:

> Their direct work is to offer opportunities to all the students for the devotional and practical study of the Bible – the study which brings one into a deeper knowledge of the Father and closer communion with Him, and the study which fits one for effective Christian service.[26]

Fowler further described the "new branches" put out by the collegiate wing of the Young Men's Christian Association. They included the international work of the Young Women's Christian Association, and the Volunteer Movement for Foreign Missions, which "first took shape" during the college summer gathering at Mr. Moody's school in 1886. The statistical summary Fowler gives is an impressive testament to the "Y's" influence over the space of the preceding 18 years:

> [The Intercollegiate Y.M.C.A.] has influenced at least three thousand young men in choosing the Christian ministry as their life profession, has led many thousands to become avowed Christians, and has trained many more for Christian service in every branch of professional and business life. Today it is furnishing the world an object-lesson of religious unity.[27]

It is no wonder that Raph, serving in the heart of these influences, was so deeply moved to reach, teach, and equip young men to serve the Lord with their lives.

As Intercollegiate Secretary, he was responsible to care for Boston University, Massachusetts Institute of Technology, and the Harvard Medical School and Pharmacy. Through his association with the Harvard Medical School, Thomas sensed the leading of God into service as a medical missionary. Years later he explained that he "felt the call to Medicine, always you understand with the prior call to the ministry and the medical asset always to be subservient to that service, just a means to an end . . ."[28]

GRADUATION AND THE BEGINNING OF THEOLOGICAL TRAINING

Raph graduated from Harvard in 1896. With his undergraduate work successfully completed, he entered Newton Theological Institute in the Fall of 1896. Newton Theological Institute was founded in 1825, and it stood as the oldest Baptist seminary in the US. One of the major drawing cards for young Raphael to attend Newton was the presence of his father, Dr. Jesse Burgess Thomas, as its esteemed church history professor.

In 1868, Rev. Alvah Hovey, DD, LLD, became the president of Newton, and he remained in that position until his death on September

6, 1903.[29] Hovey was a stalwart of the Faith, who in both his lectures and writings displayed a deep respect for the accuracy and authority of the Bible. He was also Raph's professor of theology.

THEOLOGICAL TRAINING UNDER DR. ALVAH HOVEY

A Sketch of the Life and Ministry of Dr. Alvah Hovey

Hovey was born in Greene, NY, on March 5, 1820. He graduated from Dartmouth College in 1844, and Newton Theological Institution in 1848. He was granted a Doctor of Divinity Degree by Brown University in 1856, and a Doctor of Letters degree by Richmond College and Dennison University in 1876. After preaching in New Gloucester, Maine, in the years 1848 to 1849, Hovey was ordained in Boston in 1850. He served as an instructor and professor at Newton Theological Institution from 1849 through the Spring of 1903, the year of his death. Among the professorships he held were those of Church History, Christian Theology, Christian Ethics, General Introductions, and Apologetics. His publications included *A Memoir of the Life and Times of Isaac Backus* (1858); several published essays on theological subjects, including *Future Punishment*; *Outlines of Christian Theology: For the Use of Students in the Newton Theological Institution* (1870); *The Bible* (1873); *State of Men After Death* (1874); and *Manual of Systematic Theology and Christian Ethics*, which was published in 1877.

Hovey was greatly loved and celebrated. After his death, several articles were written about him in issues of the school's new journal, *The Newtonian*. As a teacher, he had influenced generations of students, helping them to develop their theologies. It is not clear from the documents that remain in the archives of the Institution whether Dr. Hovey's *Outlines* and *Manual* were still the textbooks of choice after 1899, when Dr. Nathan Eusebius Wood replaced him as president and professor of systematic theology, or not. Wood was not a graduate of Newton Theological Institution – his theological degree was from the Baptist Union Theological Seminary in Chicago – and it is certainly possible that he selected another text.

Alvah Hovey's Position on the Return of Christ

At first glance, it will appear strange to detail Hovey's teachings concerning eschatology, that is, the doctrine of the future, or the things to take place in the end times, as prophesied in the Bible. The need to focus on this part of Raph's training will become clear in later chapters when the doctrinal foundation of the Association of Baptists for the Evangelism of the Orient (ABEO), Raph's first years of ministry with the ABEO in the Philippines, and his relationship with the doctrinal statement of the mission are discussed.

Despite his interest in the state of man after death, in his *Manual of Systematic Theology* Dr. Hovey devoted only eighteen pages to the doctrine of the last things. The second advent is discussed in less than three pages, and he devotes that space to an inquiry as to whether "the return of Christ, spoken of in Acts i.11, will precede or will follow the period of a thousand years described in Rev. xx.1 sq. . . ."[30] He explains that many of the ablest German and English expositors believe in the pre-millennial advent of Christ [the return of Christ to establish the Millennium, His thousand-year reign on the earth] as an event, predicted in Scripture, which is soon to occur. However, he sees those holding that position as being divided into two classes.

The first of these believe that at Christ's return "the righteous dead will be raised, the living believers changed, and the wicked who are alive on earth destroyed, so that Christ will reign on the earth with his saints in their glorified bodies a thousand years: then all the wicked dead will be raised and judged." The other class holds that "the righteous dead will be raised, living believers changed, and yet the race be continued by natural generation; all, or nearly all, who are born being converted very early in life. In the millennium, therefore, Christ will reign with his saints in their natural bodies." He further explains that both classes hold to a change or renewal of the earth at Christ's coming, but he concludes that the difference between them is the degree of completeness of the renewal (the former class being those who hold that it will be more completely renewed).[31] The rest of the brief section on the Second Advent is taken up by a refutation of both views.

The American Baptist Publication Society published a volume by Dr. Hovey on Eschatology in 1888. After his explanations of the premillennial and postmillennial views, and describing the strengths and weaknesses of each view, Dr. Hovey wrote the following interesting summary:

> While therefore I am constrained by my reading of Holy Scripture to believe that the theory of postmillennialists is beset with fewer difficulties than the theory of premillennialists, I heartily admire the enthusiasm, devotion, and learning of many who belong to the latter class. In evangelical and missionary labor they have no superiors. If they attach more importance to the visible presence of Christ, or to the influence of the raised saints, in bringing sinners to repentance, than I suppose is warranted by the Word of God, yet their belief does not interfere with a zealous use of the truth as it is in Jesus.[32]

While it is fair to question whether the brief and incomplete summary given by Hovey of the various views is adequate, it is more important to recognize that the amount of attention given eschatology in most schools in the nineteenth century was limited. His refutation of the views given, coupled with the sense of relative unimportance of the fine points of doctrines of "last things," was possibly all that was necessary to bring the students to acceptance of the commonly taught amillennial or post-millennial positions.[33] Briefly, the amillennial position is that there will be no thousand-year reign of Christ upon the earth. The post-millennialist believes that Christ will return at the end of a long period of growth of the Church through conversions of people throughout the world.

For those interested, information about other Baptist theologians who downplayed millennial or pre-millennial teachings around the time of Raph's studies at Newton is available in Appendix 3.

TRANSITION TO MEDICAL TRAINING

Although he enjoyed his studies and had every reason to be encouraged that he was finally receiving the biblical training that would add to his effectiveness in responding to the spiritual needs of those he would serve, Raph discontinued his studies at Newton in 1899, taking advantage of a scholarship to enter Harvard Medical School.

CHAPTER 3

Medical Training and Back to Theology

But when Jesus heard that, he said unto them, They that be whole need not a physician, but they that are sick. —Matthew 9:12

MEDICINE IN THE LATE 1800'S

Physical illness and remedies

What was the practice of medicine like when it was studied by Raph at the end of the nineteenth century? The last half of the century was one of dramatic change in the science and art of medicine. Though many of the pharmaceutical, surgical, and therapeutic treatments will seem primitive, many of the foundational principles and practices of modern medicine were established during this period.

In the last half of the nineteenth century, antiseptic practices were finally recognized as a must in medical treatment and surgery. Oliver Wendell Holmes (1809–1894) was the Parkman professor of anatomy at Harvard Medical School from 1847 to 1882. In 1843, he read a paper entitled "On the Contagiousness of Puerperal Fever," a disease that had killed a great number of pregnant women. The disease had often been passed on to pregnant women by the hands of doctors who had examined other women infected with the bacteria, or who had been involved in postmortems before examining the women. Based upon his recognition that doctors themselves were the source of the infection, Holmes recommended both their abstaining from these practices, and washing their hands in calcium chloride. A few years later, the Hungarian physician, Ignaz Philipp Semmelweis (1818–1865), through his study of the mortality of women who had suffered with Puerperal Fever, concluded – and demonstrated through his antiseptic practices – that the fever was a kind of blood poisoning (septicemia) that could be prevented. Both Holmes and Semmelweis were opposed by many in the medical establishment, but eventually their practices were adopted, saving untold lives. Joseph Lister (1827–1912), because of his studies of septicemia, tetanus, and gangrene (especially those contracted in hospitals) spent years developing improved dressings for wounds, chemical antiseptics, and better procedures for preventing infection in surgery. Following his 1867 textbook on antiseptic principles in surgery, he wrote many papers through the end of the century describing his studies and techniques.

Louis Pasteur was born in 1822 and died in 1895. His studies, together with those of Robert Koch (1843–1910), led to the acceptance of the germ theory of disease.

In 1895, Wilhelm Roentgen, speaking at a meeting of the Würzburg Society, presented his discovery of "x-rays." It was from that time on that the medical applications of the discovery became clear.

Of great importance to Raph, and to missionary doctors throughout Asia and Africa, was the fact that in the same year, 1895, Ronald Ross demonstrated the development of malarial parasites in the mosquito. What is not as generally known is that Ross acknowledged the work of Dr. Patrick Manson as having "actually solved the problem." Remarkably, Dr. Manson came up with the theory in a quiet corner of Asia, on the Chinese Amoy Island, located at the mouth of the Jiulong River and opposite Taiwan. The island was one of the treaty ports opened after the war with Great Britain, from 1839 to 1844, for foreign residence and trade.[34] He was known as a "Father" of tropical medicine, and we will meet him again as founder of the London School of Hygiene and Tropical Medicine, in which Raph enrolled twice. Dr. Sidney W. Rivenburg also collaborated with Dr. Ross in combatting malaria. He ministered to the Angami people as a missionary in Nagaland, Northeast India.[35]

Regarding pharmacology, a comment from Roberts Bartholow in his *Treatise on Materia Medica* is enlightening:

> The domain of Pharmacology is rapidly enlarging by the contributions of chemistry and by the new remedies brought forward by dealers with a view to profit. When a new remedy is announced, its physiological actions are immediately studied and defined. Clinical experience is then acquired, and in all parts of the world the new agent is applied to the treatment of diseases, and a verdict rendered after trials that very often give an erroneous notion of the real powers of the medicament. The earliest announcements are not unfrequently given forth by medical *quidnuncs*, who are more enthusiastic than logical, more sensational than exact, and more concerned to advertise their own doings than to give expression to faithful observations.[36]

Despite the quackery mentioned by Bartholow, and the vigorous sale of home remedies, a gradual increase in the development of truly efficacious medications was also apparent.

Mental illness and remedies

Although the brain and nervous system were gradually becoming better understood toward the end of the nineteenth century, the treatment of mental illness was still at a very controversial and experimental stage. Asylums, into which those who were deemed to be mentally deficient or affected were quietly placed, were thought to be the most humane and effective institutions for the treatment and rehabilitation of the mentally ill. However, from institution to institution the experimentation and treatment varied greatly, and they were often anything but "humane." Until his death in 1893, the French neurologist Jean-Martin Charcot was still parading mentally ill patients (and probably some frauds) before audiences to demonstrate the variety of mental states among them, and to attempt to "treat" them.

In 1888, Dr. David Ferrier (1843–1928), a specialist on the physiology of the brain, was one of the witnesses before the "Committee of The London County Council on A Hospital For The Insane" (1888):[37] This is how Dr. Ferrier characterized the status of the treatment of the mentally ill in his day:

> We have learnt a good deal of late years with regard to the objective functions of the brain, viz, the functions of motion and sensation, and their disorders, but as regards the subjective functions of the brain —the psychological aspects of cerebral activity—I think I may say we are practically in total ignorance. Much has been written on the symptomatology and classification of the various forms of insanity; but I think we really know nothing whatever with regard to the physical conditions underlying those manifestations. Until we are able to correlate mental disorders with their physical substrata, and this we are very far from being able to do, we cannot be said to possess any real knowledge on the subject, and therefore investigations and means of research calculated to elucidate these problems are greatly to be desired.
>
> I do not think that the present system of asylum management, under which the medical officers have not only the medical care of a relatively enormous number of patients, but also a host of administrative—many of them trivial—duties, is at all calculated to promote advance in this direction ; and I have not the slightest doubt that a hospital for the insane, in which insanity shall be studied in the same manner and with the same scientific methods as are applied to general diseases in our hospitals, would greatly enlarge our knowledge on this subject, and, as a natural consequence, lead to more successful methods of dealing with it.

Dr. Ferrier's assessment of the knowledge of the functions of the brain and the treatment of the insane was still accurate at the time of Raph's enrollment at Harvard Medical School.

CHAPTER 3

HARVARD MEDICAL SCHOOL

In 1899, Harvard Medical School was still the pacesetter for reform in medical colleges of North America. The first real reforms had taken place in 1871 under the leadership of Harvard President Charles W. Eliot. In the words of military surgeon and historian of medicine Fielding H. Garrison, Eliot "raised the entrance requirements of the Harvard Medical School, lengthened its curriculum to three years, and graded it, providing at the same time better facilities for clinical and laboratory instructions."[38]

William Lambert Richardson, an obstetrician, was dean of the Medical School from 1893 to 1907. During his tenure, advanced entrance examinations were introduced. It was his predecessor, however, Dr. Henry Pickering Bowditch (served 1883–1893), who had encouraged the construction of laboratories to increase the effectiveness of training in the research aspects of medicine.

Sir William Osler (1849–1919), whose brilliant career included professorships in medicine in Canada, the United States, and Oxford University in England, visited Harvard in 1877 to familiarize himself with the methods of teaching and standards there. In an article he wrote about the Harvard Medical School, he concluded that:

> It is a matter for surprise that some of the leading colleges in the United States have not followed the good example of Harvard. No doubt it would be accompanied for the first few years by a great falling off in the number of students, and consequent diminution in income and this in many instances is avowedly the chief obstacle to so desirable a step. One or two of the smaller schools have adopted the grading system . . . These are indications that the medical schools in the United States are being stirred up to some sense of the requirements and dignity of the profession they teach. It is high time.[39]

Harvard Medical School turned down a gift of half a million dollars to become a co-educational institution – a gift accepted by Johns Hopkins in 1894 - but the school became recipient of "princely sums of money" from J. Pierpont Morgan and John D. Rockefeller in 1901, the latter a million dollar gift given to the medical school apart from the funds used to set up the Rockefeller Institute.[40] At the end of a visit to Harvard in 1909, Osler was most thankful for the changes that had occurred in the "last ten or twelve years."[41]

This, then, was the up-to-date medical teaching center where Raphael was to spend three years until granted his MD in 1902. Nothing survives in written form of his experiences in medical school. As a diligent student in a demanding program, he probably had little time to "publish" his experiences. It is too bad, because this was not only an interesting and important part of his life, but it was also a fascinating time in the history of Harvard Medical School. At the time Raph was a medical student, Kenneth M. Ludmerer wrote an article regarding the potential of the school as seen by Huntington, Rockefeller, and other philanthropists who gave substantial amounts of money to the Medical School program.

> In 1901, Harvard's benefactors realized that the tasks to be accomplished in medicine greatly outweighed the discoveries that had already been made. They knew that the definitive treatments remained few, despite the substantial progress that had occurred in the understanding of disease mechanisms. Nevertheless, the philanthropists remained undaunted in their willingness to support medical research. They believed that with the proper application of scientific method, even more glorious discoveries would be forthcoming in the future. Such sentiments were widespread among educated Americans of the period, but no one stated them more clearly than Eliot. The medical achievements of the nineteenth century, to Eliot, were a "clear prophecy" of "greater blessings to come." A medical school "must always be expecting new wonders." It was this promise of future discoveries through research, more than satisfaction with what had already been accomplished, that inspired the donors to Harvard Medical School.[42]

INTERNSHIP AND RETURN TO NEWTON

From1902 through 1903, a full 22 months, Raph experienced another eventful period of his life as an intern at the prestigious Boston City

Hospital. Though his internship there gave him "hope of a fair standing in the profession," Thomas was not distracted by the potential of a lucrative medical career from the path of missionary service that had brought him into medicine.

He undoubtedly had many stories from his residency there. One he wrote of much later was in the context of describing an American in the Philippines who was climbing a tree – "not because he was chased by a carabao, but because he was pursued by "wrigglers with pink tails." The mental condition of this fellow reminded him of the experience at Boston City Hospital. As he tells it, he went into Ward E

> where the alcoholic addicts were sequestered, and one said to me "Look there," pointing across the room. I looked and saw nothing but another bed. I said, "Yes, and what of it?" He looked fiercely across at the unoffending bed and whispered harshly, "There's a form there; there's a form." Just an hallucination of a fevered brain, but for him something awful.[43]

He resumed studies at Newton in 1903, the same year that the school began publishing its journal, *The Newtonian*.[44] Occasionally, the Professors were listed, and the following were there at the time of his return: President and Professor of Theology Nathan Eusebius Wood; Professor of Introductions and Apologetics, Alvah Hovey; John Mahan English, Professor of Homiletics and Pastoral Duties; Charles Rufus Brown, Professor Biblical Interpretation and Old Testament; Professor of Church History Jesse Burgess Thomas; Frederick Lincoln Anderson, Professor of Biblical Interpretation and New Testament; Winfred Nichols Donovan, Assistant Professor of Biblical Interpretation and Old Testament; and Samuel Silas Curry, Acting Davis Professor of Elocution.

The Professors frequently hosted the 50-some men in the three classes (Junior, Middle, and Senior) in their homes, and, when Raph was in his father's home, he was apparently encouraged to sing. According to *The Newtonian*, at the Thanksgiving banquet of 1903, Raph was the soloist, singing "All Through the Night."

His thesis topic reflected his assumption that God was preparing him for ministry in China. It was entitled: "Some Aspects of Oriental Religion."

In that thesis, he summarized what he believed to be the proper approach to be taken by missionaries toward the belief systems of Confucianism, Taoism, and Buddhism, in the following (handwritten!) words:

> Summing up, then, we notice that, in introducing and maintaining these old religions, tendencies are outstanding, which should be recognized by those who are engaged in similar enterprises. Compromise with ... other religions is dangerous, and if principles are jeopardized by it, unpardonable. Compromise with the essentials of obedience to doctrines of a religion, for purpose of proselyting, popularization, or easing of conscience, means degeneration and death. Pandering to popular desire to win favor, and externalism, manifest in excessive ritual or works as a basis of merit are both dangerous. Equally dangerous with the extreme tendency of excessive introspection or excessive reliance on merit through works, is the tendency toward the indifference of mere perfunctory morality.[45]

He was one of the commencement speakers at graduation and chose as his topic "The Strategic Importance of Japan in the Evangelization of the World."[46] This could well have signaled the presence of another influence toward choosing a field in East Asia. During his Senior year, Dr. A. A. Bennet of Yokohama, Japan offered some courses of lectures. His lectures covered "all phases of mission work in Japan, dealing with the country and physical conditions, manners of the people, the progress of Christianity, etc."[47] There is no record of Raph's having taken that course, but since it took the place of several other classes in missions, it is likely that he did. In his speech, sounding forth a very positive, if naïve, assessment of what God was accomplishing in this land that had been opened to Protestant evangelism only 50 years before, Raph explained the reason for this late arrival of Japan upon the scene of world evangelism:

> Nor are we surprised when we find the land thus providentially opened in the "fullness of time," to discern that the nation, who have been centuries upon centuries for this day, are a "chosen people" of God. Like the

> Hebrews, they appear to be especially adapted to God's service. The keen and tenacious mind, the unusual vigor and endurance, coupled with coolness and courage, which have put them in the lead as soldiers, are but a few of the uniquely striking characteristics of this "peculiar" people. But, more than all the rest is stamped upon Japanese character, the one supreme quality which God required of the Hebrews: loyalty, unquestioning, thoroughgoing loyalty. This crowning virtue, in which the Hebrew eventually was found deficient, blossomed again in the feudalism of the middle ages, only to wither once more in the desert of popery and regal tyranny. But it has remained for the seclusion of this lovely island to keep sweet and pure for ages upon ages this national virtue, that above all others is well-pleasing to God.

It is true that Japanese believers had the loyalty and tenacity to have a major impact on their society. Yet, sadly, at the very time that Raph presented Japan as a place of great hopefulness for the gospel, the impacts of rationalism and militarism were eroding the positive effects experienced in that first half-century.

Although he had set his sights on Asia, as we shall see, Raph was directed to a country he had never considered.

CHAPTER 4

The Asia Raph Thought He Knew

A time of war, and a time of peace. —Ecclesiastes 3:8

Since in "the old days" missionaries generally went to the fields to which they felt called or led by God without having previously visited that part of the world, Raph was not unique in his thoughts about service in Asia. In preparing for China, and speaking about Japan, Raph utilized newspaper reports and first-hand accounts from Asia that were fascinating and confusing from the perspective of shifts in political power, and exciting from the perspective of the "advance" of Christianity.

While he was an underclassman at Harvard, The World's Parliament of Religions held in conjunction with the Columbian Exposition of 1893 took place in Chicago. Its purposes included the following: bringing together representatives of the "great Historic Religions" of the world, providing a forum for the presentation of the similarities of religions, to indicate the impregnable foundations of Theism and belief in immortality, and to provide for the accurate setting forth of the beliefs of each of the religions.

Paralleling as it did the development of the Student Volunteer Movement, this interest in foreign cultures and religions – whether positive or negative in impact from a Christian perspective – encouraged many young men to consider serving God in Asia. Books published through all the major denominational presses, Fleming H. Revell Company, and

The Missions Study Reference Library (published by The Young People's Missionary Movement), were springing from the presses to describe the nations from a Christian perspective, and to spread the news of God's victories through the lives of missionaries and national believers around the globe.

Through accounts of the ministries of Dr. Robert Morrison, Miss Aldersey, Medhurst, Mr. Goddard, J. Hudson Taylor, and so many others during the fruitful years of Protestant ministry in the nineteenth century in China, that country became an attractive Asian field. While many Chinese people were coming to Christ, some of the leaders of the country were suspicious of foreigners from countries that had historically made excessive demands and had shamed China, even if the motives of the foreigners seemed good.

China also found herself embroiled in wars with surrounding countries, especially during the years of Raph's college and graduate training. In 1894 and 1895, the Japanese won a war with China that forced open treaty ports, resulting in the independence of Korea, and Japanese control of Formosa and the Liotung Peninsula.

The island of Taiwan is located close to the coast of mainland China, south of Japan and north of the Philippines. In 1895, the Republic of Formosa was formed on the island, the name coming from the Portuguese explorers who had discovered the uncharted island and named it "beautiful island." When news of the Treaty of Shimonoseki arrived at the island, the people formed the Republic as an act of defiance. According to the Treaty, Taiwan was ceded to Japan, so the short-lived Republic died when the Japanese arrived at Tainan, the capital, later in the year. A missionary to Formosa wrote:

> Another problem facing the mission in North Formosa is the coming of the Japanese. We have no fear. The King of kings is greater than emperor or Mikado. He will rule and overrule all things. We do not speculate. We do not prearrange. The Japanese question must be faced, as all others have been faced, with plans flexible enough to suit the changed circumstances, and faith strong enough to hear the voice of God across the storm. There will be difficulties, dangers, and trials before things are adjusted,

> but Formosa is given to Jesus and the purposes of God shall be fulfilled.[48]

European nations actively sought to partition China, including – and especially - neighboring Russia which, between 1895 and 1898 received a lease to a portion of the Liotung Peninsula, including Port Arthur. Through this, they received the right to build the Trans-Siberian Railway across Manchuria, and to build railways through China to port cities. Understandably, a great number of reforms were undertaken in China to protect her sovereignty. One of the rescripts was so poorly thought through that it created resentment among foreign missionaries and Chinese nationals. Mob violence, including attacks on foreigners, increased until the Boxer rebellion broke out in 1900. Missionaries were killed or forced to run from China, and many Christians were killed during the rebellion.

The Russo-Japanese War broke out in 1904. On the part of some Chinese thinkers, this was a conflict between the yellow and white races, and the Japanese were recognized as an imperial power. The Japanese became concerned about the Russian interest in controlling Manchuria and the northern part of Korea. They looked for a way to get an agreement from Russia concerning those geographic concerns, but the Russians dawdled, and the Japanese finally concluded that war was the only option. Their victories in that war encouraged those who envisioned a continental empire to seek control over Korea, the removal of Russian troops from Manchuria, transfer of the Russian-leased portion of the Chinese Eastern Railway, and even control of Sakhalin Island (north of the northernmost large island of Japan, Honshu).

The Japanese colonialists had eyed Hawaii and the Philippines for years, but they remained neutral when the United States occupied the Philippines after the Spanish-American war. They felt that it was better to stay on the good side of a non-hostile power. Japanese, British, French, and American imperialism were in balance in Asia. Yet the Japanese eyed a greater sphere of Japanese colonial influence in northern and south-east Asia.

The best description of the Japanese attitudes toward the Philippines and the rest of Asia "to the south" is that of Sven Matthiessen in his careful study of Japanese Pan-Asianism and the Philippines. He describes two major points of view among the Japanese from the late nineteenth century to the end of World War Two. One point of view was, simply put, that of those who desired to prevent the advance of the United States from the Philippines, Hawaii, etc., to the control of Japan and other parts of northern Asia. The other "Pan-Asian" perspective saw Asia as an area of peoples with racial, ethnic, and geographic similarities that made them a family. As Nishimura Shinji (1879-1943) believed, the Philippines could be integrated into "a Japanese dominated Co-prosperity sphere and . . . that for Japan, 'going to the Philippines is like coming home.'"[49]

Concerning the people of Japan, Raph exclaimed in his speech that "The keen and tenacious mind, the unusual vigor and endurance, coupled with coolness and courage, which have put them in the lead as soldiers, are but a few of the uniquely striking characteristics of this "peculiar" people."[50] He was right about the characteristics of these beautiful people, and it was these characteristics plus their loyalty to emperor, country, and manifest destiny that was changing and was to further change the face of Asia throughout Raph's life. Christian leaders who had been trained in missionary schools were influencing the modernization and priorities of the nation. Interest in Christianity had increased dramatically from the 1850's through the first fifty years of evangelization.

But Raph's notion of the Japanese people as chosen people of God would prove to be difficult to support over the decades to come as the influence of Christianity waned while Bushido was stretched to cover modern military aspirations.[51] However, in defense of what Raph wrote, it must be admitted that others whom he read, and by whom he was taught were writing the same things. Ernest W. Clement, Principal of Duncan Baptist Academy in Tokyo (later part of Kanto Gakuin University), and author of the *Handbook of Modern Japan*, wrote in 1905,

> And when we take into consideration how much Christianity has done for Japan in fifty years, we feel quite warranted in prophesying that within this twentieth century Japan will become practically a Christian nation.[52]

If only they had been correct!

CHAPTER 5

The Preparation of Missionary Doctor Thomas for the Philippines

Lead me in thy truth, and teach me: for thou art the God of my salvation; on thee do I wait all the day. —Psalm 25:5

FROM CALL TO LEADING

Before his graduation from Newton, on April 27, 1904, Raphael submitted his application to the American Baptist Missionary Union (ABMU).[53]

In the application, Raph revealed several interesting facts about himself. When asked about the languages other than English he had studied, Raph responded that he had learned Latin, Greek, French, German, Anglo Saxon, and Hebrew. He described his facility in the languages as "Fair," though he continued to enjoy his reading of Greek classics through his life. He could not play the piano!

Raph wrote that he served as acting pastor at two churches: East Freetown Baptist Church, East Freetown, Massachusetts, for "a year or two;" and acting pastor at Salem Baptist Chapel, Salem, Mass., for one and a half years.

When one considers Raph's later experience in the Philippines, two interesting questions in the application form are #25,' "Do you believe that personal effort to lead souls to Christ is the paramount duty of every missionary?" and #26, "Do you purpose to make such effort the chief feature of your missionary career, no matter what other duties may be assigned to you?" Raph responded "yes" to each question.

He was a total abstainer from all forms of alcohol, opium, cocaine, and other drugs. He believed that he could cheerfully acquiesce in "the decision of a majority." In response to a question of whether he would bear responsibilities calmly and cheerfully, Raph wrote "Fairly."

In the somewhat comical way that people assess others in this world, two of the references whose names Raph had given, both doctors with whom he had worked during his internship, described him quite differently regarding the matter of his tactfulness.

George H. Monks, MD, whom he assisted while at Boston City Hospital, wrote of Thomas on May 9, 1904, that he ". . . could hardly be considered as belonging to the highest grade of assistants, though he seemed interested and anxious to please. He seems a very nice fellow, and intelligent, though I should say he lacks tact. However, he might present entirely different characteristics under different circumstances."[54] Elliott P. Joslin, MD, wrote on the contrary that "He has considerable tact, and those under him were glad to work for him."[55]

George W. Creesy, of Salem, Massachusetts, a trustee of the North End Baptist Chapel, where Raphael served while in his first two years at Newton, gave a thoughtful account of the young servant of Christ. Regarding Raph's disposition and ability to harmonize with other workers, Mr. Creesy wrote, "Mr. Thomas has a very smooth and even temperament and is not easily disturbed by his surroundings. If more of the students possessed such a nature as his, there would be far less of disturbances in the church."[56] Of his ability as a teacher, preacher, and evangelist, Creesy wrote that Raph "was very successful as a teacher in the Sunday-School, having a most interesting class, and I know he was well repaid for his labors both preaching and teaching. Through his efforts a number were led to Christ and are now workers in His vineyard."[57]

Mr. Creesy also believed that for a young man, Mr. Thomas "had in him the making of a good leader," and his opinion as to the applicant's fitness for foreign missionary service is worth quoting at length:

> You will find him admirably fitted for the work, and if you conclude to accept him you will make no mistake, because when he enters into his work he is always forgetful of self in the earnestness of his efforts in the Master's cause – and as you see, I can hardly say enough in his behalf.[58]

There is no clearer statement from that era concerning Raphael's doctrinal views than that made by the Rev. Everett D. Burr, DD, Pastor of First Baptist Church in Newton Centre:

> Mr. Thomas has given evidence in all his public utterances which I have heard, as well as in his private conversations of a living faith in a living Christ. He is in my judgment a firm believer and earnest advocate of what we are pleased to call the evangelical position.[59]

This same Pastor Burr testified that one of his first experiences upon going to First Baptist Church was finding "Mr. Thomas at the bed side of a sick young man." Burr continued, "He has done a great deal of delicate personal work. I know of no mistakes which could justly be attributed to him." His concluding opinion as to Raph's fitness for foreign missionary service was emphatic. He wrote, "I think it is the one thing he ought to do. His whole yearning is for this."[60]

Raph assumed that the most needy field would turn out to be China, but God had something else in mind for Raphael. Just three days later, on April 30, Raph sent a hand-written letter to Mr. Dutton of the ABMU in which he excitedly described his long talk with "The doctor from the Philippines," Dr. Lerrigo.[61]

On April 29th, Dr. Lerrigo, freshly returned from the Philippines after his child had died and his wife had experienced serious medical complications, spoke at the Newton chapel. After that chapel session, Raphael and the doctor huddled, then walked together for hours. In writing of his "call" to the Philippines years later[62], Raph explained:

> the call came as follows. It was clear and clean cut. I had to accept. I thought I was heading for China. I had already decided that the "call" was where the need was

> greatest and the workers fewest. That was just plain "horse sense". It has always seemed strange to me why doctors wait for a special call to go to the foreign field under such circumstances. They should demand, rather, a special call to stay home. But my call came as follows. Dr. Lerrigo, a Baptist Missionary to the Philippines, spoke on Newton Hill. I happened to hear him: unusual for me to go there for the outside speakers, but this time I went. He spoke on the need for a Medical Missionary to take his place and "carry the torch" in Capiz, Philippines. He had to return. I had heard of the Philippines but that was all. I had no conception of what they were like or of my going there. Now the call came. I decided to go. Then I learned that the Secretary of the American Baptist Missionary Union, Dr. Thomas Barbour, had been trying to catch me on the telephone that day to inform me that they felt I was needed at this outpost. That was all there was to it. I had decided at Northfield that when God called I would respond, wherever the call might lead me. The call came and I responded. It was as easy as that.

In his April 30th letter, Raph wrote, "The work there appeals to me strongly and I should like nothing better than to put my life right into it – provided that the Board should care to send me."[63] Dr. Barbour, and later the Board of the ABMU, assured him that they cared to send him, appointing him on May 9, 1904, as a missionary to Capiz, Philippines.

This decision was also reflected in the June 1904, issue of *The Newtonian*, in which a list of those members of the senior class who had been called to a definite field of service included the two words "Thomas, Phillipines [*sic*]."

ORDINATION

Having completed his work at Newton Theological Institute, Raphael had to complete one more formal step before leaving his American church and the United States. He was to be examined for ordination. One of the invitations sent, on September 5, 1904, was to Dr. H. C. Mabie of Fremont

Temple. It read, "Dear Sire, You are invited to be present at the council to be held at the First Baptist Church – Newton Centre, Mass. Saturday Sept. 10, 1904 at 3 P.M. – for the purpose of recommending brother Raphael C. Thomas for ordination into the Baptist Ministry. Yours sincerely, M. Grant Edmands, Asst. Clerk."[64] The council recommended ordination, and on September 11th, 1904, he was ordained by the First Baptist Church of Newton Centre, Massachusetts.

He was examined concerning both doctrine and practice. The examiners needed to know that he was a firm believer in the fundamentals of The Faith, and orthodox in his doctrine. He illustrated the unshakeable firmness of his faith throughout his life, but a statement made near the end of his life clearly shows that he was also unwavering in his faith. In a letter written late in the 1950's Raph wrote that, to him as an evangelist, the doctrines concerning salvation are those of greatest interest. But he added that if anyone should challenge the Deity of our Lord (with the Virgin Birth), His vicarious atonement, His bodily resurrection, the final authority of the Bible, and the New Birth, he would "rise up in wrath!"

Reverend Raphael Clarke Thomas, MD, sailed for the Philippines on October 25, 1904, from San Francisco.[65]

CHAPTER 6

The 'Preparation of the Philippines' for Dr. Thomas

Let them give glory unto the LORD, and declare his praise in the islands. —Isaiah 42:12

BEAUTIFUL PEOPLE

Fiercely loyal, warm, compassionate, friendly, beautiful; these words only scratch the surface of all that could be said about the people of the Philippines. Those who have spent time in the Philippines, and those who have had the privilege of making friends with Filipinos and Filipinas, universally agree that they are delightful people.

The green, gorgeous beauty of their islands is marred only by the large areas in and around their cities where the poor have constructed lean-tos of wood, cardboard, and scraps of cloth. Jesus said, "The poor you will always have with you," and these islands of poverty within the thousands of islands of the Philippines are heart-breaking reminders of this truth.

The people Raph met, though poor, were willing to do anything to extend hospitality. They did everything they could to promote and maintain good relationships. They were careful not to offend and would avoid confrontation. However, if they were offended, especially if it were before their peers, they would at least avoid the offender for a long period of time. On the other hand, if one had done something – especially something considered to be important – for a person, the person helped would sense a very great debt (*utang na loob*) to the one who helped. One can easily imagine the result of the cure of a life-threatening physical problem by a doctor! The recipient of the help would often go to great lengths to reciprocate in any way possible.

Ruth Woodworth, a missionary to the Philippines with the Association of Baptists For Evangelism in the Orient (ABEO), arrived in early 1934. In her book, *No Greater Joy*, she provided a brief, but delightful, description of the people, their generosity, and their love for beauty:

> Filipino people are very kind and hospitable. I have never met such generous people, always wanting to give you their best. They often brought us delicious fruit, vegetables, crabs, shrimp – anything they thought we would like. They also love beauty. Their balconies and walks are lined with pots of bougainvillea. I have always loved flowers and gardening, so with the help of two students I used Monday, our day off, to beautify our grounds [at the Bible Institute]. At one time I had nine different shades of bougainvillea.[66]

Such descriptions from those who have come to know and love the Filipinos could fill these pages.

Though many areas of the Philippine islands are seldom explored by outsiders, retreat and recreation centers abound for those who want to experience the hospitality of the people. Roman Catholic and Protestant influences are clearly seen throughout the islands, Yet, the "deep south" island of Mindanao, with its proximity to the largely Muslim population of Indonesia, has been a hotbed of pro-Islamic resistance against the government and religions of the rest of the people to the north.

LOCATION

The Philippine archipelago is located on the western rim of the Pacific Ocean. It consists of 7,107 islands stretching nearly 1,000 miles from north to south. About 10% of the islands are uninhabited. The three major island groups are Luzon, Visayas, and Mindanao. The capitol of the country is Manila, located on the northernmost large island, Luzon. Manila is nearly 2,000 miles south of Tokyo, 700 miles southeast of Hong Kong. The Philippine islands are due east of Vietnam, and north of Indonesia. Papua/ New Guinea is to the southeast.

The island of Panay, where most of Raph's story in the Philippines takes place, is a roughly triangle-shaped island in the Visayan Sea; one of the thousands of Visayan Islands. To its south is the Panay Gulf, and to its west is the Sulu Sea. All these bodies of water are part of the large geographic entity known as the South China Sea.

LANGUAGE

Both the location of the islands and the early history of the people groups found in the Philippines have resulted in a great variety of languages and dialects. There are more than 170 languages listed for the Philippines, including many Austronesian, Malayo-Polynesian languages. Because of the long Spanish, and more abbreviated American occupations of the country, Spanish and English language influences are understandable. Between those occupations, in an early attempt to form a Philippine republic, the Provisional Constitution for the Republic of the Philippines (Constitución Provisional de la República de Filipinas) was approved on November first of 1897. Article VIII designated Tagalog as the official language of the Philippines.

Raph and other foreigners were exposed to new languages each time they travelled any distance, especially when visiting inland areas and smaller islands. The languages they would have encountered included Hiligaynon (Ilonggo), Cebuano (and its dialects), Ilocano, Kagayanen (Cagayano), Sulod (Bukidnon), and many others. They frequently took translators with them who knew the dialect of the people, or whose dialect was close enough to theirs to get by. There were also many whose English was good enough, or whose ability to talk in a kind of pidgin language with gestures helped conversation, medical treatment, or communication of the gospel to take place.

NATURAL BEAUTY

Anyone who has been blessed with an opportunity to visit the Philippine Islands will willingly report that they are beautiful. The mountains, seas, forests, fruit, rice terraces, animals and people all overwhelm the tourist with sights and smells that are both amazing and overwhelming. Tropical cyclones (typhoon) and volcanic eruptions add ferocious elements to the tranquil beauty.

Raph wrote the following description of some aspects of the great beauty of the Philippines:

> I never tired of the wonders of the tropics. Monkeys cavorting in the tree tops, brightly colored parrots darting about, huge bats swarming overhead and clouds of locusts, and in the sea itself the most marvelous exhibition of corals and fish of striking contrast of colors astonish an Occidental. There are broad reaches of coral bank off Mindanao, where the water is crystal clear and one can see many feet into its limpid depths. Once I saw a shark, a big fellow, just below the surface, though this time it was from the safety of the deck of the Gospel Ship (our Fukuin Maru): but more of that ship later.

COMMUNITY LIFE

In a helpful article published in 1956, John H. Romani described the primary unit in "the hierarchy of Philippine local government:" the *barrio.* It is believed that the *barrio* developed from the Malayan *balangays* (named after the boats they arrived in), which were small communities of family groups started as these people migrated into the broad island country that would become the Philippines. When the Spanish arrived in the Philippines, they initially worked with and through the authorities in the *balangays.* In time, however, the authority was stripped away from the chiefs of the *balangays,* who became tax collectors, and the communities were formed into *pueblos.* The "*barangays*" became *barrios,* with "lieutenants" as their headmen. The Americans changed the local governmental situation little, changing pueblos to municipalities, but leaving the *barrio* when it was in proximity to municipalities as the sub-division. The lieutenant was then referred to as the chief administrative officer of the *barrio.* The barrio, with its clusters of houses and families, served as the center of social activity and the chief source of identification for its members.[67]

HISTORY

At this point it is necessary to shed some light on the history of the Philippines, particularly upon the arrival of two foreign religious influences that came to dominate portions of the archipelago.

Although counter-theories of the peopling of the Philippines from the north and south have been proposed, based upon the archaeological, anthropological, biological and linguistic evidence, it appears that Polynesia was probably first populated through Southeast Asia by people originally from South China. When the first "Austronesians" arrived and began to populate the islands is a matter of debate among scholars, though they think the movement from South China began around 6,000 years ago.[68] There are ethnographically determined differences between various groups of people in the Philippines, so points and times of arrival probably varied.

Before the Spanish era, various sea-faring peoples became aware of the Philippines, notable among them were the Chinese. In his work on the Chinese and Arab trade in the twelfth and thirteenth centuries, Chau Ju-Kua described the Philippines, referred to as Ma-I. He referred to Calamian, Palawan, and Busuanga as the San-su (three islands) in the same account.[69]

Islam traveled with Arab traders to the islands of Borneo and the Sulu Sea beginning about the ninth century, AD. Its influence grew in that region, spread to Palawan in the north, and Borneo in the west. However, Islam appears to have been introduced in Mindanao not from Sulu, but from Johore around 1515, with the arrival of Sharif Muhammad Kabungsuwan and the Samals. According to Philippine Muslim history, Kabungsuwan spread Islam in Mindanao through proselyting, military conquest, and diplomacy.[70]

Yet, apart from the tenacious folk-religious customs of the various people groups in the Philippines, the strongest religious force in the country for centuries radiated from the Roman Catholicism introduced to the country when Ferdinand Magellan arrived in 1521.

In a recent study, Philip T. Hoffman described the rulers and leaders of the European continent as being engaged in a 'tournament' with one another that affected the people of the rest of the world. "The prize for the rulers engaged in this grim contest was financial gain, territorial expansion, defense of the faith, or the glory of victory."[71]

The two powers that dominated the Asian sphere were Portugal and Spain. During the extended period of discovery by sea of lands south, west, and east of these countries, from the early-1400's to the late-1500's, ancient routes by land to India, Central, East, and Southeast Asia, were supplemented with long sea journeys. To avoid continuing conflict, a compromise was agreed upon in 1494 that limited these two sea-powers to separate areas of exploration, colonization, and exploitation of the people and goods – including the valuable spices - of the lands they discovered. A line of division was drawn west of the Cape Verde islands, which are in turn located west of the great bend of western Africa. The Portuguese received Africa, and Spain received 'the New World' and a lot of water (or so the Portuguese thought). For the Portuguese, this was fine, because it allowed them to explore Africa, and gave them the southern passage, discovered by Bartolomeu Dias in 1488, that would take them to India. Beyond India, they hoped to discover the Spice Islands in Southeast Asia. For the Spanish, this arrangement gave them full access to the western lands discovered by Columbus, including, as they thought, the island of Japan (Marco Polo's *Chipangu*], and possibly India.

The Spanish explorer Balboa first laid eyes on the Pacific in the early 1500's. Most of the energies of the Spanish in "the New World" had been used up in battles to colonize and control that region of the world. Magellan, who had served the crown in Portugal, India, and in battle with the Arabs, had originally approached the King of Portugal with a bold plan to find a Western route to the Spice Islands. King Manuel, who disliked Magellan, and who had other problems of his own, refused to support the expedition. Magellan left Portugal, emigrated to Spain, and developed a relationship with a powerful family that helped him when he approached the House of Commerce with his plan. He included, this time, an assurance that he thought the Spice Islands would be in the Spanish portion of the world. After numerous audiences, Magellan, and a fellow-Portuguese, were given a contract in 1518 to find islands, mainlands, and rich spices.[72] He sailed with five ships and 275 men. The story of his voyage, including the discovery of the Straits of Magellan, Guam, and the Philippines is fascinating, especially in that the explorers went so far over broad stretches of ocean with no idea of where they were going!

Magellan and his diminished crew arrived in Cebu Island in 1521, but there was no permanent settlement until 1565; first in Cebu, and later in Manila. Colonization by Spanish government representatives, and Christianization by the friars, went hand-in-hand. Land grants to colonizers, and the organization of regions and peoples within the islands, were accompanied by both harsh methods and social transformation. The gradual increase in domination of the church accompanied the trappings of colonialism.[73]

By the end of the nineteenth century, anti-colonial feelings, syncretistic offshoots of Roman Catholicism, and demands for a greater Filipino presence in the priesthood, all fed the forces of nationalism. Though it was years in the making, with Jose Rizal as its inspirational leader, the National Revolution reached its zenith from 1896 to 1898.

Rizal, whose writings extolled the religious freedom he had experienced in Europe, became a martyr to the cause in 1896. He was angry about the way in which his people had been treated for hundreds of years and horrified concerning the low estimate frequently given of his people by many of the modern writers who described them. In his book, *The Indolence of the Filipino,* he described the so-called *indolence* of the people as not a cause, but an effect; the result of the domination of the Philippines by the Spanish. Rizal wrote,

> The ancient writers, like Chirino, Morga and Colin, take pleasure in describing them as well-featured, with good aptitudes for any thing they take up, keen and susceptible and of resolute will, very clean and neat in their persons and clothing, and of good mien and bearing. (Morga). Others delight in minute accounts of their intelligence and pleasant manners, of their aptitude for music, the drama, dancing and singing; of the facility with which they learned, not only Spanish but also Latin, which they acquired almost by themselves (Colin); others, of their

exquisite politeness in their dealings and in their social life; others, like the first Augustinians, whose accounts Gaspar de San Augustin copies, found them more gallant and better mannered than the inhabitants of the Moluccas. "All live off their husbandry," adds Morga, "their farms, fisheries and enterprises, for they travel from island to island by sea and from province to province by land."
In exchange, the writers of the present time, without being better than those of former times, neither as men nor as historians, without being more gallant than Hernan Cortez and Salcedo, nor more prudent than Legazpi, nor more manly than Morga, nor more studious than Colin and Gaspar de San Augustin, our contemporary writers, we say, find that the native is a creature something more than a monkey but much less than man, an anthropoid, dull-witted, stupid, timid, dirty, cringing, grinning, ill-clothed, indolent, lazy, brainless, immoral, etc., etc.

To what is this retrogression due? Is it the delectable civilization, the religion of salvation of the friars, called of Jesus Christ by a euphemism, that has produced this miracle, that has atrophied his brain, paralyzed his heart and made of the man this sort of vicious animal that the writers depict?

Alas! The whole misfortune of the present Filipinos consists in that they have become only half-way brutes. The Filipino is convinced that to get happiness it is necessary for him to lay aside his dignity as a rational creature, to attend mass, to believe what is told him, to pay what is demanded of him, to pay and forever to pay; to work, suffer and be silent, without aspiring to anything, without aspiring to know or even to understand Spanish, without separating himself from his carabao, as the priests shamelessly say, without protesting against any injustice, against any arbitrary action, against an assault, against an insult; that is, not to have heart, brain or spirit: a creature with arms and a purse full of gold .... there's the ideal native! Unfortunately, or because the brutalization is not yet complete and because

> the nature of man is inherent in his being in spite of his condition, the native protests; he still has aspirations, he thinks and strives to rise, and there's the trouble![74]

By the year 1898, the revolution against Spain was declared over by Filipino General Aguinaldo, who proclaimed Philippine independence.

As a result of the defeat of the Spanish fleet in the same year, and the victory of America in the Spanish-American war, the Philippine Islands were ceded to the United States by Spain. The nation that had helped the Philippines throw off the bondage of Spain now found itself in a Philippine-American war that continued into early 1902.

Despite the opposition of those who were longing for self-government, many representatives of the United States worked hard to provide services to undo the depressing effects of the preceding centuries of colonial rule. Raph wrote,

> The ex-soldiers from our Army were filling in the need for teachers in the schools already in the making. The United States educated the nation well. At first, however, some of the teaching was a bit crude. For example, an American Provincial Superintendent of Schools reported to me that one of his early Filipino teachers was asked about his methods of "nature study". He immediately told little pupil Juan to "Go out and bring in some nature." Juan responded with alacrity and reappeared with a little sprig of something in his brown fist. "What is this?" said the teacher. Juan replied: "This is some nature." Then the teacher went to the mantel and took down a scrawny little potted plant. "What is this?" he queried again. Juan replied as before: "This is some nature." "But why do I hold it on my hand?" persisted the teacher. Juan now replied: "By reason of its beauty". With that the Nature Study ended.

NATURAL AND HUMAN CALAMITIES

The physical location and tropical climate of the Philippines places it where many natural calamities have taken place. Annual visits from typhoon and occasional volcanic eruptions are the most dramatic, perhaps, but in the Philippines of the early twentieth century, there were many others.

W. Morgan Shuster (1877-1960), a graduate of Columbia University, and of their School of Law, spent several years as a collector of customs in Cuba and the Philippines after the Spanish American war. He lived in the Philippines for eight years. The following, from a lecture he gave in 1909, is his description of the conditions in the Philippines that, in his opinion, made the Filipinos poor, fatalistic, and dependent:

> One result of our règimè in the Philippines has been to teach us something of the enormous physical obstacles which of themselves are a great drag upon the work of uplifting, morally, intellectually and materially, the Filipino people. One must live years in the islands to realize fully what these obstacles are. The natural languor produced by a warm and comparatively changeless climate; the torrential rains and ensuing floods, which annually wipe out whole river towns, ruin crops, carry away bridges and obliterate the best constructed roads; typhoons which blow down scores of houses, level whole fields of hemp and groves of cocoanuts, destroy the growing rice, and wipe out the food supply on which thousands of people depend for their support; droughts which every years, in some province or provinces, produce similar unfortunate results; rinderpest, which decimates the work animals; enormous swarms of locusts which devour growing crops in a night; fires, which, owing to the highly inflammable nature of the houses, frequently sweep an entire large town; to say nothing of occasional onslaughts of cholera, small-pox and bubonic plague, although these latter troubles have now been almost entirely conquered.[75]

Some of Shuster's language helps one to recognize the paternalism of the so-called altruistic attitudes of the Americans in the Philippines after 1898. While throughout his address, Shuster attempts to defend the Filipinos from the calumnies made against them, his confidence in the Anglo-Saxon race to instill, dignify, create, give, and teach them is patronizing:

> We are attempting to raise the material, moral and intellectual standards of more than seven millions of people, to instill into them the Anglo-Saxon ideas and methods, to dignify honest toil, to create in them a national spirit, to give them a common language, and to teach them, by practical but gradual experience, to be at some future date the arbiters of their own destiny as a people.
>
> A more high-minded course for a great and powerful nation to pursue towards a weak and dependent people whom the fortunes of war had cast into her hands, can hardly be imagined. I believe that it is wholly unique in history, and I venture the prediction that it will remain so for a long time to come. Charity and altruism among nations are not nearly so contagious as with individuals.[76]

Contemporary historian James Bradley writes of the "benevolent intentions myth" that was believed by most Americans but questioned by many in the Philippines.

> One of the most famous stories about McKinley is how the president confessed to a visiting delegation of Methodist ministers that he fell to his knees and prayed for enlightenment and that God told him it was his duty to uplift, civilize, and Christianize the Filipinos. The story might not be true, but it captures the benevolent intentions that McKinley injected into U.S. foreign policy. McKinley understood that to his electorate, imperialism was a dirty word, and so he made Americans believe that their nation's boldly imperial moves were instead efforts of great compassion and sacrifice. If the average American felt pity for Others, he had a Christian duty to help.[77]

Sadly, the behavior of many of the U.S. envoys and troops in the Philippines was anything but benevolent. Justifying their behavior by the "manifest destiny" of the Aryans to practice social evolution, civilian and military leaders turned a blind eye to the torture, rape, water-boarding, murder, looting and burning of villages of the "ignorant blacks" by the American troops.[78]

The description given of Iloilo in 1900, written by John Marvin Dean, is helpful to understand the physical condition of this important city experiencing recovery in 1904. Dean was looking for a building for use of the YMCA, which had been encouraged by the U.S. Secretary of War.

> [General Hughes, commander of the Department of the Visayas] assured me that it was out of the question as the town had been well-nigh destroyed by the insurgents upon evacuating and such buildings left standing as were suitable for government use were all occupied, some being rented at high figures in order to obtain sufficient accommodation for headquarters, department offices and officers' quarters. This I found to be true. Iloilo, although the second city of importance in the Islands on account of it being the port of entry for Negros sugar, Cebu hemp and Panay rice, could only boast of a population of ten thousand. The town, for it does not deserve the name of city, stretches along a flat sandy point between the Jaro River and the Strait of Iloilo. The insurgents had occupied the town for some time and only withdrew, when the place was bombarded by an American fleet, after firing the larger part of the houses and shops. In consequence of this wanton destruction Iloilo presented a very mournful appearance when I first walked along its streets.[79]

NON-CATHOLIC CHRISTIANITY ARRIVES

Although earlier Christian influences had brought several Filipinos to Christ, and some churches into existence, it was in this period from 1898 through 1902 that non-Catholic Christianity burst upon the scene. YMCA., Presbyterian, Methodist, Baptist, Episcopalian, United Brethren,

Congregationalist, and Christian and Missionary Alliance missionaries, among others, all arrived during that period.[80]

Before the arrival of the missionaries, in an 1898 meeting of mission board officials in the United States, the boards hammered out a comity agreement. In order to avoid overlapping and duplication of effort, the country was divided up among them.[81] In 1901, the Evangelical Union of the Philippines was formed. It existed "for the purpose of securing comity and effectiveness in their missionary operations."[82] For example, the Presbyterians agreed to work in the Luzon provinces south of Manila, dividing the work in the Visayan provinces with the Baptists.[83] This was to have a profound effect on Raph's ministry. The following brief article in the May 1907, issue of the *Baptist Missionary Magazine* is an early example of that effect:

> Dr. R.C. Thomas, of Jaro, is substituting for a time at the Presbyterian hospital at Iloilo while the physician in charge is in China. This is a good illustration of the cordial relations which exist between the Baptist missionaries and those of other denominations in the Islands.[84]

Although 1900 is usually given as the year in which Baptist missions had their beginning in the Philippines, it is probably more appropriate to go back to the period of God's preparation of the men who would arrive in Iloilo that year. Braulio Ciriaco Manikan y Miralles (born in 1870), usually known as Braulio Manikan, left his preparation for the Jesuit priesthood and the Philippines to study civil engineering in Europe.[85] In 1898, Manikan, who had visited various Protestant churches in Barcelona, was introduced to the Reverend Eric Lund, a missionary to Spain under the American Baptist Missionary Union.

Lund was born in Sweden and attended a Lutheran school near his home, Bethel Seminary in Stockholm, and then the Mission Institute in London. While at Bethel Seminary, he became convinced that baptism by immersion was the only biblical method, and he joined the Bethel Baptist Church. While studying at Harley College in London, Lund became burdened for missions, and recognized the importance of translating the Scriptures. He was strongly influenced by Charles Haddon Spurgeon and Adoniram Judson. In 1877, Lund went to Spain at the invitation of a classmate from that country. He was persecuted and imprisoned, and in response to his report upon returning home, the Swedish Baptist Foreign Mission Society was founded in 1881. Lund and his wife were sent to Spain as the missionaries of the Society, and it was there that Lund met Samuel Smith with the American Baptist Missionary Union, who referred Lund to the mission for financial support. It was through the influence of Lund and a Christian businessman, Mr. Armstrong, that Manikan came to Christ.[86] Manikan was determined to return to return to the Philippines as a missionary but was prevented for a time due to lack of finances and the Spanish-American war.

While he was waiting, he worked with Lund in translating some tracts and the Bible into the Hiligaynon dialect. While this collaboration was under way, Manikan was teaching Lund his language, and Lund was teaching him theology and Baptist tradition.[87] Lund had reported the baptism of Manikan, and their efforts in Bible translation, to the ABMU. Despite Lund's reluctance to leave Spain, the two men were appointed by the ABMU to become their first missionaries to the Philippines, arriving there in April 1900, and beginning their ministry in Iloilo in May. Curiously, Lund had expressed a desire that the first Baptist missionary to come from America should be "an educator," but the Board refused, emphasizing that the first worker should be an evangelist.[88] This kind of tension became familiar to Raph after he arrived.

CHAPTER 7

Missionary to the Philippines

A wicked messenger falleth into mischief: but
a faithful ambassador is health.
—Proverbs 13:17

JOURNEY TO A NEW LIFE

In 1948, Raph prepared a brief autobiographical article entitled "A Philippine Medical Missionary Harks Back." His characterization of the article allows some of his humor and personality to shine through:

> This is to be a sketchy autobiography. It must be sketchy only as it covers a period of years to "hit the high spots" and answer the question: "Does it pay to become a Medical Missionary?" Naturally, it is very "self-centered", as autobiographies are bound to be. It also must have plenty of movement. That is characteristic of automobiles and also of autobiographies. If they are to be followed through by any reader, they must not lag. I will try to bear that in mind.

From the point of view of a biographer, many essential details were left out of his autobiography, but the "Snapshots" he included are useful in their display of his outstanding memories of his life and ministry in the Philippines. In this and some of the following chapters, Raph's brief autobiography will provide much of the "local color."[89]

AT SEA

The most delightful way to experience the long sea voyage from San Francisco to the Philippines begun in October of 1904, is to let Raph tell the story. Those who have taken extended trips on ships will appreciate some of the personal details, but it is his observations of stops along the way that are especially interesting. The people who make their homes in other countries than their "home" should take copious notes of their first experiences, because after a while, familiarity takes away the newness of things seen.

> We embarked from San Francisco on the Steamship China, of the China Mail – a Line long since defunct, but a proud link in the chain of Steamship Lines that kept the flag of our Country flying thru the years, when it was almost blotted out by competition of other nations.
>
> The voyage was longer than it is now and the accommodations not so luxurious. My roommate, a fellow missionary for the Philippines, Henry Weston Munger, grandson of Dr. Weston formerly President of Crozer Theological Seminary, and I were to share our stateroom with a Frenchman. As everyone knows, the French fear a draft. Consequently, this man closed all the portholes and we nearly suffocated. We were righteously indignant (righteous indignation is permitted even to ministers) and Henry went to remonstrate with the Frenchman endeavoring to have him accept some other berth. Later Henry met me with rueful demeanor and told me that the man had refused indignantly. Just then a gentleman passed and Henry said: "There he is now". "Why Henry", I replied, "You did not speak to that man, did you?" "Yes," he said, "why not?" "Because," I answered, "it is not the

> right man." And it was not. It seems he was the occupant of the Apartment De Luxe, engaged at a fancy price. He thought Munger was trying to oust him. It is strange how such a triviality stays by me after the years of important events, but such is life.
>
> It was one of the bright spots, and I am determined in this recital to emphasize them. On the whole a missionary's life is full of happiness; overwhelmingly so. Why not emphasize it? The average critic of missions never does. He should! Another trivial event that is stamped on my memory is when one of the Celestials (for a large part of the crew were Chinese still sporting the long blue gowns and the pigtail) leaned over my shoulder at the dinner table, when I was bravely trying to appear composed, although my reaction to the meal was anything but comforting as we steamed out of the Golden Gate and met the tossing about of the waves, and said "Sleesick?" I gave him one glance and he disappeared, pigtails flying, through the buttery door.

In this time of one-day journeys to Asia by air, it is difficult for anyone to appreciate the length of a sea journey from the West Coast to the Philippines. It consisted of shipboard life of more than a month – with a brief respite in Hawaii - and the possibility of numerous stops after the eventual arrival in Asia. Raph provides an interesting description of major Asian ports in 1904. It is apparent that he wrote these reminiscences long after the event, because he tends to pepper his remarks with events that took place during and after the Second World War.[90]

> We stopped at Honolulu, Yokohama, Nagasaki, Shangai and Hong Kong. Customary snapshots of these well known Oriental and Occidental cities would be slowing down the pace. It might be well, however, to catch a brief glimpse of Japan, as it was. Nagasaki, for instance, was an interesting port because of the fact that the [Japanese] there held the coveted position of coaling ships more rapidly than at any other port. They swarmed up the

bamboo ladders; men, women and children, passing the tiny baskets of coal from one to another, for all the world like a swarm of ants. That was in 1904, long before Nagasaki was blown apart by the Atom Bomb. Shanghai, as well, was a peaceful but very odoriferous City. The saying among the passengers then was instead of "go ashore and see the sights", "go ashore and have a smell". They were right. I have smelled assafoetida and H2S in my profession, but Shangai outdoes them all. In the old City of Shangai, I saw a coffin with its grisly contents by the side of the walk: evidently the coolies tired of carrying it. No wonder the City was unsanitary.

Hong Kong, also, was a proper English City. The coolies obediently trotted along with their English Lordships, bearing them aloft on the sedan chairs to the substantial abodes on the terraced hillsides of this modernized Chinese City. The trip upwards toward the Peak was a stiff climb, and these coolies had to sweat. But that too was before the [Japanese] took over. The blast of the small cannon as they shot at a floating target in the harbour, as we sailed away to the Philippines, lingers in memory even now as a harbinger of what was to follow when real war came.

ARRIVAL IN THE PHILIPPINES

After Raph arrived in the Philippine capitol, Manila, he still had a considerable trip by sea near many of the myriad islands that make up the Philippines. As fascinating as these other sights were to Raph, he saved plenty of descriptive fervor for his arrival in the country that was to be his new home and his place of ministry for decades to come. There is nothing like the experience of awakening for the first time in the land, and among the people of the land, where a missionary has prepared to serve. Months of packing, preparation, and travel behind him, Raph was ready to experience for the first time the beautiful people of the Philippines!

His first paragraph references the Spanish-American war.

Manila, as well, was peaceful. There was little to remind one of Dewey's victory, save the few sunken ships in the harbour. The old Walled City, now ruined by bombs, was intact and lovely. The City of Manila itself was really a modern city. Now it is overrun and devastated. But I was not out for sightseeing, though glad to accept it if it came, and we were off on our last lap of the journey to Iloilo, on Panay Island, one of the same Visayan belt that Leyte is in. Everyone knows all about Leyte by this time, because of the War, but Panay is less well known. I know it best.

The voyage from Manila to Iloilo took two days and a night. It was a lovely sail. The perennial green of the islets we passed, with their sandy beaches, lined with picturesque fisher's huts of bamboo; and swaying coconut palms shading them, were everywhere. Here and there a fisherman, straining at the net, up to his waist in the waves, enlivened the picture. But for the most part there was a peaceful quietness that soothed and relieved the customary nervous tension of American jangled nerves. We already felt the soporific influence of the Orient, where they are said "never do today what you can put off to tomorrow." I was still irked by the urge to get to the field and to work: yet I was not so over eager as to forget to be alert to every passing exhibit of this Orient I had entered. The flying fish that broke the surface and splashed in again a long distance ahead; the porpoises that raced at the prow of the rather slow steamer; the gulls screaming overhead and the passengers themselves, my future neighbors, all claimed attention. Yet over it all peace seemed to reign. Such was the Orient then.[91]

AFTER ARRIVING IN ILOILO PROVINCE

In the last paragraph, Raph mentioned the sense of urgency he had to "get to the field and to work." We can only imagine the enthusiasm with which Raph finally came to Iloilo at the end of this first long journey to the Philippines. However, that was not to be the end of his travels. He was soon to be exposed to the time-consuming, uncomfortable travel realities in early twentieth-century Panay.

> On arrival at Iloilo, Capital of Iloilo Province, on the Island of Panay, I was whisked to Jaro, nearby, where the missionaries were deciding upon my designation. They sent me to Capiz, some eighty kilometers north, as the crow flies. (There was no railroad then. I saw the first spike planted later for this one and only railroad in Panay.)
>
> My journey to Capiz, Capital of Capiz Province, was typical of many subsequent trips by water. It was a smoky little craft, without any staterooms or dining room. We slept on the deck, and as it was cold we dug up a dirty piece of canvas to cover us. We snuggled up to it affectionately, a real "friend in need", and next day the Filipino boy who was with me discovered this ship had carried a cargo of lepers to Culien, the Leper Colony, on its previous voyage. I watched myself carefully for some time after that, you may be sure, but escaped contagion. As a matter of fact, I discovered later that Leprosy is rarely contracted by a Caucasian over there. It is less contagious than is usually supposed.
>
> We landed at a dilapidated wooden pier and were rapidly transferred in a *kilis* that a sailor once dubbed a "bone rackin consarn with the door aft", along a dirt road full of crab holes, to the home of Joseph C. Robbins, later to become for two years the President of the Northern Baptist Convention. But Joe and I had been mates at Newton Theological Institution, and now were just "pals" on the same job. The home was a delightful one. Mrs. Robbins was the best of hostesses, and I was then a bachelor. I appreciated such home life. Having a good appetite I also appreciated the good meals she served, especially "devilled crab". (I never knew the Devil could furnish such appetizing provender. Was especially amazed to see him attempt it in a missionary home.)

Eating crabs, deviled or not, was not the greatest of the experiences Raph and Joe were to have in Capiz.

> Joe and I taught the Filipino youngsters the great American game of baseball. We may have pitched to little Roxas, later President of the Republic, as his home was in Capiz. Who knows? Such chances come to a missionary to mould the future of a nation. For even lighter pastime Joe and I were in the habit of batting bats out of the windows, when they tended to swarm in and terrify Mrs. Robbins. We had a pretty good batting average, as the windows opened the whole side of the house – the small diamond panes of oyster shell, the customary window panes out there, which let in the light, without the glare – but had these bats been like those we saw hanging by their claws near the Crystal Caves of Dumalag, we might have done even better. Some of them are enormous. One ... had a wing spread of over five feet. Believe it or not! But bats, centipedes, cockroaches, ants galore, never dismayed our American women. They killed the roaches and put the sugar away from the ants!

Anyone who has had the experience of living for a while in Asia can well imagine the sizes of the bats and roaches the missionaries were dealing with. When baseball bats were not available, a lampshade on the head and a tennis racket in hand would do the trick!

A COLPORTAGE WAGON TOUR

In July of 1905, Raph experienced another highlight of his first term: an eighteen-day exploratory trip to the extreme south of Negros Island. His fellow-missionary Charles L. Maxfield (1872-1935), who arrived in the Philippines in the same year as Raph, described what he titled as "A Colportage Wagon Tour" in a letter to friends and supporters in America. The party consisted of 5 students from the Baptist dormitory, two colporteurs, a cook and the two missionaries. They visited the towns and villages along 70 miles of the sea coast and then went inland to visit towns along the foot of the mountains.

The colportage wagon had been supplied by friends of Mr. Maxfield in America, and two local ponies provided the horsepower. On either side of the wagon, messages had been painted. On the one side, in Visayan, was written *Ma-ayong Balita*, and on the other side, in Spanish, the phrase *Las Buenas Nuevas.* Both phrases declared the purpose of their trip, to declare "The Good News." Maxfield remarked that to the children the jingling bells and the "novel American wagon" were comparatively of as much interest as Barnum's circus would have been to American children.

While they stopped for only an hour or so in some villages, in each village, in only a few minutes, a gathering of the people would provide a good hearing for the preaching of the Word of God. It was Holy Week, and most of the people from the farms were gathered in the towns and villages for the processions that would form in the evening. If they preached in the evenings, after the processions, an audience "of a thousand or more" would be available in some places.

They sold nine hundred printed editions of the Gospels, thousands of tracts, and many English and Spanish Bibles. The faith of the ministry team was increased by both the desire to hear, the eagerness to buy, and the "intelligent questioning" of the people with regard to "the Way of Salvation."

Mr. Maxfield's description of the work of Dr. Thomas, his colleague, provides an early view of the physical care and spiritual concern Raph lavished on those he met.

> Dr. Thomas not only healed bodies but he drove the arrow of conviction for sin to many hearts and applied the balm of the Gospel to the wound. Believing as he does that the disease of sin is more deadly in its effect than sickness of the body it is not surprising that he often went beneath the surface and made plain the fact that much of the sickness was due to disregard of the laws of nature or disobedience to the laws of God. Even better than the medicines given were the wholesome hygienic talks given at the clinic and many who care for medicine were made to see that vicious habits were destroying both body and soul. And many who had but a little while longer to live were guided to the Great Physician. Believing as he does so much in the

> Great Physician, we can feel not less confidently that he left many of his patients happy in Christian hope.

He added that even larger towns were without a doctor, and there was little knowledge of sanitation and hygiene. Contagious diseases and plagues were "almost as fatal to children as was the edict of Pharaoh." The need for a medical missionary was great!

Raph had already decided to give a large part of his time to touring in a similar way through "the four districts of Panay, Conception and northern and southern Negros." Maxfield admitted that such a ministry would be hard on the body, but there was no question about the need of such work. He estimated that they could reach all the large places in those districts, ministering to the needs of two hundred thousand people in thirty days. During the eighteen-day trip he was describing, twenty-three hundred people were treated "and nearly every kind of sickness and disease from slight fevers and pulling teeth to the setting of a broken arm was considered." Maxfield expressed his joy that "each of the fields in the islands may have the presence of a medical missionary" during an annual tour. He closed the letter with an admission that more families were needed to reach out to over two hundred thousand people, and the hope that more families would soon come.[92]

VISIT TO MINDANAO

Raph was determined to know of ministry possibilities throughout the region in which he was to serve. Below, he describes an early investigation of the island of Mindanao. After describing a hair-raising experience at sea, Raph tells of an encounter with the Moslem residents, frequently called Moros at that time, who were the ancestors of the Muslims on Mindanao today.

> Before the hospital in Iloilo was erected, however, I felt the urge to see more of the medical possibilities elsewhere. I discovered that Mindanao held those who used the Visayan language, and I was wondering if my call might lead me there, or at least lead others there. I also wished

> to bring back some young man who might be trained for service there later. This I was able to do, but never was able to persuade our Board to go in and "possess the land," which would have been possible I believe at that time. I had sampled the medical work in Capiz and found it satisfactory. I now wished to investigate Mindanao, the second largest island in the Archipelago.
>
> Eventually I caught a Transport that was journeying south. I say "eventually" purposely as it was recognized that ships rarely sailed on time. Transports were especially desirable, as they took missionaries at a dollar a head: most convenient method. It was appreciated. We finally started and arrived en route at Cebu. From there I took a side trip to Mactan, close by, where Magellan was massacred. It was a quiet spot, and there was a small monument to commemorate his death, but how inadequate for such an event. From there we sailed south to Mindanao, to Camp Overton, on the north shore. The day before I landed I was informed an American soldier had been attacked by a Moro, who had sneaked up on him unawares. He saved his rifle by discharging it and thus summoning help, but the Moro hacked off his hand. The commander of the post was courteous, and I was permitted to go to the west coast in a launch. Once there I journeyed about, healing the sick and looking over the territory, with occasional jaunts by canoe thru the mangrove swamps.

Since Raph mentioned the account he had heard of the Moro hacking off the soldier's hand, it would be good here to mention that before he left for the Philippines, Raph's brother had given him a pistol to protect himself against "wild animals." Raph mentioned that he had seen none except the python. Actually, the pistol became more of a nuisance than a help. When he was traveling on small boats, the only way to get out of the sunlight was to go into "the tiny doghouse affair on the stern," but soon several Filipinos in the boat would pile in with him. The pistol was a lump he had to lay on in those tight quarters, so he was happy to hand the pistol over to the Constable when he completed his trip. He never used it again!

CHAPTER 7

Not only did Raph see the place where Magellan was killed, he was also told that near the place he was visiting, Jose Rizal, "the George Washington of the Philippines," was imprisoned for a time before he was taken to Manila and was assassinated. The "dreary isolation" reminded him of Napoleon's imprisonment on St. Helena. Raph remarked that "Rizal truly was a remarkable man and a loyal patriot. The Filipinos may be justly proud of him!"

> After skirting the western shore, in many places wooded to the very water's edge, we had to cross a body of water to resume our journey to the east. We found a canoe and paddler, and Dunato – my Visayan boy who was especially addicted to writing indifferent sermons but harmless pastime – and we started on the trip to the next shore quite a distance away. At first we got along famously, and then trouble began. Night fell and the sea rose and soon we feared we would flounder [founder]. Dunato and I took to paddling as the native with us was a sluggish fellow, perhaps a tube enthusiast, for they always are uncertain: but in spite of all we could do we progressed very slowly. The sea became more angry and I became concerned. I shouted to Dunato: "Can you swim?" He replied calmly: "No" (*Indi* in Visayan). But it did not seem to bother him at all: nothing seems to disturb such Filipinos! (But this is not true of the upper class Mestizo. Spanish blood seems to make them especially sensitive and excitable: though Chinese Mestizos are not so. Many of the successful businessmen are of this class).
>
> However, we did not upset, and we paddled hard, but not hard enough. For just as we approached our destination we saw the ship come in and depart: I "had missed another boat," a catastrophe down there. However, we made port and I did what I could in a medical way, and then we secured a parao (or two masted dugouts with bamboo outriggers) and finally reached Iligan, where a market was being held.

Raph's comment about a "tube enthusiast" is probably a reference to opium smoking, which was a vice brought to the Philippines from China.

Open markets are common in the Philippines, and nearly every kind of fruit, vegetable, meat, and trinket can be found in them.

> At this market I really had experiences. The Moros (Mohametans) were fierce looking fellows, with their filed and blackened teeth, brightly colored, tight-fitting trousers, and close-fitting colored shirts. They were obliged to leave their murderous bolos and krises outside, as they could not be trusted to wear them, as they are hot tempered and irresistible when infuriated. Running amok is well known down there. It is terrific. They kill all they meet until they in turn are cut down. It is said that General Wood gave the American soldiers a thirty-two revolver at first, but when a Moro nearly "got him," though peppered with thirty-two caliber bullets, he gave them forty-fives. But when bartering these wild Mohametans seemed tame enough. In fact, one of their maidens, evidently a Chieftain or Datto's daughter, treated me very nicely. I wished to purchase a bamboo splinter, brightly colored, that was shaped to fit her long fingernail to protect it (the custom there where they allow one of them to grow long). She appeared to be scandalized when I offered her money for it: but later, half hiding behind her dad, she pushed it out to me gratis with a sweet and seductive smile. I was younger then!
>
> This was a real triumph, matched only by the days when as Major of the Newton High School Battalion, I discovered the girls "fell heavily" for my brass buttons and tinseled epaulettes. Now, even the Moro maidens appeared to be susceptible to a mere duck suit, but I had no desire to remain and be carved up by a "boy friend" of this Datto's daughter. So, after adding to my pile of souvenirs – and Mindanao was a great place for them, as Moros are adept in pounding brass into kettles and ornaments, as well as expert in making brilliantly colored bamboo articles and filigree silver work – I was ready to leave.

CHAPTER 7

North of the big island of Mindanao in the Southern Philippines is a small island called Camiguin. Raph was told that there were forty pianos on the island. That sounded interesting to him because he thought that musical people would have a lot of imagination and would be interested in the story of the gospel. He was waiting for the steamer to take him back to the island of Panay.

He arrived on the island and spent some time doctoring their bodies and talking about the Lord Jesus. But the time arrived when he had to go back to Mindanao to catch the steamer. Yet, wouldn't you know it, a big storm came up, and the Filipino boatmen would not go out into the storm. He tried his best to persuade them, but they refused to budge.

Finally, he offered one boatman enough dinero to tempt him to take Raph out in his boat. The waves were high, and the wind was strong. About halfway across, Raph saw a boat that was in trouble. The boat was laboring hard, and he thought it would sink. So, Raph started hollering over the howling wind to the boatman, telling him to turn back and help the other boatman. He seemed to be completely deaf to what Raph was shouting. He just grinned and kept on his way, fighting the waves. Raph was very upset and sure that a tragedy was happening before his eyes. The boat filled with water and quickly went down.

What Raph didn't know was that the water was only waist deep! He could not believe his eyes. There was a coral shelf that ran out from the island, and the man really wasn't in great danger! Raph was both embarrassed and quite upset with his own boatman. I guess it was the grin, and the fact that he didn't tell the good doctor that there was no great danger.

A NOTE ABOUT MISSIONARY ATTITUDES

While most missionaries have lovingly cared for the people they have served, sadly a not-uncommon frame of mind (and very un-Christlike) was that of a condescending paternalism. The following are examples of that attitude:

> "The torpor of mind in heathen countries is inconceivable to one who has all his life lived in a Christian land; almost

> nothing encourages me more than to hear a question asked that shows inquiry, that evinces a thought or a reflection. It is an evidence of life, a sign of resuscitation? I could willingly dispute all day long with them, but there is none who thinks enough to carry on a dispute, none who defends his religion or his customs. This remark may of course be subject to some limitation, but the fact remains, they generally and chiefly act because their ancestors did so."[93]

> The mind of a heathen is dark enough, -too dark to describe to you a long work of patience; and persevering labor is necessary before the fallow ground, with the luxuriant growth of vicious weeds now flourishing on it, can be upturned or made soft, even with usual success. Our sufficiency is of God. And if the hearts of sinners at home, in Christian America, are so obdurate, will it be surprising if the consciences of the heathen are scarred with a hot iron.[94]

As much as Raph came to love the Filipinos, he was a product of his age, and – especially early on - he partook of the patronizing language that accompanied the work of Europeans and Americans among the "uncivilized."

> This also is quite Filipino. They have learned through the years to obey and not to contradict their betters. The teachers we missionaries had of the Visayan language would be very slow to correct us if we insisted we were right. They would agree although they knew we were wrong. This obedience now is changing. The Hukbalahaps [communists] are learning differently. Let us hope that this clash of years of docile obedience and the newfound independence and self-determination may become properly adjusted without "frustration" as the psychologists might phrase it, due to the clash of conflicting "conditioned reflexes." The Filipino must become "integrated". Then all's well, we hope.[95]

CHAPTER 7

During the unfolding of his story, it will become apparent that as time went on, Raph's admiration for the people of the Philippines knew no bounds; and any negative paternalism was swallowed up in the most profound love of a father for his "children" in Christ, friends, students, patients, colleagues, and fellow believers.

CHAPTER 8

Early Medical Ministry in the Philippines

Life is short, and Art long; the crisis fleeting; experience perilous, and decision difficult. The physician must not only be prepared to do what is right himself, but also to make the patient, the attendants, and externals co-operate. —Hippocrates[96]

In the Baptist Missionary Magazine for April 1905, J. C. Robbins provided an article entitled "Capiz Spells "Opportunity," The Populous Province a Waving Harvest Field for Doctor and Evangelist." He wrote with enthusiasm about Raph's coming to the field.

> Our Baptist work is making steady progress and the coming of Dr. Thomas means much to us. At a reception given to him last night more than 200 of the principal people of the city, including the governor of the province, were here to greet him. Ever since Dr. Lerrigo left we have prayed for a doctor for this field, and now our hearts are full of thanksgiving. Our need for a physician was most urgent; for not only were the poor people without medical aid, but the missionaries and other Americans were helpless in case of accident or severe sickness. The

> doctor had not been in Capiz twenty-four hours before patients were here for treatment. As Ladislaw, one of our native preachers said the night that the doctor arrived: "We have everything that is needed now; on our right hand, the Bible with medicine for the soul; on our left hand, a physician with medicine for the body."[97]

His concluding paragraph clarifies the exciting "Opportunity" he is referring to:

> The outlook is most hopeful, and the word of the hour here, as all over the Philippine Islands, is " opportunity." Within a few days, delegations from nine towns and barrios have been here requesting visits from the missionary and the doctor. While it is true that Bishop Rooker was better received in this province than anywhere else in the islands, it is also true that the people, understanding that they are no longer compelled by the government to attend and support the Roman Catholic Church, are breaking away from it in large numbers. Now the responsibility rests with American Christians to say whether they shall drift into atheism or become true disciples of Jesus Christ.

THE CONDITION OF MEDICAL WORK WHEN THOMAS FIRST ARRIVED

Gleaming hospitals and surgical suites were not available to the early medical missionaries. In fact, the medical missionaries often travelled long miles under difficult conditions, but it was worth the effort! Charles W. Briggs, an American Baptist missionary in Panay and Negros during the time of Raph's arrival, authored a small book entitled *Missions in the Philippines*. He described the need as the doctors found it.

> Medical work has been found very helpful in removing prejudices and in commending the gospel to the Visayans. Dr. P. H. J. Lerrigo and Dr. R. C. Thomas have both been welcomed in towns that were otherwise apparently closed

> to mission work and influence. Both of these doctors testify to the sore need of a physician within the call of the missionaries themselves, in addition to the appalling need among the Visayans. Some of the large towns and their surrounding barrio district, comprising 50,000 or more inhabitants each, are entirely without a doctor. Nearly all of the Visayan people must bear their pains unaided, or suffer at the hands of quacks. The few Filipino doctors in the large centers know but little of compassion and do practically no charity practise. They generally refuse the most urgent case, unless an exorbitant price is forthcoming.
>
> In such conditions the available services of a skilled doctor, with the love of Christ and of men in his heart, is a boon that commends itself to many who would otherwise spurn the message which the missionary brings.[98]

A MEDICAL TREK WITH JOE ROBBINS

Raph loved to take trips into lesser known parts of the country, and to provide medical help to the people in a variety of forms of clinics. Raph described a district medical trip he took in the hills of Capiz with his comrade in adventure, Joe Robbins, in whose home he lived in 1905.

> Joe Robbins and I started off one morning in the gray of the dawn, as it is very hot out there, only eleven degrees above the Equator. We were astride two shaggy little ponies, tough little brutes that had a will of their own. Once conquered, however, they would obey. .... One of the [the bearers] had shouldered a teter pole of bamboo, with a baby organ balanced at one end and a heavy telescope basket of equal weight at the other, a burden that made me stagger, though accustomed myself to athletics. He was to carry this burden at the mincing gait they use, for twenty miles or so, through a tropical sun and receive a magnificent wage of forty centavos, or

twenty cents in our money at the end of the trail. (Yet some call the Filipino lazy!)

With our pith helmets in place and our white duck suits, with the thinnest of underwear under them, and sunglasses adjusted, we start off at a smart pace. We rattle across the dilapidated wooden bridge, passing the coral stone buildings used as jail and *municipio*, or town hall, and on past the rows of bamboo shacks lining the roadway, with here and there an upper class house of better material, two stories, with lower level appropriated by calesa, a little two wheeled carriage – and pony and *cochero*, or coachman. Such surroundings as these are typical of all the Philippines, except Manila, the only really large city. There, one sees plenty of up-to-date stone buildings and modern conditions.

We pass out into the country where we find coconut palm trees lining the roadside, and betel nut palms with their fruit hanging high like clusters of grapes (the native "chew"), and bamboos with their feathery tops and their green trunks creaking and grinding as the wind sways them together. Here, close to the road we pass a cemetery, with its bone pile of luckless tenants ousted from their snug concrete vaults: dispossessed because of unpaid rental. (This custom long since has been done away with, but then it was very conspicuous.)

Then we pass the dwellings by the roadside and come to an isolated shack in a palm grove. It is a typical bamboo shack of a peasant or two, with a thatched roof made of nipa palm and a bamboo ladder at the entrance. We clamber up this ladder, a makeshift stairway, and find the interior as simple as the exterior. It exhibits one or two rooms with split bamboo floor and almost no furniture. The natives sleep on a mat on the floor or on a bamboo bed about as hard. The kitchen, a small antechamber, has a stove, so called, which is nothing but a rough wooden table with two cobblestones to hold the pot for the rice, the staple food of the Oriental: and below them some inflammable material to avoid a conflagration. Overhead corn is drying on the cob and in the corner a large crate holds the rice. Little else, unless we include a favorite pig dozing in the corner. (Most of the animals remain below. They raise a disturbing medley in the morning if one wishes to sleep).

We are welcomed hospitably. Filipinos are a hospitable people. They are glad to give us a coconut or two for a long drink. The water of a green coconut is the traveler's joy, a draught free from germs and food as well as drink. It is thin and sweetish in taste, like maple sap: not milky as we know it over here: while the nut itself is about the consistency of soft butter. Natives spoon it out. We descend the slippery ladder and pass on to a native market place where the natives gather from all the countryside. It is there we have our best chance to meet them. We hold a clinic: pull teeth, distribute pills: let one of our preachers hold forth and then press on to the hills, our destination.

At a river, where the bridge is gone, we swim our ponies across. The trick here is to hold them by the tail, lest they turn on you with their forefeet. Later we enter the trails in the hills thru the cogon grass that towers above us even when on horseback. These narrow slits are hot and uncomfortable. Wild pigs are hunted there by the natives. One of them got a pig with his spear and was taken to court on some charge of infringing a law: but Joe Robbins was equal to the occasion and he appeared before the judge and had it adjusted aright, as the native seemed to have been discriminated against.

Finally, we topped a hill and there on top was a little bamboo chapel, with an American flag waving above it. (That interested me. A new era!) Nearby was a shack where we were to spend the night. We turned in on the hard bamboo floor (with our nets spread above us as the mosquitoes are "public enemy number one" out there)

> and were trying to sleep when we heard a murmur in the corner. We later found that one of our carriers had been trying to convert a mountaineer!
>
> The return trip was always a stampede as Robbins was a great home lover. His little Mary, a lovely child, was always there to greet him. (She now lies in the little cemetery out there, like a number of other missionaries' children, my own included.) Such tragedies make missionary life what it is. I emphasize the bright spots, but it would not be real life anywhere without some of the dark ones.

The toll on the health of missionaries in environments with unfamiliar sources of danger cannot be underestimated. Although bodies developed immunities, and tools were developed to avoid the dangers of everything from mosquitos to elephants, missionaries from the earliest centuries of the church were exposed to harsh conditions and dangers shared with the people they served, or uniquely experienced by them for the lack of antibodies necessary to fight off illness. Many missionaries to various countries worldwide died before they were able to truly begin their work. As Raph wrote concerning the death of little Mary, there have always been dark spots in the midst of the bright ones.

It is rightly said that there is no place safer than in the place where God wants you to be, but sometimes He lets his servants share the sufferings of those around them so that they will better understand, and so that the people watching them can see how Christians live in the face of adversity. Death in these situations is a cause of grief, but it is not unfair. To the believer, death is only the doorway to home in the presence of the One they serve.

THE DISPENSARY IN CAPIZ

Raph believed that the medical work was most appropriately settled in Capiz because the Catholic opposition there was less pronounced than elsewhere. In March of 1905, he wrote "I have fallen love with this field and am unspeakably grateful to the Lord for leading me here. Had He not guided me, I should not be here today ..."[99] Due to his excitement and devotion to this work, most of the letters Raph wrote to the mission and to supporters in his early years on the field were about the hospital ministry, building and staffing the hospital, and field personnel concerns.

In his autobiographical sketch, Raph wrote of the dispensary work he did in Capiz in his usual amusing terms; terms that today might be politically incorrect!

> I shared the downstairs of the Robbins home with the calesa and pony. There was a concrete floor and a bamboo chair for the patient, and one for myself. One day a youth dashed in very much excited to tell me that a young lady in a nearby shack could not open her mouth. This was a shocking state of affairs. Just what a young Filipino lady might do when she could not open her mouth was a question, for they are capable of talking a good deal when excited my nurses taught me later; but I was taking no chances, so I dashed along with him, catching up my medical bag ready for any emergency, and on arrival I found the whole family of relatives (or *parientes* as they call them) old, middle-aged and young in the room, smoky oil lamps streaming and the girl with woebegone expression and tight shut lips, sitting bolt upright on the bed. With the sang-froid of a newly graduated Medico, who had had experience at the Relief Station, the accident center in Boston, I wooed them all out, turned out the lights and in a few minutes she was chattering like a magpie: just a case of hysteria! BUT, soon after that a *tao* came to the dispensary saying his wife was ill and wishing me to call. He was calm and unruffled and I gathered from his demeanor that there was no hurry. On calling in the afternoon I found the wife deceased and already being prepared for burial. SUCH is the lack of discrimination a Medico encounters in that Far Eastern sphere!

This is the first time the word *tao* appears in a quote from Raph. The word *tao* means *person* in Tagalog. It will appear again as it became part of his permanent vocabulary. Those who have learned and regularly used a second language will often find that some words in that language come to mind more quickly than the same word in their first language.

Raph was not through with his ministry to the people after a long day. He frequently made night calls. The following serve as "heart-winning" examples.

> Once I remember Joe Robbins and I were hurried to care for a small operation at night in a shack, where he held the flaring torch outside, while I opened a badly abscessed breast. It was a weird scene, no doubt, for any bystanders, but when one considers the pain of such a trouble and how easily it is relieved by a simple thrust of a knife in trained hands, it must have made them wonder why American doctors had not come sooner. Another high experience was when I was called to remain several days and nights in the home of a young girl who had been almost fatally injured by an explosion in road repair. She lay for days on the floor, and I gave first aid and second aid until she recovered. The gratitude of the parents was touching. They are an affectionate race. They love their children. That is where a Medical Missionary has the advantage. He wins hearts.

In November of 1905, Raph wrote a note to Mrs. Huntington of the Woman's Board about the need for medical books, especially for the training of nurses and other medical people. He was convinced that that the field was ripe for medical mission. The American doctors were offering at reasonable prices the kind of care that was usually too expensive or unavailable for common people. The gratitude of the people resulted in an attitude of trust in these medical missionaries.

HOSPITALS

One of the ministries that Christians envisioned early in the development of the church was that of healing. This was appropriate because of the healing ministry of Jesus during his lifetime, and because of the sign-gift of healing given to the apostles in the early church. Despite the opposition of some Christians to medicine because of its pagan associations, by 350 A.D., the Bishop of Antioch dedicated some buildings devoted to the care of the sick.[100] The necessity of such facilities was clear; charity demanded it.

> The concept of the church's care of "the poor" was basic to the founding of the earliest hospitals. The hospital was, in origin and conception, a distinctively Christian institution, rooted in concepts of charity and philanthropy. There were no pre-Christian institutions in the ancient world that served the purpose that Christian hospitals were created to serve, that is, offering charitable aid, particularly health care, to those in need.[101]

In 1900, Dr. Andrew Hall, a pioneer missionary physician, together with Mrs. Hall, a nurse, with the Presbyterian Foreign Mission Board, began medical work in Iloilo. He established a small "bamboo hospital." The work was needed and effective. By 1906, a more permanent concrete building had been built. Raph had written of the advisability of having the hospital in Iloilo instead of at Jaro, and a response from Dr. Barbour made clear that this suggestion had already been made and was under consideration by the Board.

In 1907, because of an agreement between the Presbyterian board and the ABFMS, Dr. Thomas became the second physician on staff. The plan for union between the Board of Foreign Missions of the Presbyterian Church in the U.S.A. and the American Baptist Missionary Union involved the payment by ABMU of a half-interest in the hospital: $7000 gold.

In the December 1908, issue of the *Baptist Missionary Magazine*, Raph described the hospital in greater detail.

> The district for which the hospital is responsible is large. It draws upon an area of 5,000 square miles, including a population of three quarters of a million people. Transportation to this main center of the islands of Panay and Negros is good. At Iloilo, as the second town of importance in the archipelago, there is a continual interchange of commercial activity. The harbor teems with shipping and steam craft from all parts of the islands.

> At present, also, railroads are being projected which will bind this main center more closely to the outer districts. Manifestly the stream of humanity drifting toward the nucleus of this wide circuit is to increase daily, and upon vessel and upon railroad coach alike we may expect patients. To receive and treat the suffering in this great host is the privilege of our little hospital. It is a rare privilege, for it means so often not only the cure of bodies but as well the cure of souls. Evangelism has a large place in the institution. Testaments are in the wards, scripture texts are given out-patients, chapel services are held in the mornings and personal workers labor at the bedside. In every way a Christian atmosphere is maintained. When a China man was found the other day departing with his Testament clutched close to his breast, it meant something. When another patient immediately joined the church when he left the wards it meant more. And when Yap, dying, faintly whispered thrice as his final message to this world, "I am a Christian," it meant still more. All these and many other hints are the straws that point whither the wind blows. They mean that Christian service is not lost upon those who suffer. They mean that the heart of a man is softened by kindness, and that such a heart is good soil for the good seed. Results have demonstrated that souls of men are reached in a mission hospital, and the Philippines offer no exception to this rule.[102]

Raph provides the following observations of Iloilo City, the Capital of Iloilo Province, and the hospital ministry as he found it.

> This city, with Cebu, represents the only large ones in the Visayas. Iloilo then had a population of about forty thousand, though today it is much larger. It was a typical Philippine town, with Chino shops in large number; upperclass houses fairly plenty; and many shacks. Later a fire burned a thousand of them while I was there and many houses of better material replaced them. The Union Mission Hospital, where I was to labor for the next twenty years, off and on, was erected in 1905, shortly after I came

> down from Capiz. It was a wooden building, with painted matting (*siwali*) walls, very inflammable, a constant source of anxiety to us all. We had ropes in the rooms for patients to escape, but just how some of the weak ones and the corpulent ones ever could do it was hard to imagine. More than once I was routed out of bed in the middle of the night to rush to the hospital as a fire raged close by, while the head nurse rallied the nurses corps, bundled up patients and prepared for a hasty exit: but the wind always veered the other way and we escaped. We thanked the Lord for that.
>
> Across the road we had a fine concrete Nurses Home. It really was an attractive building. We had two American doctors and two American nurses and later fifty Filipino nurses. Dr. J. Andrew Hall, my colleague, the pioneer medical missionary on Panay, had already started a Nurses Training School in a bamboo hospital shack, before I came. He had three nurses there before even the Government had started its school for nurses. These nurses became proficient. One of them, as I mention later, went to the Massachusetts General Hospital in Boston for graduate study and made good. One of my classmates in the Medical School, a visiting man there, told me so.

In a letter written in July 1907, Raph praised the nurses and the nursing school enthusiastically. "The little nurses in the Nurses Training School, THE FIRST NURSES TRAINING SCHOOL IN THE PHILIPPINE ISLANDS, are doing nobly. . . Six of the eleven nurses are from Baptist territory...."

Then he added the following concerning the value of the hospital ministry for evangelism:

> "The evangelistic side of this Hospital service is one of the strongest features of the work. I had heard before that a mission hospital was a favorable environment for reaching the hearts of men, but never before did I realize the truth of this fact as I do at the present. The patients appear eager for the Bible and are eager for the truth."[103]

OBSERVATIONS CONCERNING FILIPINO COLLEAGUES AND PATIENTS AT THE HOSPITAL

A required activity for the new missionary is that of watching, listening, and learning as much as possible about the people and their culture. For Raph, a new missionary doctor with lots of experience in the States but none in the Philippine Islands, much of that learning took place in the hospital, among the patients.

> Inside the hospital we had a fine chance to study Filipino nature. ... Teaching the classes was fun, however, but once or twice we ran into a snag trying to maintain discipline. They had fights on occasion, and pulled hair vigorously. Once they even attempted a strike, but that dwindled. More of that later. It ended in "decapping" and that means disgrace. No Filipino can stand that. They are very adverse to being called names, or being made ridiculous. Call a Filipino a "*babuy*", or "pig", and he would be ready to knife you. They have their own cuss words" and their own "feelin's". Once one of our American nurses was teaching a class of nurses using the blackboard. She was cleaning it with a rag and remarked, "This is all linty." They were aghast. It seems that "*linti*" is the strongest cuss word they know.
>
> In the hospital in those early days, also, when English was not so familiar as it is now, when some of the Filipinos can talk in public as well or even better than some of us can, the nurses made some funny mistakes. For example, one said a patient had "meat growing on left neck: (Referring to a tumor). Another called a nostril a "nosetrail". Another nurse, who was serving Jacob's crackers to a patient reported he had: "Three pieces of Jacob". (Cannibalism at its worst). One of the office boys reported on a card a case history of a patient who had suffered from syncope, or a fainting spell that the patient was dizzy till it make him nonsense". Some of them called pills "balls" or "pieces". Another mistake of a nurse that was not so funny for the patient, who

> happened to be an American missionary, was to give her a tablespoonful of Camphorated Oil, one of the strongest of heart stimulants, and when I arrived, not knowing what had happened, I was amazed at her condition. Her pulse was racing and she was hopping all over the bed. I sent the nurse for the bottle from which she had supposed she had taken the Castor Oil prescribed! It was a dead giveaway, for the odor of camphor could be detected almost, but not quite, I hope, across the room, for nurses' mistakes have to be softpedaled, though of course they have to be reprimanded and disciplined. If a dangerous dose is given it is almost a fatal mistake for a nurse.

Everyone likes a good story about the mistakes missionaries make in learning their new language, and the difficulties of the people trying to communicate with them in English. As is obvious from these few selections, Raph had a million of them!

SURGERY

Raph had to put every aspect of his training – and imagination – into treating his patients in the Philippines! There is no better witness to the uniqueness of the surgeon's life in the Philippines in his place and time than Raph himself. The following is his graphic and enlightening description.

> But the life of a young surgeon carries a "punch" in it that ought to interest surgeons at home, many of whom live hum-drum lives. Out there the use of the scalpel is not limited by visiting men at a hospital at home, where the interne has little chance to operate. The majority of my nurses had lost their appendixes before so very long. Once I asked them in class how many had been operated. Most gladly responded their appendixes were missing, but one replied: "Not yet!" Evidently she expected to lose hers in due time. But more important cases were plentiful. The young doctor who suffered a ruptured intestine in Typhoid

> Fever; the boy gored by a carabao horn in the abdomen, who came in with intestines spilling out, whence a round worm crawled. These recovered safely. They were real jobs for a surgeon. Cases of gall bladder disease, intestinal anastomosis, fractures of all descriptions, including the skull, elephantiasis surgery and even a ruptured spleen gave plenty of excitement for a young surgeon. Gynecology was especially interesting, as I had graduated from the New York Lying In Hospital and had also taken special courses in maternity work in Vienna. Cataract operations also interested me: I was doing them without iridectomy. Another common ailment was stone in the bladder. We accumulated a large stone pile of which we were very proud. Another source of impressive surgery was the oft-repeated removal of ovarian cysts, that at times were of amazing size. Removal of such an encumbrance proved an excellent advertisement in the barrios whence the patients came. It was a marvelous method of "reducing" with which they had not been familiar: but it certainly helped to further our missionary work. Gratitude paved the way for the minister. Elephantiasis cases, unique for an Occidental, intrigued me also. To cut out huge slices of pork-like material was interesting to say the least. But to enumerate the various surgical opportunities would be impossible: suffice it to say we had to tackle everything that came along in endless variety. What a luxury for a really interested surgeon! And an added advantage was the indifference of the average *tao* to pain. The story was current for such a peasant whose great toe was cut off by a wagon wheel. He caught up with the wagon later carrying the toe in his hand! Can't speak with authority on this, but could easily believe it!

One of the major challenges for surgeries was the lack of certain surgical instruments that were available elsewhere. For inventive, industrious physicians, that lack was not a problem in Capiz:

> Dr. Lerrigo and I took off an arm together. He had returned to the field just before I left Capiz, and as we

had no surgical saw available, we sent to town and secured a buck saw blade, coiled it up and boiled it, and found it did the work very neatly.

AUTOPSIES

Among his "Snapshots" in his unpublished 1948 memoir, *"A Philippine Medical Missionary Harks Back,"* there is one about the early days of the Union Hospital where he worked with Dr. Hall:

> We had more liberty out there than doctors do at home. Autopsies were more easy to obtain. I noticed this especially as I remembered how the famous Dr. Mallory, who conducted a course in Pathology at the Boston City Hospital while I was there, to which young doctors flocked from Johns Hopkins and elsewhere, had to give it up for lack of "material" (the doctor's off-hand way of alluding to corpses). In the *Alle Gemainen Kranken Haus* in Vienna, I remember having seventeen bodies in one day. What a difference: for all of these were subject to investigation by students. An interesting snapshot that comes to my mind is the bewildering experience of my colleague Dr. Hall, when he performed one of his first autopsies there, rather I would say, it was a case of embalming for burial. He reported the body "turned a delicate shade of green." However, the wife, a Syrian, who had told him to "make a good job of it," seemed satisfied and he escaped. Would he have done so over here? Moreover, we were not pursued by shyster lawyers who bedevil unfortunate physicians in our own fair land on fracture and other potential court cases.

THE CONDITION OF LEPERS IN THE PHILIPPINES AND THEIR TREATMENT

Leprosy in the Philippines was a major challenge for the missionary and military doctors to tackle. Raph's account of the war against leprosy includes his description of one of the great generals of the war against leprosy, the Governor General of the Philippines, Leonard Wood (1860-1927). Governor General Leonard Wood was a colorful and highly decorated officer in the United States Army. He served as the White House Physician to President Cleveland; was a commander of The Rough Riders in Cuba, with Theodore Roosevelt as his second-in-command; was Military Governor in Cuba; and fought in the Philippines before being named Governor General. He was eventually made Army Chief of Staff by President Taft.

Dr. Wood, a medical doctor by training, was a leader possessing wisdom, discipline, and compassion.

> Before closing this chapter of my experience I must mention the Oriental scourge that has harassed humanity from Bible times. The cry of "Unclean! Unclean!" has trumpeted leprosy abroad throughout the world. When I first arrived in the Philippines lepers were scattered everywhere. When I rode my bicycle to Santa Barbara, eleven kilometers from Iloilo, I was accustomed to meet a whole flock of lepers on the way to beg in the marketplace. They were a grisly horde, some of them with great sores and missing fingers and toes, in all stages of decay. In later years they were segregated in the Island of Culion: but their welfare was really seriously considered when Governor General Wood took over.

Raph knew him well, and he considered him a friend. He described the General and his legacy in the Islands respectfully:

> General Wood used to visit our hospital regularly and he was most gracious. We had something in common as he too was a graduate of Harvard College and Medical School and an Interne at Boston City Hospital: but it was not that tie that brought him to our doors so often. It was a genuine concern for the sick. He was very democratic and home-spun in his attitude. He disliked too much official chaperonage and "sneaked around" with as little ostentation as possible, just like an ordinary mortal. The Filipino officials on the contrary like to put on "lots of

dog". Once, I remember how he abruptly asked one of these newly appointed Government officials: "How do you like your new Governor?" This was embarrassing for a "politico" and he squirmed. Evidently General Wood expected it would be so, for he grinned as he put the question. He had a great sense of humor. I knew both Governor Forbes, who visited the hospital also – he too being a Harvard man, we had something in common, and Governor Dwight Davis, famous for the Davis Cup events – who was on a Harvard tennis team with me, when he and Holcome Ward were National Doubles Champions. I liked them both, but General Wood really endeared himself to me, he was so great and yet so human. Little did I realize when I saw him limping into the hospital one day that it meant he was not long for this world. The story was that he had received a head injury in Cuba and a tumor developed on the brain.

When he came to Boston later and was operated on by Dr. Harvey Cushing, and the word came that he had crossed the line, there was sincere mourning in many hearts I am sure, as there was in my own. I felt I had lost a friend! He was truly a great man, and I believe he would have made a great President. But Wood and MacArthur were not politicians. Why is it necessary for a President of the United States to be a POLITICIAN? Perhaps that is our great mistake! In the Philippines General Wood was a success, though not appreciated by some of the Nationals, because he was a strict disciplinarian. I well remember when he addressed a YMCA group in Baguio. A Filipino leader, later Resident Commissioner to the United States (whose name I will not mention, though he is in power today) cut loose after Wood had left, criticizing his remarks severely. I hope this Filipino has changed his mind by this time, for General Wood did a much needed work of discipline when it was badly needed. Another Governor messed things up badly: Wood helped to correct them!

Raph further explained that after General Wood died, his friends launched the Leper project in his place. With a two-million-dollar budget raised through a major campaign, they established treatment centers in Cebu and Santa Barbara, near Iloilo. Culion was established as the main segregation colony, and the eyes of the Leprologists of the world were on the Philippines.

At Boston City Hospital, Raph met the pathologist, a Dr. Brinkerhoff. This doctor on staff at the Bureau of Science at Manila eventually became the Leprologist at Molokai. He was involved in the establishment of the project. Also, he apparently played a trick on Raph when he arrived in Manila that will bring back memories to those who travelled to Asia many years ago. In our early years in Japan, just after arriving in country, we referred to that process as our "amoeba exchange." At his hotel, Raph was told that the water was safe to drink. Brinkerhoff took him to his laboratory and showed Raph a drop of water under the microscope; it was full of amoeba! He gave Raph time "to develop the trouble," anticipating that he (Dr. Brinkerhoff) would be comforting Raph during his first illness in the Philippines. Thankfully, Raph never developed the expected outcome of drinking the dangerous water.

ALBERTO FRANCO, PREACHER FROM LA PAZ

Though Raph met Alberto in a later term, this is an appropriate place to include his story. Raph, this tender-hearted Medico, became "Dad" to many Filipinos. The story of Alberto Franco, whose body was marred by leprosy, but whose heart could not be turned away from God and others, is perhaps the most moving of their stories.

> A Filipino boy came to us in La Paz, where he lived, from the high school next door. He began to help me at the hospital and student dispensary, joined the student church I had established at Doane Hall, helped in the boy's dormitory, and then went to the States for a year at Gordon College. After that he graduated from Southern Baptist Seminary, and returned to the Philippines where he took a two-years course in Education, at the Silliman Institute, a Presbyterian College in Negros.

Raph did not mention that Albert was a first-year student at Iloilo High School when, while attending Miss Ellen Martien's Sunday School class, he "believed and accepted the Lord Jesus Christ as his personal Savior." Mrs. Doane paid the expenses of Alberto's travel to and from America, and he stayed and worked at the home of Mrs. Peabody to make money toward his tuitions. It should also be mentioned that Alberto taught for several years at Doane Evangelistic Institute.

> Then he married one of our best nurses, a girl who had done successful graduate work at the Massachusetts General Hospital in Boston. (My classmate, a visiting man there assured me of this). One day she saw a spot on his face and asked him to have his blood examined at the official medical bureau. (This is a final test). He did so and wrote me of it, as I was home at the time. He said "Dad", - he always called me Dad! I love him like a son! When I saw the report I could not talk. I took it home and handed it to my wife and she fell faint on the floor." It read POSITIVE FOR LEPROSY. They both knew all about it from hospital experience where I frequently had to report lepers, a sad office indeed, as in the early days there was no place for them to reside, until the boat came to take them to Culion, out to the prison, a noisome place. How some of them hated to go there. It was reported that one woman jumped overboard rather than land!
>
> At first they thought of concealing it, but that would not do as they were Christians and dared not infect others. There was but one course open, admission and segregation at Santa Barbara. Alberto left wife and home and his dear little girl with another child expected, whom he never might hold in his arms. He faced it manfully, and when in the Treatment Station he became so useful that now he is an integral part of it all. In fact, a recent letter tells us that an official reported that the morale of this leper station is the best in the world, and that Franco is responsible for it! What a tribute: Does anyone wonder why I love the Filipino!

> Last time I saw him, some years ago, I could not shake hands, as that was not permitted, but his poor leprosy scarred face was shining, and it has been ever since I am sure, for his letters are most cheerful. Friends over here have given him a building in which to teach the illiterate and carry on a church. They also have given him two dormitories, one for men and one for women. The latter he has just put up at the cost of several thousands of dollars, superintending the work himself. He also has befriended little orphan boys, taking them into his home, and has tried to initiate a project for an outside settlement for ex-lepers, who are feared by neighbors as ex-convicts are here at home. He also has retained a cheerfulness and sense of humor through it all. This was characteristic of him when I knew him as a boy. I remember one day when he was in high school and helping me at the student dispensary in La Paz, we saw a snake in the grass. I said: "Alberto, is the bite of that snake fatal?" He said: "No". Then I was a bit peeved at the idea of his knowing more about snakes than I did, as I had handled pans of them at the London Tropical School. I said: "How do you know?" He grinned and replied: "Because one of them bit me." Real Filipino logic!
>
> The best report of all that has come through recently is that Alberto has taken into his little Leper Church fifty-six new members this past year. That is marvelous under such circumstances. May God bless him.

And God did bless Alberto with a long, successful ministry. On January 29th, 1933, a group of thirteen in the Leper colony received baptism at his first service, and by the close of the year nineteen had been baptized. In his written testimony, Alberto explained that "In 1935, I became symptom-free of the disease and was to be released if I wanted to, but the Lord led me to decide to remain and I did so under his leading."[104]

CHAPTER 9

Evangelism, Church Planting, and Other Ministries under the American Baptist Foreign Mission Society

If any man serve me, let him follow me; and where I am, there shall also my servant be: if any man serve me, him will my Father honour. —John 12:26

EVANGELISM

Raph's hands were kept busy in medicine, but his heart was full of love for the people, and of a desire to personally take the gospel of Christ to them. Though later in his story, it is perhaps most appropriate at this point to quote his trilogy of articles concerning "The Evangelistic Program of a Medical Missionary." The articles were printed in the *Watchman Examiner* in September 1927.

> A missionary experience of more than twenty years has convinced me that a medical missionary in the Philippines must be an evangelist. Study of apostolic methods

> demonstrates the large place laymen had in the first missionary movement. Every means, such as education and healing, served the major end of evangelism.[105]

After describing the apostolic mission of Paul in the first century, Raph wrote of the possibility of the basic elements of Paul's ministry being practiced in the Philippines:

> Such a program is possible for the Philippines, and every missionary, lay as well as evangelistic, should have a share in its direct evangelism. With these convictions, equipped with both theological and medical education, I have fitted my life into such a program. The first year, 1904, medical mission touring the hills of Capiz Province, in Panay Island, followed by two years of complete charge as evangelistic missionary of a parish of about 50,000 in Iloilo Province, offered me evangelistic opportunity. Four chapels were built at important centers, and constructive work was begun. Later, when I became associated with the Union Mission Hospital in the city of Iloilo, student evangelism was undertaken, field evangelism was given a secondary place. Hospital duties were not neglected. The hospital prospered in every way, spiritually, medically, and financially, becoming self-supporting from the outset. This left opportunity for the evangelism outside the hospital, which in some form, is indispensable for any well balanced medical missionary program. In my case, experience as intercollegiate secretary of the Boston Young Men's Christian Association had prepared me for student work, and our proximity to the Iloilo high school opened the way for evangelism of the Government students.[106]

EDUCATION

When the Presbyterian missionaries arrived in Iloilo, they had planned to start a school. Princeton graduate Dr. David Hibbard started a small school in his home, but he was unable to obtain land because of the opposition of the Roman Catholics. They were offered property in Negros Oriental, and they opened their school, Silliman Institute there.[107]

As soon as the Baptists were settled into the area, Charles Briggs did his best to present the need for a school to Dr. T. S. Barbour during the latter's first trip to the Philippines in 1901. Dr. Barbour was convinced, and upon his return to the States he approached John D. Rockefeller about the need.

In the year of Raph's arrival and based upon receipt of a generous grant from Rockefeller to support educational work in the Philippines, plans were begun to develop an industrial school and a Bible institute in Jaro. "A gift of $12,000 bought a farm of seventy acres," and on that property two large school buildings and a house for the principal were built. Tools and supplies for the courses related to various trades were also purchased.[108] When Charles Briggs was on furlough in 1903, he met Mr. William O. Valentine, who had been serving in Burma, and encouraged him to transfer to the Philippines to become the administrator of the proposed school.[109]

Mr. Valentine, a graduate of Mansfield State Normal School (now Mansfield University of Pennsylvania) and Colgate Theological Seminary, after teaching for several years applied to the American Baptist Missionary Union and become the first principal of the two schools, both of which opened in 1905.[110]

Two years after the Jaro schools were opened, the enrollment had increased to nearly 300 students, all of them living and working on campus to earn their tuition and board. The emphasis was on giving financially depressed boys training in industrial fields. They gained experience in working and in studying the Bible at the school.[111]

Raph was asked to teach Bible there on occasion, and under the watchful eye of the evangelistic Mr. Valentine, a Christian atmosphere, a thorough knowledge of the Bible, and opportunities for Christian service were provided for the students at the school.[112]

CHURCH PLANTING

In the June 1906 issue of *The Baptist Missionary Magazine*, Raph wrote an article entitled "Signal Providences." In it, he described the steps taken to procure land for meeting places in his new field of Iloilo. The need for these meeting places was great, because the Protestants were "terrorized by the intense opposition encountered there, and so widely scattered that there appeared to be little hope of securing unity or church organization without some central meeting places."[113]

Several pieces of land were sought in Santa Barbara, but the local Roman Catholic priest bought up one, and frightened the owner of another to prevent the sale. The priest had bought up several pieces of land that appeared to be useful to the "Protestants." Raph believed that the Lord had kept the best piece of land for them since they were able to arrange for a permanent lease of a piece of land, at a reasonable price, adjacent to the large Roman Catholic cathedral! They also obtained a piece of land in a nearby town, Cabatuan, with a population of 21,000 people. The most influential members of the town had forbidden anyone in the town to sell land to the Protestants to build a chapel, but a Roman Catholic landowner proved willing to rent them a strategically located piece of land for three years at the price of fifty cents a month.

Raph had spent the evening looking at another piece of property, a corner lot that seemed perfect for the building of a permanent church. Across the street, another corner lot was even better, but it seemed unattainable. Before he returned to his lodging place, a preacher, Antonio, came to him to introduce a Chinese man who was the owner of the best corner lot. Antonio told Raph that the Chinese man wanted to become a Protestant believer. He was planning to move, and he wanted to sell his property for a chapel. Raph wrote that he had been content to start "First Baptist Church" on the second-best corner in town, but God had the best corner in mind for it.

He concluded the article with these words:

> The field is an exceedingly hostile one; the Protestants have been terrorized and scattered far and wide; opponents were openly and covertly doing all they could to shut us out of the territory, and yet in spite of all that the wit of man could invent we were guided to these spots and they were ours, without a struggle, within a little over twenty-four hours of the beginning of our quest. Such an evidence of the guiding presence of the Lord in this field is more inspiring than the privilege of worshipping in a cathedral. Our little bamboo chapel will be a trifling

affair in comparison with the massive stone building beside which it will stand; but we shall be satisfied if the Lord will tarry there.[114]

THE LAW

Because Raph did not tie memories together with dates – even years – in his brief collection of written recollections, it is difficult to be sure whether the following incident was in his first or later terms. Raph was pleased to be able to say that he had never had a "ticket" in the Philippines, though he was stopped twice by the same policeman (who let him go with a warning). He was summoned to appear in court. It happened like this:

> We had an American judge out there who was from the South and probably addicted to mint juleps and other stimulants, that irritated a naturally hot temper. He took it out on me in this way. The hospital telephone jingled and I heard a voice at the other end of the line of a manifestly angry person summoning me to come to court at once. I was to bring one of our nurses with me. I had already been approached by an ordinary barefooted *tao*, who had told me of this shortly before, and I was planning to take the girl over before long: but it seems that this barefooted *tao* was the SHERIFF. That was different. I saw no badge and did not realize his dignity! I at once called the nurse, who was wanted as a witness apparently in some case, and we reached the court room just as the judge and his attendants were coming in. He caught sight of me, turned red in the face and bristled like a terrier as he shouted: "Did you resist the Sheriff in summoning this witness to court?" Then, without taking a breath or giving me any chance to reply to explain my side of it, he bellowed again: "I fine you fifty dollars for contempt of court and you are in the hands of the Sheriff until it is paid" I replied that I did not have that amount (fifty pesos it was) on my person – and incidentally whoever heard of a missionary who did – and I requested the privilege of telephoning for it. This was granted and later the money came. Then I

> took my chair and sat down squarely in front of the judge and stared fixedly at him. He stood it for a time and then sent a boy down to say I could retire to the next room if I wished: but I refused. Perhaps I was again in "contempt of court," but I was enjoying it. Not so the judge. He fidgeted and apparently was ill at ease. Later I wrote him a letter explaining that I was not willing to allow it to stop there, but intended to write details of the incident. I knew it would hurt the work to leave it without any rebuttal. He wrote back, apologized to the court, and returned the money. Poor chap. It was just a fit of temper. Later he came to the hospital with a malignant disease of the throat. I sent him to Manila and they sent him home to die. It all was just one of the comical incidents to me, this court case – but this later experience for him was a real tragedy. He was not so very old, but did admit he smoked excessively, a common cause of cancer of the mouth.

FIRST FURLOUGH

At the end of his first term of service, Thomas boarded a ship bound for Seattle. He arrived there on November 15, 1907. His furlough was to prove to be an eventful one. In addition to his speaking engagements, in 1908 he arranged to take a course in the School of Tropical Medicine, in London, now known as the London School of Hygiene and Tropical Medicine. The school was founded by Sir Patrick Manson who had served as the Medical Advisor to the Colonial Office. The school opened its doors on October 2, 1899.

> And we surgeons had tropical diseases as well as the ordinary rank and file of occidental disease, most of which we had also. On furlough I . . . graduated from the London School of Tropical Medicine [[115]]: studied under Sir Patrick Manson and the rest of the celebrities over there. I discovered I was in the fluke region (a type of intestinal parasite), but a Medical Missionary has no time to become famous.[116]

CHAPTER 9

In the Summer of 1908, Raph also took a course in the New York Lying-In Hospital; excellent practice and preparation for deliveries and child-care!

An even more momentous event was to take place during that furlough During that same summer, a young woman was applying to the American Baptist Foreign Missionary Society (ABFMS) for acceptance as a missionary to the Philippines as Raphael's fiancée. Her name was Winifred Mae Cheney.

CHAPTER 10

Winifred

House and riches are the inheritance of fathers:
and a prudent wife is from the LORD.
—Proverbs 19:14

THE HIDDEN HEART OF A ROMANTIC

Since he was a true product of his generation and faith, little of his "love life" found its way into Raph's letters and his autobiographical sketch. Perhaps it would be helpful to present some of his thoughts regarding "the way of a man with a maid" from *The Medico*, the unpublished novel he attempted in later years.

Raph tells the story this way. The hero of the story, Dr. Thorne (of Harvard Medical school), had an arranged meeting with a college junior, Rose. She was excited to date a handsome doctor, with dreams of a future in a big American city with her husband a successful surgeon.

While he was dating Rose, the story goes, she introduced him to a young nurse named Elsa. That same evening a Filipino doctor plead for doctors to help the people of the Philippines, and Elsa beautifully sang "I'll go where you want me to go, dear Lord." It was in that meeting that Thorne realized God's will for him to go to the Philippines as a medical missionary.

So, he came to Rose one day with the news that he believed God was leading him to serve as a missionary in the Philippines. She could not agree and refused to go, but Thorne was convinced God wanted him to go. So, heartbroken, he sadly burned her letters and went on.

Sometime after his arrival in the Philippines, Thorne received news from his mission agency that a nurse was at last coming to help with the work. The nurse was Elsa. At first, their relationship was very professional, but in time they fell in love with each other. A jealous individual, who had observed the Americans and knew of their growing relationship, in hopes of finding a way to prevent them from falling in love, tricked Elsa into thinking that a skin problem she had was leprosy.

Unable to think of how to break this news to the man she loved, Elsa had said nothing to Thorne about the leprosy. In a moving scene in the story, in a small boat on the river, Thorne attempted to express his love to Elsa. Elsa's resistance to discussing their love confused Thorne, and it was then, to explain her resistance, that she admitted to him that she had leprosy, and that they could never be married.

As the next chapter begins, Elsa tries to explain to Thorne how she had come to know of her condition, and how she had tried her best not to break his heart with the news. The Doctor who had confirmed that her spot was leprosy was the very man who had launched the jealous plot to make her think that she was a leper, and by this to force her to eventually go to live with the lepers in Culien. She tells him for the first time that she was orphaned, and that the sale of the family home had made her rich. She wanted to give her whole fortune to support Thorne's hospital when she went away. The story continues:

> The man groaned aloud, but still he sat dazed. The whole picture was now coming to him, the heroic sacrifice of this girl, who had done more than die for him, she had lived for him, a life of brave comradeship while this horrible secret was here. He lived the whole thing over again, the life of self-restraint when she loved him all the time, but dared not show it because she thought he loved another girl, yes he saw it clearly now, idiot that he was not to have guessed that before . . . she had taken up her bitter cross to bear it bravely to the end. It all came to him now so

> clearly, and at the very moment that he had learned her real nature, her heroism, she was to be snatched from him.
>
> Suddenly his whole being flamed up within him. He burst out in a wild inarticulate cry. He clasped her in his arms and kissed her feverishly on the mouth, on the hair, again and again. He shuddered and held her close. She struggled to be free, then yielded to his caresses.
>
> "I wonder if it can be wrong?" she breathed. "No, Elsa", was the solemn response, "Our marriage is registered in Heaven, Darling. So help me God, never will I touch a woman as I now hold you." She sighed softly, and again he heard the whisper, "O Roger, I love you." Silently a chill wind blew over the water, and a dampness crept about them.

This is not the end of the story. The jealous doctor, in a fit of remorse, finally admits to Thorne that he had lied, and that the skin condition was another that is common in the Philippines. Thorne leads him to Christ and promises him his personal forgiveness. A friend of Thorne who had come into town, a specialist in diseases of the skin, examined Elsa the day before she was to leave for the leprosarium, and confirmed the fact that she did not have leprosy. Thorne's joy was boundless, and so was Elsa's!

The story demonstrates that under Raph's reserved, customary silence concerning personal things, there was a romantic, passionate heart; and so should every heart be that is passionately in love with God, the love of his life, and his fellow man.

This is the heart that found the maid whose last name was to become his.

WINIFRED CHENEY

Winifred was born July 14, 1881, in Ganges, Michigan. She described her Christian experience and the growth of her desire to serve the Lord in the Philippines in a letter accompanying her application to the ABMU[117]

"Rev. J.P. Haggard. Secretary ABMU

My dear Mr. Haggard – You have asked for my Christian experience.

I cannot name the day I accepted Christ as my Savior – I think I always believed in Him – although I did not accept him openly until the spring 1893.

I have been interested in the church or anything connected with the church always. So when Rev. Chas. Maxfield, who has known me from childhood, went to the Philippines and told me of the need there for Dom. Science teachers, I had a strong desire to go.

I felt, however, I needed more experience in teaching before leaving the states. Now, I believe you understand why I must go as I feel the Lord has led me in His own way.

Very Sincerely Yours,

Winifred M. Cheney"

By the time she had made application, Winifred had "entertained the desire" to become a foreign missionary for about five years. She had led many children in her Sunday School class to Christ. She gained the experience in teaching she felt she needed by teaching Manual Training and Domestic Sciences for 3 years at the High School in Lyons, NY, the same subjects in Houghton, Michigan for one year. She had also worked as the YMCA house secretary in Binghamton, NY, in 1904.[118]

One romantic, fascinating, and little-known glimpse of the early relationship of Raph and Winifred was recorded by Rev. Henry Munger, and later mentioned by Alfredo Franco Barile in his book *Recollections*.[119] Barile wrote:

In 1906, Rev. Henry Munger noted in his Chronology that when Rev. Lund came back after his furlough, he brought his daughter Elena with him. Miss Elena Lund

> knew the art of Swedish sloyd and brought her experience to the Jaro Industrial School. This system of woodcarving by hand was originated in Sweden and was introduced to the Filipino students by Miss Elena. One of Miss Lund's co-teachers in sloyd or industrial arts was Miss Winifred Cheney, a native of Kalamazoo, Michigan, USA. When Dr. Thomas started teaching part-time at the Jaro Industrial School, Bible Department in 1906, he fell in love with Miss Cheney . . .

It should be no surprise to mention that this romance was not revealed in any of Raph's formal correspondence.

CHAPTER 11

Raph and Winifred to the Philippines

Surely goodness and mercy shall follow me all the days of my life: and I will dwell in the house of the LORD for ever. —Psalm 23:6

Raphael and Winifred were married in Kalamazoo, Michigan, on September 16, 1908. Less than four months later, on January 5, 1909, the young couple sailed from New York on the beginning of their first voyage together to the Philippines. After their arrival, Raph was once again designated to the Union Hospital in Iloilo.

Major events and changes in names of various Baptist missionary ministries took place in the years from 1907 through 1918. For example, the American Baptist Missionary Union became the American Baptist Foreign Mission Society in 1910. This information is summarized in Appendix 2.

HOSPITAL MINISTRY RESUMED

The needs were great, and the number of patients receiving treatment from the gentle hands of the two physicians at the Union Hospital and at their clinics was large. The following excerpt is from the 1909 edition of the Annual Report of the American Baptist Missionary Union. It draws our attention to both the great need for and high valuation of the hospital ministries.

> Full consummation of the union with the Presbyterian mission in medical work, to which reference was made in the report of last year, and completion of the new hospital in Capiz are outstanding incidents in reports of this form of work. A half interest in the hospital erected by the Presbyterians in Iloilo has been purchased by the Union and Dr. R. C. Thomas, now returning to the Islands, has been designated to this work in conjunction with Dr. Hall of the Presbyterian Board. Two American and eleven Filipino nurses are associated with the physicians in this work. Reports of the past year indicate that the normal capacity of the hospital, thirty patients, has been proved somewhat elastic, not less than forty-four being accommodated at one time. The hospital has already won a place for itself among the people of all classes, and with two physicians in residence will be able to render greatly increased service. The work of building at Capiz, while in charge of a responsible contractor, has naturally made considerable demand upon the time of Dr. Lerrigo. He reports nevertheless a very considerable increase in the number of treatments. An additional burden assumed at the request of the civil authorities was that of oversight of a temporary hospital established during the epidemic of cholera.[120]

Raph and Dr. Hall so appreciated the help they received from their hospital staff, especially their faithful nurses. Though written a few years later, the following description by Amanda Klein, who was working in the hospital during Raph's second term, gives a taste of the hospital ministry from the perspective of an American nurse who worked in the Union Hospital:

> Among our patients are included the rich and poor of many nationalities. We have the distinction of being the

> first Mission Hospital in the islands. Our training school for nurses was two years in advance of the government one in Manila and one year ahead of St. Paul's Hospital in Manila. Our staff consists of two American doctors and two American nurses; the Presbyterians and Baptists are in the union. The training schools for nurses have been standardized and only women who are ready at least for high school can enter training. In our pioneer days some of our nurses were only first and second grade girls, so you can imagine the task that was ours and you would be amazed at the things wrought by eternal vigilance. The Filipina nurse is gentle, kind, patient, ambitious and untiring in her efforts and service. ... All who have read other articles on nursing in mission stations know that many of the cures here are little short of miracles to the humble sick poor.[121]

Staffing was always an issue at the hospital, and the recruitment of missionary nurses was crucial. Raph had given some thought as to the type of woman who would be ideal for the work of a missionary nurse. Here is the list of qualifications he prepared for the Mission:

1) Robust physique
2) Missionary spirit
3) Youth – under 30, if possible, to better grasp the language
4) Reticence concerning hospital matters outside of the hospital
5) Education, college training, if possible, ability to teach (Training school must be a powerful evangelistic agency)
6) Capacity to manage, superintend . . . and train, rather than devotion to nursing herself.
7) (unexpressed) ... the less likely of marrying, the more likely of her being desirable.

Though the language Raph used in point 7 will seem odd, he must have meant that one aspect of a nurse that would make her more desirable for the job would be her being less likely to leave it for marriage.

HINTS CONCERNING MISSING MISSIONARY COOPERATION

Dr. Barbour from the Mission had visited the field in 1909, and after his return he wrote to Raph about two missionaries whose incompatibility had caused Raph and the rest of the missionary team to feel that it was inadvisable for them to work together. One of them asked about the possibility of working alone, with no responsibility in the Mission Conference (the leadership team on the field). This kind of incompatibility may seem surprising to people who assume that those who have committed themselves to serve the people of, say, the Philippines, should also be good at serving each other in Christ. Sadly, though this would be ideal, and it is what Christ would want, that kind of unity and cooperation is not always found among missionary colleagues. They are, after all, humans – made children of God by the grace of God – and subject to single-mindedness, narrow-mindedness, jealousy, and inconsistency in spirituality and lovingkindness.

Problems that develop early on can be the result of unchecked culture shock, or transition stress. This reaction to the changes and stresses involved in taking on a new culture can be severe. One hundred years ago, there was little understanding of the prevalence and destructiveness of this complex of problems. In other cases of incompatibility, it is not cultural adjustment that is the problem; rather, it results from deep personality differences, unwillingness to compromise, and failure to love selflessly and fervently.

Raph mentioned to Dr. Barbour that four individuals had spoken of the possibility of resignation, and he personally "felt how inevitably trouble seemed to be coming to this mission. You [Dr. Barbour] speak of establishing brotherly relationships and a spirit of mutual cooperation, but much as I long for it, I do not see the light ahead."[122]

MINISTRY OPPORTUNITIES, 1909 THROUGH 1911

In his second term, Raph's ministry energies outside the hospital were divided between exploration, traveling dispensaries, evangelistic outreaches, supporting church planting efforts, and field administration issues. Quite enough for the average person, but Raph was not average. Ministry to students began to grow as a priority in his mind.

In December of 1910, Raph wrote a beautiful description to his supporters of a lively, lovely Christmas celebration in Iloilo:

> Service at Pavin chapel [a small school building they hope will become a church building] – at dark – lanterns twinkling, stars bright overhead and clustered thickly. It seems as though they were brighter and more plentiful than at home. A stand of bamboo set up. Paper dangling. Young speakers punching the air. Between recitations & Scripture verses were songs, and very good ones indeed! The Filipino loves music, and is capable of holding a tune when some from other lands might lose it. Santa Clause was also there to give out gifts to the children. The best gift of all was the glad tidings we hope will be prized by these humble villagers.[123]

In a prayer letter at the beginning of June, Raph described a communion and baptism in the river at the church of Santa Barbara. Seven gave their testimonies and were baptized in the river, including a blind woman. They sang hymns and the account of the baptism of our Lord was read from the Visayan Testament. Some on the shore called out negative comments about the events of the baptism, but most were respectful, and Raph hoped that some "took them into their hearts to ponder upon them."

Also in June, Raph wrote to Dr. Barbour about the dormitory at Capiz (the Iloilo dormitory). He wrote that Mr. Maxfield had gone to Bacolod, and the work of the dormitory had been turned over to him. Raph was "very enthusiastic." He added that

> work among the students is, to my way of thinking, about the most promising line of work open to us. While the Presby[terian]s have a better building, and theirs is only a bamboo hut, it is in a better location and I am hoping for improvement of quarters when the Board can approve.[124]

In the Ninety-fifth Annual Report of the American Baptist Missionary Union (1909), a lengthy description is given of the dormitories and girls' schools in the Philippines. It was the success of these ministries to boys and girls that encouraged Raph to devote himself more to their development in Iloilo.

DORMITORIES AND GIRLS' SCHOOLS

The dormitories for students attending the Rizal Institute, or government high school, in Bacolod report a year of marked success, accommodations for both boys and girls being taxed to their utmost capacity. The great significance of this work lies in the fact that in these dormitories, conducted under Christian influences, the boys and girls are introduced to a social life and atmosphere wholly unlike anything that most of them have known in their previous environment of idleness, suspicion and immorality. The new conditions awaken a quick response in these impressionable young people. Dr. Steinmetz writes that a gentleman in Bacolod remarked to him recently that the young people in the mission dormitories have a very different appearance from the other students.

The new manliness and womanliness developing within is manifesting itself not only in the faces but in the conduct and intellectual attainments of the pupils. Six of the boys have been baptized and others would come but for the opposition of parents. A dormitory of similar character has been maintained during the year by Mr. Briggs for forty-one boys attending public school in Iloilo. The missionary spends two evenings each week with the boys in Bible study, songs and prayer, and the students regularly attend Protestant services in Jaro or Iloilo on Sunday.

Girls' Schools

The home school in Capiz, conducted by Miss Suman, celebrated its entrance into the new building with a very happy Christmas festival. Originating in the desire to care for a few homeless little girls, the service of the school has broadened until quite a number of children, including

> both girls and boys, are provided with a Christian home and are given regular instruction preparing them to enter the public schools. A woman's Bible training school was opened in Jaro in the middle of June under the direction of Miss A. V. Johnson. Of fifty young women who presented themselves, coming from seventeen different towns and barrios, forty remained until the school closed in December. Plans are now being perfected by the Woman's Society of the West for the opening of a school for girls of the higher class in Iloilo under the care of Miss Bissinger. Mrs. Steinmetz, aided by three native teachers, has continued through the year the successful kindergarten established in Bacolod, an attendance of fifty-five being reported.[125]

AN INCIDENT IN NEGROS

Travel to meet new people, to have new adventures, and to share the gospel, as we have seen, were a regular part of Raph's life in the Philippines – as were erupting volcanos, typhoons, mud-flows, and religious fanatics! This adventure involves the latter.

> One outstanding incident in Negros, a part of my medical district where I toured frequently, concerned Papa Isio, a ladrone leader who was said to have a thousand adherents in the Canlaon district. That is a volcano, said to be 8000 feet high, I understand. We climbed it, up a rough mountain trail, and felt sure it was high enough anyway. They caught Papa Isio, some said it was done by a ruse that covered a lie, and he was imprisoned in Bacold, the Capital of the Province. I saw him there and he was a sad looking little vagabond, wizened up, with ferrety eyes and a mean face. The story was that he had almost supernatural influence with the ignorant mountaineers, naming one of his followers "God" and creating a smudge with a damp fire, from which this white robed figure would emerge. It was this control that kept those wild bandits in check. But now he was trapped. His day was over. One of the

> tenientes, an American lieutenant, gave me the knife of Valentin Guilleromo, the chief lieutenant of Isio. It was an ugly looking weapon, no doubt with a sordid tale of murder and treachery if it could have spoken. It joined my arsenal-the attic abounds in such souvenirs, but where this one is now I do not know: the memory lingers![126]

A life lived well among generous people will often result in an "arsenal" in the attic, on the walls, or in the basement. Frequent moving results in the unloading of some of those treasures along the way.

A PRECIOUS GIFT AND PAIN

Concerned about his wife, Raph wrote to Dr. Barbour on February 22, 1910, telling him that they needed to leave their present house. He emphasized that it was "urgent" since the house was "a serious menace to health." The reply was that there were no funds for a mission house, so they remained where they were for the time being. Later, the Board prompted the Philippine Property Committee to make money available from their emergency fund to build a kitchen and porch on the Thomases' house in September of 1910.

The couple was blessed with the birth of a lovely daughter, Winifred Eastman Thomas, on July 3, 1911. In an August prayer letter, Raph wrote, "One small event, chiefly of importance to ourselves, and perhaps too personal a matter to mention in a general letter, is the addition to the mission force a small girl, to be known in the future as Winifred ("Winky") Eastman Thomas. We trust she will be a good missionary."

This happy event was not an unmixed blessing, however. Raph wrote to Dr. Barbour of the circumstances of the birth and the impact on his wife, Winifred:

> You probably heard of the birth of our child Winifred Eastman Thomas. It was a great joy to us, but with the great joy came great sorrow as well, for Mrs. Thomas has been in the hospital ever since. The baby was born July 3rd, and we feel it will be weeks yet before Mrs. Thomas will be able to leave the hospital. I am a physician and not

> easily frightened – but I am frank to say that I regard it a miracle that my wife escaped with her life. She was at death's door . . . a scarcely perceptible pulse, and black vomit. We both believe the crisis was passed because of prayer.[127]

Because Winifred's health continued to deteriorate, plans were begun for a long health cure for Mrs. Thomas, and a study trip for Raph, in Europe.[128] Raph's estimates for the cost of the trip are amusing today. He figured that they would spend 6 to 8 months in Europe, hopefully living on $3.50 a day. His greatest concern was that Winifred would receive adequate medical care. Raph's final words in the August letter are worth remembering: "We both feel that the Lord has been very good to us, better than our deserts, and we are trusting Him to bring back renewed health and vigor for further service."[129]

A TRIP FOR HEALTH AND STUDY

They sailed from Iloilo on February 6, 1912, and journeyed through Hong Kong, arriving in Berlin, Germany on March 17. Raph was involved in study and medical practice there and enjoyed a visit from his parents. Two and one-half months were spent in medical study in Vienna, Austria.

In 1910, the first edition of the *Manual of Tropical Medicine* by Aldo Castellani and Albert J. Chalmers, became available, and it was undoubtedly a textbook used by Raph at some point in his studies and/or work in the Philippines. In the 1919 Third Edition of that text, the authors attributed the rise of tropical medicine to several factors, including increased information flowing in from exploration of the tropics and more effective use of the tool of the microscope to identify causes of disease. The Philippine Islands were listed in the Tropical Zone, which runs in a band above and below the equator. The introductory chapters include descriptions of the effects of the temperature and humidity of the Tropical Zone, including influences on temperature, respiration, blood, digestion, growth and skin.[130] Before describing the causes, pathology, symptomology, prognosis, diagnosis, treatment, and prophylaxis of different types of tropical diseases, the authors reminded the readers that various populations serve as sources of the diseases. There are those who are true indigenous natives, those who are immigrants, and those who are descendants of an amalgamation of both groups.[131]

In addition to those diseases that arose within the environment and ecosystem of the Philippines, how many of the diseases treated by Raph and other physicians in the Philippines were introduced by Europeans and Americans? He undoubtedly would have learned much about, and added plenty to, the discussion of tropical medicine during those two and one-half months.

This became one of the most memorable of seven furlough trips during which Raph attended clinics worldwide, then returned to the hospital to practice the new knowledge he had on behalf of the people of Iloilo, and of Negros Province, where he set up infirmaries.

The family then spent three months in Barcelona, Spain, in language study. In his letters during this period of absence, it was apparent that the needs of the work in the Philippines were on his mind. Constant mention is made of the need to send a nurse to Iloilo to relieve Miss Klein. On December 9, 1912, with Mrs. Thomas feeling much better but the baby ill, the family of three arrived in the United States.

RETURN TO THE PHILIPPINES

Six months later, their time away from the field came to an end. Mrs. Thomas was much improved. The family visited the West Coast, and then sailed from San Francisco on June 26, 1913. Their arrival at Iloilo was a month later, on July 28, 1913. Raph jumped into the work right away.

In November, having had a chance to see the changes that had taken place in his absence, Raph wrote a letter to their supporters in which he expressed his belief that the progress made in the development of the Philippines had been "satisfactory." He wrote

> Americans are likely to expect too much of these Oriental people in the way of immediate development. They have done very well, considering the short time of American occupation and we are optimistic for the future if sufficient time is given for education and evangelism, before the

> reins of government are given into their own hands. … The best parts of Americanism, a pure Christianity, is being tendered to these people who have known no such blessing in the past. . . . Without this feature [evangelism] we would have little confidence of success of this or any other nation.[132]

Raph's comments were not intended to be disparaging of the Filipinos. While the influences of the American occupation of the Philippines were certainly not all positive, Raph's statement was intended to emphasize his enthusiasm concerning the growing positive influences of education and evangelism on the people of the Philippines.

He was particularly excited about the work in the dormitories, especially because the students were busily using them! Here is how he described the situation in the dormitories in Iloilo, Bacolod, and Capiz:

> Practically the work has been full of promise. The students patronize the dormitories and many of them have been reached by the Gospel. Not as many have made an open confession and been baptized, because of the difficulty of breaking away from established systems, and because of adverse influence of parents and friends, but the number who have come out openly has been satisfactory "first fruits."[133]

Both difficulties Raph describes in this letter are among the most understandable and troublesome of those experienced in cultures where religious traditions are deeply engrained, and where group and family ties are tight. It is easy to understand that Roman Catholic opposition to "Protestant missionary work" would be a continual source of tension. But for those who are comfortably settled in the practical freedoms of choice and movement in an individualistic society, it is more difficult to understand the pressures faced by children, and even adults, who "stick out" and become "nails that must be hammered down" through expressing to family and friends their faith in Jesus Christ and their willingness to publicly testify of that faith through baptism.

WINIFRED "FALLS ASLEEP" IN JESUS

Mysteriously, between their return to the field and December 22, 1913, Winifred's health deteriorated once again. With no further indication as to its cause, Raph wrote to Dr. Franklin, the Foreign Secretary who replaced Dr. Barbour, of the death of his "beloved wife on December twenty second." He wrote,

> I was unwilling for a cablegram to be sent, lest by any mischance the news should reach her mother before I could write here. As she is sensitively organized, I feared the shock for her.
>
> It is my ambition to have a memorial building erected in her honor, and to perpetuate her work, which she was carrying on with me among the students, and mean to put the matter before the conference at once. If they see fit to grant me the privilege of securing funds for such a building (if the Board consents) I shall count it my greatest privilege to set about it.
>
> The blow has been a crushing one, but God is good, and His loving hand is sustaining me. . . . It is a sad Christmas for me, but for others I pray it may be a happy one. Very sincerely yours, Raphael C. Thomas."[134]

Mr. Huntington, the Assistant Secretary of the ABFMS. sent a letter to Raph in 1914, containing the following resolution:

> That the Board of Managers have learned with deepest sorrow of the death after a brief illness in Iloilo of the wife of Rev. R. C. Thomas, MD. Although her service on the field had been comparatively brief, Mrs. Thomas had endeared herself to the members of the missionary company and had already manifested her deep interest in missionary work by active and helpful participation in the work in Iloilo, particularly the dormitory work for students. The members of the Board and the officers at

> the Rooms desire to express to Dr. Thomas their heartfelt and brotherly sympathy in view of his great loss.[135]

Years later, writing to Winifred's mother about some items he had sent from the Philippines to her and to his daughter, Raph revealed some of the inner thoughts about his first wife that had remained with him through the years:

> It seems only yesterday when her sweet spirit went to be with Jesus. What a tie that is to bind us to the other Land. I am sure this will be a treasure for Winifred [Winky] to see. . . . Now I think that time has made it easier for you and it will be not so hard to stand the emotional strain of awakened memories. For me they are sweet and tender. But I know there is always a bitter with the sweet of such memories if we look backward rather than forward. It is the forward look that makes them the sweetest.[136]

In January 1914, the conference approved Raph's request, and they asked the Board to permit him to use 25,000 pesos ($12,500 in U.S. currency) from friends for the erection of a dormitory for boys at the Iloilo High School. This was already on the list of approved projects, but they moved it up the list. Raph explained that the dormitory work "enables us to take advantage of the thorough educational system established by our government, by evangelizing and regenerating the youth the government is educating." Winifred had been working with him in this ministry, and through making it [the girl's dormitory] a memorial, he would "ever have the solace of feeling that she was still working with" [him].

Two further school related issues were on Raph's mind at the beginning of 1914. He championed the establishment, on property with a house already present, a Bible school "of their own," supervised by the Board's own missionaries. In addition, in support of his friend and cherished colleague, Raph wrote to Dr. Franklin that Mr. Valentine's record argued for him not to be replaced in the Jaro school.

The question of how long Raph would have remained in the Philippines after the death of his wife, Winifred, is impossible to know, since another event intervened to accelerate the decision-making process. A telegram from E. S. Harrington to Baptist Foreign Mission Rooms, dated February 28, 1914, described Raph's father as being seriously ill. Harrington asked if the Board was willing to have Raphael return to the States.[137] Secretary Franklin replied that would take Thomas five or six weeks to reach Boston. He stated that the Board would doubtless approve a leave of absence if Raph should believe it advisable, but that he (Franklin) did not have the authority to promise payment of the expenses of the journey. He suggested that the Board would probably expect Thomas to bear the cost of the journey because of his recent return to Philippines.[138]

Raph's brother, Leo, corresponded diligently with Dr. Franklin concerning the condition of their father in March 1914. He reminded Dr. Franklin of an agreement Raph had made with Dr. Barbour that Raph would be permitted to return to the States if his father became seriously ill. Now, with a motherless baby, it was necessary for him to return sooner. He mentioned that Raph's colleague in the hospital, Dr. Hall, had hinted that the hospital could be run as a "one man" job. Leo felt that Raph "needs more toning up" than he was able to do during his last furlough. In fact, Leo wrote, "I believe he is homesick and remaining in the spot where he has lost his young wife depresses him." Leo perceptively commented that "He is not one to run from duty nor to think of himself when the work may suffer."

In illustration of that last point, Raph wrote on the March 23 that he was back to Capiz for the first time in 8 years. He was performing operations on the way, and on the way back. He "rode with the doctor on his motorcycle . . . not at all like riding on a carabao."

CHAPTER 12

Ministry in America

My soul melteth for heaviness: strengthen
thou me according unto thy word.
—Psalm 119:28

Despite some improvement in his father's condition, and the certainty that his travel expenses would not be covered, Raphael decided that he would sail on the S.S. Persia, leaving Manila April 30 and arriving in San Francisco on May 24. In his correspondence with Dr. Franklin, he wanted to make it clear that his decision was made after conferring with Dr. Hall, with his full approval, and with that of the other missionaries.

After the safe arrival of Raph and his daughter, little Winifred, in Port Chester, New York, he wrote a letter to Dr. Franklin in which he stated that his greatest concerns were that the Board would meet the travel expenses of his child, and that they would permit his name to stay on the roster of the mission even if it becomes necessary for him to engage in some other calling than that of a missionary for a time.[139]

REPORT AT THE JUDSON CENTENNIAL

Raph was asked to give a report of the ministry in the Philippine Islands, on June 24 and 25, in an address at the ABFMS Centennial celebration of the life and ministry of Adoniram Judson, missionary to Burma. This address is perhaps even more powerful because of the experiences that had preceded his departure from the Philippines, and the prospect of an extended period before his return to serve there. Only those who have returned home from years of labor among people they have come to love deeply can truly understand the burden they bring home with them, the intense desire to communicate to others as much as possible the needs of those people, and the thirst for news of the works of God among them, that fill their hearts. Raph began with words that sharply clarified the freshness of the scenes of his address in his own mind:

> I have just landed from the archipelago, ten thousand miles away, and though my heart is full, it is difficult for me in five minutes to give you the keynote of the Philippine situation.

He proceeded to give several examples of subjects concerning which he might speak: the medical work in the 60-bed hospital in Iloilo; the hospital in Capiz; the pathos of the medical work; and tours into the mountain districts. The illustrations of each of these must have held the attention of his audience, all of them invested in prayer for missions, in a powerful grip.

> I could perhaps describe the parting of old Si Loy, who had come down from the hills ill with a fatal malady, and as I sat by his bedside and saw the smile which illuminated his countenance in that last hour, it was a lesson concerning the value of medical missions that was worth while . . . if for no other reason than to allow that saint to depart to his home under such conditions.
>
> The little child who came into my office not long ago, a child of four or five years perhaps, totally blind because some kind friend had put some medicament into the eyes to cure some other disease and destroyed her sight forever. It was a lifelong lesson to me of the results of ignorance from merely a medical point of view in those far-away lands.

> A picture stands out before me now of one of those little islands in a distant part of Capiz, where an old, old man had been waiting for ninety years – he said he was ninety years of age and he certainly looked it – waiting at ninety years for the promise of Israel, and when we witnessed his confession it was one of the most beautiful that I have ever heard – complete, simple, and satisfying. And when he was buried in baptism in a little rocky chalice in the side of a hill with a view looking over the plain with its palms and its rice-fields, and gathered about . . . were those simple mountain people, I said to myself, "This is a triumph."

Raph also made a case for what he declared to be the "most important of all the issues in the Philippines right now: the education of the leadership of those people.

> Educated, evangelized, regenerated leaders is the demand of the Philippines to-day, and I am exceedingly optimistic concerning the work of our government in that country if the church will do her part in raising up leaders who have integrity and ability, who are Christ's men. If such leadership is not raised up I am exceedingly pessimistic concerning the future of the Philippine Islands.

He spoke of the character of the young men who need to be prepared to serve Christ and their country, giving more than one example, but the most moving is the last: Ilario Castilio.

> He was a blind boy. He passed about the streets of Capiz groping his way, but he was led to Jesus Christ when his soul was illuminated with the gospel. His first effort was not to lead one to Christ who was his superior, but he went to the poorest one he could find, a poor boy who was crawling about the streets, a cripple. He led him to Christ and they were both buried in baptism in the blue waters of the bay. It was a beautiful scene – I can never forget it – the blind boy and the cripple, hand in hand, as they passed into the waters and were baptized in the name of Christ. The work did not stop there. He went to the

> Bible school, and Mr. Lunt, the leader of the school, said he had more brains than all of the rest of the students put together. I loved to look at his face as he sang the hymns. He knew them by heart, his memory was so retentive. I heard him preach one of his first sermons; the text was suggestive – "I am the way, the truth, and the life." He said, "Jesus Christ is the only one who has ever been to heaven, consequently he is the only one who knows the way." How beautiful a tribute from a blind boy concerning the great guide, Jesus Christ! The last I heard of him, he was doing itinerant work in the hills, being led by the hand and preaching the gospel of Jesus. If a blind boy, a mere Filipino, can do that, what is possible for these bright young men who are being educated in the high schools, the secondary schools, and colleges if we but give them the gospel of Jesus Christ in its power to conquer?[140]

What was the impact of this message? What is the impact of any message from the heart of a man or woman of God who has seen God work in the lives of others to change them forever? Often the result is that others finally see the needs the mission of God is intended to meet, and they cannot be restrained from giving themselves to God for any purpose He might have for them.

THE "OTHER CALLING"

That calling "other than being a missionary" that Raph had mentioned to Dr. Franklin, became two "callings." Both were offered him soon after his return to America.

The first was the call of The Second Avenue Baptist Church, of New York, extended to Raph to be their pastor beginning with the first Sunday in September 1914. His salary was to be $2300 a year, which would enable him to live and to help him support his parents. The district was a slum area, and he had a church of many nations. Fettler started a Russian church there; Italians, Poles, Hungarians and Estonians had their own congregations and pastors; and they had a Chinese Sunday School [which Raph believed to be the first one in New York].

Except for the Buffalo area, Raph's area for house visitation had one of the largest populations in New York State, and it was made up almost entirely of people of Jewish heritage and Roman Catholic Italians. He had passed the church many times while an intern at the New York Lying In Hospital and heard the outdoor preaching from the steps of the church. It was a large one, formerly attended by the Colgate family, before the area became a slum.[141] R.S. Pierce, a well-known outdoor preacher and chalk-talker in New York, had been at the church. Raphael's salary from the mission ceased at the beginning of September.[142]

In November, Raph proposed to Dr. Haggard the establishment of a training program for missionary doctors to better prepare them for medical work in other countries. He proposed that the school be established in the Parish house next door to the church, perhaps to be from held January through May. It would require a reliable physician and a trained nurse. Raph would take part. Diplomas would be given to those who complete the program. He mentioned that rooms could be sought for the attendees at the YMCA.

Haggard considered this a great plan meeting a great need, "but the all-important preliminary consideration is money" – and he felt confident Raph could not secure the funds. Sadly, even the best of proposals run aground under the assumption that God will not provide the needed resources. Raph suggested that the missionaries be queried about their thoughts concerning the need for such a school, but the ambitious project was not adopted.

During his ministry at Second Avenue Baptist Church, in 1915, Raph's beloved father passed away. Raph had always considered his father a role model, and he was thankful that he was able to be at the bedside of this great man when he died.

Years later, Raph described in his letter his attitude concerning the work at Second Avenue Baptist Church:

> I loved the work: I had a chance to do public speaking [and] the combination with medicine was ideal; the opportunity to work with so many nations was attractive for a missionary; the slums itself was right in line, as it was right close to the Bowery![143]

The second "calling" was as a physician, since he was also asked to be on the staff of St. Mark's Hospital,[144] across the street from the church. He was sought out by the two leading surgeons on the staff of the hospital, both graduates of Harvard.[145]

It was during this time of dual service in America that God brought the second Mrs. Thomas into his life. Her name was Norma.

CHAPTER 13

Norma and Her Unique Mother

Then shall the virgin rejoice in the dance, both young men and old together: for I will turn their mourning into joy, and will comfort them, and make them rejoice from their sorrow.
—Jeremiah 31:13

BIRTH AND FAMILY: THE ADVENTURE BEGINS

On June 1, 1883, Norma Rose Waterbury was born in Yercand, India. Her parents, Norman and Lucy Waterbury, were missionaries under the American Baptist Missionary Union. They had arrived in Madras on November 11, 1881. Norman made excellent progress in learning the Telegu language. After only three years of study, he took part in the development of the Telegu New Testament. Lucy thoroughly enjoyed interacting with women of all castes, and she became aware of the work of the Woman's Foreign Mission Society through the gifts they sent to help in the work in Madras and the surrounding villages. The couple had two children, Norma and Ernest.

Sadly, not long after Ernest's birth, Lucy was widowed in India. In a tribute to Mr. Waterbury, Rev. J. F. Burditt wrote the following in November of 1886:

> Only in April last, referring to the departure of some of our missionaries, he wrote me, "I have always wanted to complete ten years before furlough, but God alone knows the future." God has given him, much sooner than he planned, a never-ending furlough from all impediments and trials, and doubtless a still more glorious and blessed service. He did not "save his life" and so lose it." . . . His generous sympathy, his cheering words, his prayerful help, no longer present with us, every difficulty and discouragement seems so much greater, the loneliness of this wilderness so much more lonely . . . may [the Lord] grant speedily a new undershepherd for the bereft flock, and vouchsafe to the widow and the fatherless the consolations succor, and peace that we fain would, but are utterly powerless to impart.[146]

NORMA'S UNIQUE MOTHER

Because Lucy McGill Waterbury Peabody is to have an important role in the rest of this biography, it is vitally important that more of her story be told.

Lucy was born in Belmont, Kansas, on March 2, 1861, to William and Sarah Jane McGill. Her parents took Lucy's older brother Albert and her to Pittsford, New York. Her older brother died, and that created a greater bond in her heart to her younger siblings. When she was twelve, her family moved to Rochester, New York, where she attended high school.[147]

A classmate of Lucy in the No. 12 School wrote a delightful description of Lucy McGill as a new student there when they were in their last year of school before high school. Here is a part of that description:

> One day came a new girl! And such a girl! At 15, Lucy McGill was easy to look at, and particularly attractive as she was directed to seat near mine. I well remember her pretty clothes. ... the black velvet bands ... added greatly to her red cheeks, and long black curls. We soon became fast friends as we had the same enthusiasm for passing, and a congenial sense of humor.[148]

The teacher was apparently in a bad mood that day. When he came back and found out that a change had been made to a lesson sentence on the board, he told the person or persons responsible for doing it to stay after school. Lucy, her new friend, and a boy in the class had been complicit; they came forward, and were expelled! Mrs. McGill was no comfort to the girls when they came to explain what had happened. Lucy was scolded and told that she was to go and apologize the next day. Her friend's family had discovered that the teacher had already repented of his action and asked the principal to let them back in the school; so, they laughed hysterically at the girls' tears. The two apparently eventually went to high school together, and her friend confessed that, since they sat near each other, "all I recall of our high school days was an unending session of whispering!" Evidently, they learned something for they both graduated. They had to read their final essays to a group. Lucy wrote on Adam Smith's *Wealth of Nations.*

Her friend's parents adored Lucy, and while she was teaching at the School for the Deaf (where the father was a member of the Board) she was frequently invited to stay at their home. It was during that time that she fell in love with her Sunday School teacher, Norman Waterbury, who already had missions on his mind.

In 1886, after Norman's death, Lucy returned to the United States and settled in Rochester, New York. She privately taught deaf children in her home, and received some help from her sister-in-law, Mary Waterbury.

The Woman's Foreign Missionary Society invited Lucy to speak on foreign missions at a meeting in which Helen Barrett Montgomery also spoke concerning home missions. Both were "scared" though "there were only women in the noon meetings." Later, at a Board meeting in Scranton, Pennsylvania, Mrs. Gates, the Secretary of the Woman's Board insisted that Lucy give up teaching to join her as Assistant Secretary of the WFMS. The Board backed up that request in 1889, and she and the children moved to Boston. Later she became the Secretary, and eventually was made the Chairman of the Literature Department of the WFMS. Though she remained extremely active with the Woman's Foreign Missionary Society for decades, serving as a corresponding secretary and vice-president, no one could have predicted that she would one day be the first president of what came to be called by some: "Mrs. Peabody's little mission."

Lucy was to become "Mrs. Peabody" after her children had finished college. She had met Henry W. Peabody, a widower, at the Boston offices of the Woman's Baptist Missionary Society. He was then the President of the General Board of the Baptist Missionary Union.

Henry Peabody was born on August 22, 1838, in Salem, Massachusetts, and he worked his way from the counting house at Williams and Hall, China and Indian merchants, through clerking at Samuel Stevens and Company to a member of that company's firm. Samuel Stevens and Company were involved in international trade with Australia, India, and Africa. The Company ran into trouble in the years following Peabody's entering the partnership. By the time he retired, in 1866, he had lost a major part of his earnings. With the help of his brother, Alfred, who provided the seed money for the venture, Henry started a new trade business: Henry W. Peabody and Company; with offices in many strategic locations. He had his own fleet of ships, the "Australian Line," and was a major supplier of jute, burlap, and other fibers, from India, Pakistan, the Philippines, and other parts of Asia. After the death of his first son, he became a devoted member of the First Baptist Church of Salem, Massachusetts, and a committed supporter of foreign missions.

Henry Peabody and Lucy Waterbury were married on June 16, 1906. Their marriage was sadly very brief in that Mr. Peabody became incapacitated after the death of his son, Alfred, in 1908, and he died on December 7 of that year. Though alone, Lucy was now financially independent, and able to pour herself into Christian work and Women's endeavors.

In 1912, Lucy and Helen Barrett Montgomery worked together to form the Committee on Christian Literature for Women and Children in Mission Fields. In just the first decade, four magazines were supported by the Committee, including *The Women's Messenger* (A Magazine in China), *Happy Childhood* (also China), *Light of Love* (Japan), and *Women's Magazine* (Latin America).[149] Lucy founded *Everyland, The Magazine for Boys and Girls*, which presented the work of missions in a readable way for children. She wrote a very popular book in that series entitled *Just Like You; Stories of Children of Every Land; a Picture on Every Page* (1937) and served as Chairman from 1902 to 1929 of The Central Committee on the United Study of Foreign Missions, which published well-written, illustrated textbooks for women's groups. An example of those textbooks is

The Woman and the Leaven in Japan, authored by Charlotte B. De Forest, and published in 1923.

She spoke in churches and grand assemblies, was involved in the temperance movement [for this see her book, *Kidnaping the Constitution* (1934)], and travelled extensively around the world, often in the company of Helen Barrett Montgomery. She was a champion of women's rights [see her book *A Wider World for Women* (1936)], and she frequently wrote and spoke of political and foreign policy issues. Some of the information about Mr. Peabody and his life came from a privately published memoir she wrote.

All things considered; Norma's Mom was quite a woman!

NORMA'S LIFE ADVENTURE CONTINUES

Norma was baptized in 1893 at First Baptist Church, Newton Centre, Massachusetts. Her education was first at Radcliffe, then at Vassar College, graduating with an A.B. in 1904. She taught German for one year (1905-1906) at Walnut Hill School, and then moved into the Peabody household after her mother's remarriage. She was a church member at First Baptist Church, Salem, Massachusetts, though not a regular attender because of absences in Europe and Asia; and had joined Mt. Auburn Church in Cincinnati, just before sailing for the Philippines in 1916.[150]

After a world tour, in 1913 she was employed to write the Junior Study Book on Missions for the Central Committee on the United Study of Missions, *Around the World with Jack and Janet*, which was used in 1915 and 1916. Norma went to New York to take graduate studies in Bible at Teachers College and Union Seminary in the winter of 1915 – 1916. It was at a Baptist Church in New York[151] [most likely The Second Avenue Baptist Church] that she met Raphael C. Thomas.

As part of her September 1916 application for missionary service, Norma described her Christian experience and motivations for missionary service:

> My Christian experience has not been unusual. From childhood I have been under strong Christian and missionary influences at home, and my conversion was

> merely a natural coming into the church at ten, when I was old enough to understand what it meant.
>
> I have known a great many missionaries and have always thought the missionary's life the most worthwhile, although I have never felt especially fitted myself for teaching or preaching.
>
> Since my trip around the world, when I saw the need and the great variety of occupations open to a missionary besides teaching and preaching, I have felt differently. It may be that I can do an important work by making as ideal a Christian home as possible and by being a friend to the people in their homes. I also hope that I may be able to make the work known and interesting to people in America by writing about it.
>
> My motives for entering upon missionary work are, in short, simply to make my life as strong an influence for good as I can, and I feel that there is the greatest opportunity to do this on the foreign field.[152]

Norma was described as deeply spiritual, an earnest student of the Bible, tactful, easily adaptable, patient, and well prepared to be a missionary. Helen B. Montgomery commented that she considered "the Board fortunate that one of its missionaries could win Norma Waterbury for his wife."[153]

On September 1, 1916, Raph wrote a letter about his return to the Philippines to Mr. Huntington (in the absence of Dr. Franklin). He wrote about booking ship passage for him and his future bride, resigning from the church, and doing some medical study ... just a few things to do! Then he wrote:

> I must have some time free after resignation for marriage and shopping, etc., at least two weeks must be left. More would be better. Then must have at least a week with my little daughter in California whom I have not seen for over two years. Tentative plans as of September 6th:

> Resignation to take place: October 31st; Leave for Long Beach: November 27th; Shinyo Maru: December 9th. Plan to go to Post Grad School about the middle of September (1 month).[154]

It is hard not to smile at the thought of two weeks for "marriage, shopping, etc.", and not to be sad about the fact that two years had passed since Raph had been able to see his daughter "Winky."

Before returning to the Philippines, Raph became a much sought-after servant of God. The Field Secretary for the American Baptist Home Mission Society, who counted Raph as one of "my boys" when he was pastoring at Newton Centre, and "an unusually fine boy," on asked George Huntington on September 16 about Raph's ministry in the Philippines since he was thinking of recruiting him for a ministry in Central America.

Early in the following month, Raph was approached in conversation, and then with two long letters, by Miss Grace McConnel about the possibility of delaying his return to the Philippines to work with the Jewish people in his area. She encouraged Raph to present this invitation to his wife-to-be and to present the letters to any administrators at the mission if they were to question this move. She wrote, "There is a light shining in the lighthouse on second avenue;" referring to both Raph's place of ministry and the work he was doing there. She also wrote the American Baptist Foreign Mission Society about this matter.

Rumor reached the Board prior to the Thomases' departure of a possible assignment to Capiz. The Board and Raph wanted him to remain at the Union Hospital in Iloilo.

Norma was appointed as a missionary by the American Baptist Foreign Mission Society, Foreign Department, on September 13, 1916. On November 11 of the same year, she and Raph were married in Beverly, Massachusetts. Within weeks, they left for the West Coast. After their visit and departure, Winky remained with her Grandparents in Long Beach.

DEMETRIE, ON THE WAY HOME

Their departure was scheduled for December, but Raph had an important stop to make before leaving for the Philippines. A young man who had worked in the hospital with Raph in Iloilo, Demetrie, was in Los Angeles. After Demetrie had completed High School, he and Raph together decided that it would be good for him to study in the United States to better prepare him for laboratory work and future ministry in the hospital. He studied for several years on the West Coast. While Raph was pastoring Second Avenue Baptist Church, Demetrie had contacted him to see if he could travel back to the Philippines with the Raph and Norma. Raph had happily secured passage for Demetrie. When he went to L.A. to accompany the young man in his travel to San Francisco, he learned that Demetrie was in a hospital, so he went to see him, having no idea how sick the young man was. The medical staff informed him that Demetrie was in an advanced stage of consumption (tuberculosis).

Raph found a man who was very different from the healthy boy he had seen off on his exciting trip to America. As he sat by Demetrie's bedside, he asked him, "Demetrie, are you sure you wish to go back with me?" Demetrie replied cheerfully, "Yes, I would like to go." He had been a stranger in a strange land, and now he wanted to go home to be with his family. Raph had visited Demetrie's home, and he described it warmly,

> I knew his people. I had visited his humble home in Negros where a marvelous maritime plain runs along the west coast, dotted by green sugar fields, and in its center towering eight thousand feet into the sunny southern sky he had seen Kanlaon (Old Man of the Mountain) a volcano that dominates the whole landscape. In a sheltered coconut grove down by the blue water that laps the shore, nestled a humble shack. It was just likes scores of others thereabouts, but for Demetrie it was different. That was his home. These were his people whom he loved. He wished to see them again and that was why he told me confidently that he wanted to sail with me.[155]

Raph knew that he would never make it. Instead, he would go through a solemn burial at sea. Yet, knowing that his condition was desperate, Demetrie said to him with a smile, "I am not afraid to die." As Raph later wrote, it was the final word "of one who knew the Lord that Great Shepherd of the Sheep who carried the lambs in His bosom and would guide one beside the still waters, and through the green pastures and even through the shadows of death." He continued,

> This I believe to be the acid test of a true Christianity. I have been by the bedside of many hundreds of patients, when they crossed over to that "Land of Far Distance", and many were afraid, some somnolent, but this boy was wide awake to what lay ahead and faced it gladly because he trusted. He and those others whom I have mentioned had this simple faith.[156]

Demetrie never sailed. Within a week he was gone. But for Raph it was a confirmation of the need for a Mission Hospital where Demetrie had learned to practice true Christianity and to make himself ready for the "acid test."

CHAPTER 14

Serving under ABFMS from 1917

Hearken, my beloved brethren, Hath not God chosen the poor of this world rich in faith, and heirs of the kingdom which he hath promised to them that love him?
—James 2:5

The newlyweds sailed from San Francisco on December 8, 1916 and arrived in Iloilo on January 8, 1917. It has already become obvious that Raphael Thomas was not one to limit his life and ministry to the locale of a hospital or a back porch. He wanted to be among the people. Yes, he desired to treat their bodies, but his heart was full of a message that had to be shared: the gospel of Christ. His exertions as a physician were paralleled by the effort he poured into finding ways to witness, teach, and add believers to the church.

SOCIETY AND FIELD ORGANIZATION

From 1917 on, Raph's relationship to the rest of the missionaries in the Philippines changed, and that story will become a significant part of the bigger story of the rest of his years with the ABFMS. Brief references have been made in earlier chapters to different elements within the organization of the American Baptist Foreign Mission Society. Since the relationships of those elements to each other and to the missionaries with the ABFMS will be mentioned more frequently from this point on, it will be helpful to describe the organization as it was in the second and third decades of the twentieth century.

The Board of Managers of the ABFMS directed its affairs, and they were the ultimate source of regulations for how things were to be done on the fields, including control of the properties. They recognized that the missionaries on the field of ministry (in this case, the Philippines) were better aware of the situation on their field, so the missionaries were given much responsibility for the day-to-day operations of the field.

The missionaries, to perform their various responsibilities as planners, educators, evangelists, teachers, physicians, organizers and administrators of churches, schools, and other ministries, co-operated under the Reference Committee of the Philippine Baptist Mission.

The Foreign Secretary was the ears and the pen of the Board, the field organizations, and the missionaries. He kept up a voluminous correspondence in a day when the typewriter and the telegraph were the primary instruments of communication internationally. It was to the Foreign Secretary, Dr. Franklin, that Raph directed most of his official correspondence from the field during this period of time.

On November 16, 1917, Raph wrote the following to Dr. Franklin,

> Inasmuch as our field of endeavor is quite distinct from that of our fellow missionaries who are engaged in evangelistic and educational service, we would prefer to make the natural separation of work official as well, and to be relieved by the Board from the necessity of voting (except on measures that distinctly concern us), and of office holding. It seems hardly expedient for us to attempt to legislate for those who are really engaged in field evangelism and educational work, when we have so little to do with it.[157]

This seems like a logical request: remove other responsibilities so he can concentrate on those he is most directly involved in. However, since it involved both a setting aside of normal policy, and a stepping away from responsibilities he held jointly with other missionaries, it was controversial.

Dr. Franklin wrote the following in response to Raph's "non-voting status" letter: "We hope you will not insist upon entire freedom from service on committees. In my judgment this would be a mistake, but we have no desire to press the matter."[158]

Raph jumped on that last sentence. He wrote,

> I assume from your last sentence that they [the Board] have tacitly consented if on receipt of this communication my opinion has not changed . . . I will refrain from voting or holding office, except as I deem it wise in matters concerning my work.[159]

This matter was not truly closed, just left in a kind of dormancy to awaken at a time when Raph was hoping to increase the spread of his outreach.

MEDICAL AND DORMITORY MINISTRY

In October, Raph produced the following report at Dunwoody Dormitory in Iloilo:

> Hospitals: One
> Number of dispensaries under Baptist auspices: One
> Cost of supplies: 10,728.78
> Beds in Hospital: 60
> Native nurses in training: 28
> Native physician: (None)
> Patients pay: 50 cents/day to 3.50/day.

As late as 1919, he described his primary areas of involvement in the work in the Philippines as his ministries at the Iloilo Hospital and Dunwoody Dormitory. This is the dormitory that they located near the Iloilo High School. Norma introduced the cafeteria service there in the same year. Greater detail is given in his January 1920 report. He reported the building of the Dispensary Building on the grounds of Dunwoody Dormitory. Also in 1920, a dormitory for girls, the Renfroville Ladies' Dormitory, was established under the supervision of Ellen Martien. The La Paz Baptist Student Center was opened in January of 1921.

They held 7 clinics a week. Boys and girls were kept separate. The usual practice was for the doctor to examine the patient, to provide treatment, and to offer a New Testament. Raph was pleased to report that the patients usually wanted the Testaments. If they did not have the money to buy them, they were asked to bring the 10 centavos when possible. Raph noted that they usually did. One hundred to one hundred and fifty testaments (and some Bibles) had been sold. Raph would talk with the interested students about the contents of Bible before they left.

Raph was also concerned that the government was not doing a proper job of taking responsibility for treatment of the mentally ill. Though this was not his medical specialty, he recognized the great need as he, Dr. Hall, and others treated the people.

The medical ministry was busy. In his annual report, Raph mentioned that there had been 3,918 patients, 930 inpatients, and 2,079 outpatients. During the same year, 1,796 patients had been treated in the Dispensary. With the size of the ministry, and the necessity of keeping patients and staff well, it was not always easy to choose who should receive treatment, and who should not. For example, an American living in the Philippines took sick. He was examined by a Filipino doctor who thought he had scarlet fever. Raph invited the man's sister to bring him to the Iloilo Hospital, but when he was brought in, he was found to have smallpox. As a result, as a matter of policy, he could not be treated there. A Catholic doctor, who knew the family, also refused to treat him. The man died at a nearby house before another American doctor arrived to treat him. Raph performed the funeral the next day. The lawyer who contacted the mission asked for a statement to the effect that they couldn't legally treat the American at the hospital because of his smallpox. While the rules were clear, it could not have been easy for the doctors to turn him away.

> Another type of patent that came to us was a shocking exhibit of the superstition that still prevailed in the hills round about. They brought in this poor woman who had been savagely hacked by bolos. This was the story. There had been a death of a child in her village and they accused her of bewitching it. Asuang, or the evil spirit, is feared out there. She was supposed to be under its influence. She was so badly infected when she came to us we dared

> not even give her a general anesthetic but cut off the arm and soon saw her pass away, a victim of superstition. But the story of this poor woman from the hills was only one to remind us of the dire need for modern medicine. Two examples of this may be cited. One day I was called to see a youth who "could not open his mouth". I was reminded of the case of the girl in Capiz, but was not taking chances, and it was lucky for me I did not. I found him with tightly closed jaws and a sardonic grin on his face and convulsive seizures that at once made the diagnosis clear. He had lockjaw. He was taken to the hospital and that night I kept vigil over him, administering constant subcutaneous injections of morphine to deaden the pain. By morning he had passed away. They say much of the soil out there is impregnated with the tetanus germ. Ponies are everywhere, which favors it. But when the story came out we were shocked again at the pity of it. One of the *practicantes* or native doctors used *Fuentes*, as it was called. That meant making incisions in the shins to let the poison out. These became infected and this was the result. A little more antisepsis with iodine, the deadly enemy of tetanus, and it might have been avoided.
>
> Another instance of ignorance followed soon after. A child was brought into the dispensary stone blind. The eyeballs were white and no rays could penetrate. The story here was that a well-meaning friend, hoping to cure some eye trouble, had put in ground devil fish, or some such irritating substance, and again ignorance did its worst.

Another stomach-turning story Raph tells is difficult to place chronologically, but this seems to be a fitting place for it to be revealed. It has to do with an American man who was ill in a town on the west coast of Antiqua, a province of Panay Island. As Raph tells the story,

> I engaged a launch and we traveled through the night to bring in the patient, who proved to be very ill with some abdominal trouble. His wife, a very attractive woman, formerly a school teacher in Iloilo, wished me to take

him to the hospital, expecting to come there later herself. (Poor woman! She came too late.) Her last word to me was: "Remember doctor, he is red-headed." Those words became more significant in the light of later events. On arrival, we examined him carefully, and called in the military physicians in consultation, but we all were nonplussed. We could not make a final diagnosis. He needed an exploratory operation. Finally, when he gave consent, it was too late. He had a well-developed case of peritonitis of origin unknown. The poor chap said to me when we took him to the operating room: "Doctor, I feel I am going to get well." He was wrong. He passed away, and we had him buried after a simple service at the cemetery. Then we heard the sad news that just after our launch left his home a great storm came up and took the roof off the house and tossed the steamer up on the bank. When the message of his death finally reached his wife the roof was off, rain pouring down and the storm raging about her. She could not find transportation for days, and when she did reach Iloilo it was with a startling request. She wished an autopsy. Her words, spoken as I left, now became even more significant. She feared he had been poisoned. He was hot-headed apparently at times, and he had made enemies. The Moros, especially, are adept in the use of poison. But anyone might use it, and she was insistent that we have a post mortem examination. There was nothing else for it. I secured the assistance of the Constabulary Doctor, an American, and he took sterile jars and we went to the cemetery and opened the tomb (they bury in concrete vaults out there as the soil is so wet), and I had the gruesome job of securing specimens of the organs. (Incidentally, I may add that traces of arsenic are to be found after death, and the symptoms of this case had some likenesses to those of arsenic poisoning). The outcome was negative. The specimens were sent to Manila <u>under guard</u>, but I always wondered if the examiners were able to stand the strain of examining them very carefully. The stench must have been terrific![160]

Exacerbating the difficulties faced by the medical personnel were some problems they shared with the people of the Philippines in general. By October of 1919, the food shortage was becoming difficult, especially because the islands never produced enough rice to meet the needs of the islanders. The foreign "sojourners" in the land were experiencing higher prices and a scarcity of affordable food.

EVANGELISM AND CHURCH PLANTING

The house where the Thomas family lived was in a little area of homes called "Renfroville." The houses were named after Mr. Renfro who had built them near the High School. That was Raph's explanation of the name; in the description of the Renfroville Church that follows, another proposed explanation for the name is given. Since the house was in "a perfect spot" and was near the High School and Dunwoody Dorm, the Reference Committee in the Philippines asked the Board to consider buying the Thomases' house. It was in the vicinity of that house that Raph, colleagues, and students started a small student congregation that became the Renfroville Church.

The Renfroville Church

Raph occasionally mentioned "The Renfroville Church" in his letters. The church still exists, though now it is called the Baptist Center Church, in Iloilo City. On their website,[161] the history of the church is described as follows:

> In Iloilo the Baptist mission opened the Jaro Industrial School which is now the Central Philippine University with a School of Theology. In La Paz, along Luna Street, a Student Center and a Baptist Missionary Training School for women were opened. The work in the Center was started by Dr. Thomas and co-workers succeeded in winning more young people to the saving knowledge of Jesus Christ.

> In 1920, when there were already several baptized students, Dr. Thomas organized a small student congregation. It was named "RENFROVILLE CHURCH" . . . Its services were held in a student center, with Dr. Thomas as pastor. The Student of the Missionary Training School formed the church choir. About 5 years later, Dr. Thomas organized a Visayan congregation which met in a temporary nipa chapel fronting La Paz Plaza. A few years later, the two congregations merged. Thus in 1936 as special service were held in the Student Center, solemnizing what they termed "marriage" or union of the Renfroville Church and the La Paz Baptist Church, thereby forming the LA PAZ BAPTIST STUDENT CENTER CHURCH. Every Sunday it held an early morning Visayan service and a mid-morning English service. A student pastor conducted the Visayan service.

Raph was followed by Dr. Alton Ezra Bigelow, Rev. S.S. Feldmann, and, in 1932, Dr. Ernest Ackley, who was assisted by Rev. Jesus Vaflor who led the Visayan Service.

A few of Raph's morning and evening messages from the period of 1915 through 1917 still exist in draft form, and it is obvious that he loved to preach the Word of God to the students, and to the churches.

Evangelistic Clinics and School Evangelism

The work in Santa Barbara, a few miles from Iloilo, where the leprosarium and a purchased piece of land adjacent to a Catholic Church mentioned earlier were located, was prospering. Medical clinics were small, but the "evangelistic clinics" were well attended. For example, in 1919, a typical Saturday might have as many as 60 patients present, the majority of whom were children.

On December 5 of 1919, students from Jaro Industrial School, Dunwoody Dorm, and other institutions, gathered for special meetings, and many desired to receive Christ. There were about 50 believers in the High School, and many baptisms were administered.

CHAPTER 14

EDUCATION AND LEADERSHIP TRAINING

After his arrival in the Philippines in January, Raph wrote of his concern that the education policy of the Jaro was not cooperating with the Government Educational policy. Raph's concerns about the leadership and policies of the school at Jaro went back to observations from his first term on the field. He was disappointed that despite the desire of many of the field that Mr. Valentine continue to lead the Jaro school, officials of the Board and the Philippine Reference Committee insisted on the installation of Dr. Alton E. Bigelow. Since these concerns will be described more fully in Chapter 18, it will suffice to mention that it was from this time that more of Raph's time was spent in evangelistic and educational ministries outside of his work at the hospital.

The work at Doane Hall in Iloilo was special to Raph. In 1923, Mrs. Marguerite Doane in honor of her father, provided a gift to enlarge the community center (known as "The Hut") into a main auditorium, classrooms and reading rooms. The building was renamed Doane Hall.

This ministry included the dormitories, the large hall where meetings of the Student Church could be held.

Also in 1923, Dr. Thomas, in collaboration with the WFMS, organized Doane Hall Evangelistic Institute in the facilities of the La Paz Baptist Student Center. The purpose envisioned for this one-year program was to provide training in Bible, preaching, and evangelism for its students, many of them coming from the High School student work. The first graduating class (1924) of this one-year program consisted of two men from the Dunwoody Men's dormitory: Serafin Perez and Manuel Escarilla.

In 1924, 8 students, including 3 women, were enrolled, including Mrs. Nonato, who served with Dr. Thomas in Doane Hall Baptist Church. In that same year, Miss Helen Hinkley and Miss Bessie Traber arrived to be part of the missionary faculty.[162]

Governor General Wood had agreed to speak at the dedication of Doane Hall in October of 1923, but it was necessary for him to go to Manila at that time so he was unavailable. Raph wrote that the service was a fitting memorial for William Howard Doane. Included in the activities at the Hall were a Student Center for the "physical, mental and spiritual welfare" of the students, reading rooms, a rest room, game rooms, a cafeteria, a debating club, and church activities. The ministry was not without opposition, since the Acting Bishop of the Diocese there had been one of the most energetic young priests engaged in student work, and he was still doing his best to prevent their progress.

Raph has left us an alarming account of some of the tougher boys – and tougher situations - he and others met in dormitory life:

> As former Major of a High School Battalion, I was able to work off some of their superfluous energy by military drill: but enough remained to be bothersome at times. There were some rowdies who were teaching the boys pugilism nearby, and some of these athletes in the dormitory were husky enough to enjoy it. One day the boy in charge of the dormitory phoned me I was needed. I certainly was. They were on the verge of a "free for all". One boy, a good one, was sitting on the bed, and another, a ruffian type, was threatening him. I was young then and able to take care of myself, but I did not like to be mixed up in a row. I looked the ruffian squarely in the eye and suggested he take his hat off and we would have a word of prayer. To an American tough this would be just "nuts": a great joke: not so a Filipino. The toughest of them seem to have a sense of reverence we are losing over here. Anyway, the hat came off and we had the word of prayer: then I gently urged him downstairs and outside. My boy in charge feared to remain in charge that night: so we had the Chief of Police stand guard. Later I learned that there were knives and brass knuckles in some of the lockers of the boys, and that the one I had faced down told the Chief: "I was about to give Dr. Thomas a blow."
>
> Another close call I had with one of these boys was when we were having a picture taken of the Doane Evangelistic Students (this was a school I had established for Christian workers, in connection with Doane Hall, a large center for work with the High School students, a hall capable of seating a thousand on occasion). I had charge of the Students Church there, with hundreds in attendance. This boy had wandered off at the critical moment when the picture was to be taken. Unthinkingly, I said what every

> American would understand meant nothing: "Where is that boy? Is he crazy?" I forgot all about it, but apparently he did not, for that evening the boy in charge of the dormitory brought him to my home. Then I noticed this boy who brought him sidled away precipitately. The boy he had brought talked as though he was choking with rage. Then he exploded with the comical remark: "Why did you call me such? Why did you call me such? I was amazed. Of course I did not know what he meant. He was one of our best boys: a fine, big, upstanding, rugged chap; but a thorough gentleman: yet now he was like a wild beast. Then Franco, the boy who had brought him explained. He said you called him "crazy". Then I understood and laughed it off: but it might have been a tragedy, for a Filipino enraged cannot seem to think: he is out of his head. One teacher was stabbed in the abdomen I know, and how many others have been attacked I do not know. I do know, however, that one husky American principal of this High School was forced to knock a boy down while we were there. But once they have the explanation and cool down, they become normal. This boy did, and after that no more trouble. But it was a close shave. Franco told me later: "He had a knife". Lorenzo Porras, a colleague of mine, was stabbed to death on a fake call. He was a brilliant student, having come over here and returned after twelve years with five degrees in higher education. He was a doctor, lawyer, educator and two other degrees granted. He helped me in the hospital and later was in charge. A sad ending at last.

The story of the boy Raph had unthinkingly referred to as "crazy" is a reminder of the mistake of causing someone to "lose face" in a culture in which honor and shame are highly valued community characteristics. Raph's response of "laughing it off" was hopefully not in the presence of the angry young man, for that could well have left a permanent breach in their relationship. Most likely he explained the American idiom. Within the context of this lengthy quotation from Raph's autobiographical article, he made it clear that he understood the danger of publicly insulting a normally friendly, gentle Filipino.

CHAPTER 15

1917 to 1923, A Period of Losses

A time to kill, and a time to heal; a time to
break down, and a time to build up.
—Ecclesiastes 3:3

THE WORLD AT WAR, AND WAR WITH A PANDEMIC

Raph and Norma had arrived in Iloilo on January 8, 1917. On February 3, the United States severed diplomatic ties with Germany. On April 6, 1917, the United States entered the World War 1. On November 7, Lenin's communist government came into power because of the Bolshevik revolution. On December 9, Jerusalem fell to the British army.

1918 was also, by any measure, a momentous year. In January of the year, World War I continued to grind on, with battles on nearly all the continents. Not until November 11 was the long and painful "war to end all wars" formally declared to be over.

In March of 1918, in Kansas, a soldier reported to sick bay with flu-like symptoms, and he was followed by dozens of others. It was there that the "Spanish Flu" was first recognized. This proved to be the worst pandemic in recorded history. It was the result of the spread of an H1N1 virus with genes of avian origin. The CDC estimates that one/third of the population of the world was infected, and between 50 and 100 million people died of the flu. 675,000 Americans died of the virus. One thing that encouraged the spread of the virus was the reality of World War I troop movements. As was the case in the Covid-19 pandemic, many people were sickened and died within hours or days. There were no antidotes, no antiviral medicines, and no vaccines; so, handwashing, putting the sick into quarantine, disinfectants, and avoiding public gatherings were the only measures that helped. These measures will seem familiar to anyone who passed through the pandemic in the 2020's.

Though numerous studies were made of the virus worldwide, the coverage in the American-occupied-Philippines, was less than adequate.[163] In fact, the medical experts in the Philippines declared that the worst was over after the first wave, and because the information provided was inadequate, the second wave of the flu was worse than the first. Due to population densities, it is no surprise that China, India, and Indonesia were the hardest hit in total numbers of deaths, numbering in the millions. The Philippines lost between 70 and 90 thousand people to the virus. The death toll in Samoa was the highest on record, with the eventual death of 25% of the population of the islands (lower on the American occupied island because of better quarantine restrictions).

The influenza came in waves in the Philippines, and the ages of those hardest hit in each wave were different. The first wave was in June, 1918, and the second from September to the end of the year. The death rate in Manila alone doubled from 1917 to 1918. The third wave was in 1919 as the curve of infections gradually flattened.

Raph did not write much about his participation in treatment of the flu in the Philippines, but what he did mention was terrifying:

> I passed through the terrific epidemic of Flu that cost so many lives out there. They died like flies, so fast they dared not record them at the *municipio* I heard, lest people become panic stricken. I was soaked in it, having to remain one night in a tightly sealed room, while a patient was dying. I did it to please a native doctor: but praises be I never caught it!

On August 11, 1919, a fatherless man came to the Dispensary. Raph wondered if he was one of those bereaved by the recent epidemic of Spanish

Influenza or cholera or smallpox, since "all had been raging here with frightful mortality." A young boy came by the dispensary with a black band on his arm for a brother who had died of cholera. The boy could not afford a Testament, so Raph gave him one.

Many countries declared independence during the first world war, but many of them were quickly embroiled in new wars threatening their independence. The Philippines remained U.S. territory, and it was in that connection that Filipinos participated in the war. Philippine historian Al Raposas wrote an interesting article concerning the little-told story of the participation of the Filipinos in the first World War.

> The Philippines was dragged to World War I, the Great War as it was known before 1939, simply because United States joined the war (in 1917). Since the Philippines was American territory, it is obliged to help her so-called Uncle Sam. If America's contribution in the war is small, the Philippine contribution is, logically, smaller.[164]

> So, what were the contributions? Raposas wrote,

> The Philippines actually funded, and built, for the United States one destroyer (USS Rizal). USS Rizal is the first and only American warship named after a Filipino, Jose Rizal.[165]

The commitment of manpower to the war is an interesting story, especially since it explains why Raph did not write much about World War1 from his vantage point in the Philippines. It was not for lack of interest in world affairs; he wrote extensively about World War2. Perhaps it was because he was heavily involved in ministry in the Philippines where the war was felt less except by those who were conscripted, those who were building for the war effort, and those who lost loved ones in the war.

> One more thing the Philippines did for America during the Great War was the drafting of Filipinos for the US National Army. The colonial government had the quota set to 15,000. The Philippines provided 25,000. This became known as the Philippine National Guard (PNG).

However, the PNG never saw action. Filipinos who did set foot in Europe during the war were enlisted in the American Expeditionary Force (AEF). The most famous of these Filipino soldiers was Tomas Mateo Claudio, who died at the Battle of Chateau-Thierry in June 1918. He was the first Filipino casualty of the war, followed by around 50 more Filipino deaths until the First World War ended in the same year.[166]

PERSONAL LIFE AND LOSS DURING THIS MOMENTOUS PERIOD

For Raph, 1918 and 1919 were also years of personal loss, in that his sister, Medora Carlota Thomas, died in 1918, and his mother, Abbie Ann (Eastman) Thomas died in 1919. It was hard for Raph to be so far away from the rest of his family as he and they grieved.

In August of 1919, Raph wrote a touching account of those troubled times to their supporters:

> I saw an interesting example a day or so ago of how ready the patients are to read the Bible. In the men's private ward, are patients representing three nationalities, side by side. The first bed holds a stalwart Japanese. The next accommodates a bright young Chinaman and the next a Filipino youth. One day I noticed the Japanese man was reading one of those impossible books that are typical of Japan. They always make me think of the old story about little Ikey who first saw such a book and when asked if he could read it he replied, "No, but if you will bring me my flute, I think I can play it." As I do not know Japanese, I was unable to read the title, and was a little in doubt as to which end of the book to look for it anyway, but I was morally sure it was not Biblical. I asked the man if he would like to read the Bible, but he said he could read only Japanese. Then the Chinaman beside him passed over a Gospel the nurse had given him, written in Chinese, and the Japanese said the letters were all the same. A

Gospel was given him and he seemed quite pleased. I feel pretty sure he will take it with him, for they do that as a rule. Miss Leeson was telling me she gave some Chinese Gospels to a Chinese private patient a while ago, and as he was tuberculous, she hoped he would take them along, and sure enough he did. He packed them up with his [things] and carried them off. We just had another private patient who has been with us weeks. He did the same. They seem hungry for the Word. This man sent in a check for some 700 pesos just after he left, so I think he paid us a fair price for our services, but if the money brings him an intelligent grasp of God's Word, he will have priceless possession in his Bible. – To resume our tour through the ward – the Filipino in the next bed to that of the Chinaman also was asked if he cared to read the Bible and he seemed quite willing. So all three nationalities, side by side, were reading the Good News.

We have just been having another catastrophe. I never saw a time when there were so many. Epidemics, earthquakes, rice shortages, etc., and now a regular cyclone. They say it lasted a minute or so, but the paper reports 45 houses wrecked, more or less, and a great loss of money. Several were injured, and one killed. The whole back part of Mr. Berger's (the Presbyterian missionary) house was blown down, and the house behind it, the one in which I used to live was turned over on its side. The path of the cyclone was zig-zag and where it went it tore off roofs and ripped out the sides and fronts of houses, and in the plaza it twisted great trees up by the roots, and created great havoc generally. I was called up at midnight to treat the victims. One of them, a boy from Silliman, was too badly injured and he died that night. The others suffered minor injuries only.

The students' Dispensary has been open now for about a week. So far we have averaged something like five patients a day. It will take some time for the students to get in the habit of coming, but we already have some good chances for personal work. The students are ready to talk

> religion as well as medicine, and as we have a good stock of Testaments, and several religious meetings to which to invite them, we believe it will soon be a felt force.
>
> We are glad to say that three of our nurses have been examined for baptism, and will be baptized as soon as the storm permits. We have had a storm for three weeks or so. We are rejoicing that these girls have taken this stand. We hope for others soon.[167]

During their first term together in the Philippines, Norma wrote a sequel to her book *Around the World with Jack and Janet*, this time putting the twins, Jack and Janet, in the Philippines. The book was commissioned to be done in a short time, because an author who had planned to submit a book to The Central Committee that year became unable to do so. The book included several fascinating photos that illustrate the people and their lives in the Philippines.

CHILDREN

The Lord blessed the couple with two children (not named Janet and Jack!) during their first term in the Philippines together: Marguerite Mather Thomas, born on May 22, 1919, in Iloilo; and Jesse Burgess Thomas, born on December 7, 1920.[168] Just a few months later, on April 12, 1921, eager to share these beautiful little ones with their Grandparents, the proud parents and their young children sailed from Iloilo. They disembarked on May 16, 1921, at Vancouver, British Columbia.

A Syrian doctor took over the hospital ministry during their absence, and Miss Martien, described by Raph as "a wonderful woman and devoted to the work," was left to cover the work in Iloilo. Born in 1868, Miss Martien had been dean of women at Stetson University in Florida from 1906 to 1918. After joining the Woman's Board of the ABFMS, she had served as the Matron of Doane Hall in Iloilo.

During his time in the States, Raph hoped that Mr. Maxfield would be able to return to the Philippines to cover the student work in the La Paz district of the Iloilo work, but his sailing was delayed.

CHAPTER 15

At the completion of their time in the States, the Thomas family sailed from Vancouver on June 15, 1922, to begin their second term together in Iloilo. They arrived there on July 10th. Some of the missionary activity of that term will be described in the next chapter, but it is necessary here to mention one more loss the family experienced.

Less than a year after their arrival, on May 4, 1923, their beloved Marguerite became ill and died in Iloilo. She was buried in the American Cemetery, next to Raph's first wife, Winifred. Raph wrote to "Mother" (Mrs. Peabody) that life would never be the same again (thinking at the same time of an experience they had already shared with another couple who had lost their little girl). But he added that the experience of losing Marguerite would bind Norma and Raph "closer to Him and to Heaven to have our little daughter happy over there on the other side."[169] In the same letter, he described Norma as "brave as a lion," "sensible and self-sustained throughout," and "strong beyond most women." Gardening was an outlet for her, and Raph encouraged her to buy whatever she needed for household or gardening supplies, for "any outlay now would be economy if it keeps her happy."

Raph also admitted to Mrs. Peabody that he was struggling to have the same "energetic relish" in the opening of the school year as he had anticipated. He found the "method of drowning out sorrow by hard work" good, but hard in a hot country where the energy to be creative was sapped quickly. He knew that in work with students "one has to keep bright and cheery. We can do it even now, but it seems like the story of the Punchinello who had to be "funny" even in times of sorrow. But the Lord has been very good to us, and we know it is all right, and bless His name."

Mabelle Rae McVeigh, Foreign Secretary of the Woman's American Baptist Foreign Mission Society, wrote Raph on June 23, 1923, and mentioned how terribly shocked they were when they received word concerning the death of little Marguerite. They had a prayer service for the Thomas family immediately after they heard. She wrote:

> All of hearts were grieved with you, though we knew that the Everlasting Arms were strong enough to uphold both you and Mrs. Thomas. It was my pleasure to see little Marguerite at a meeting in Boston, and I shall never forget her beauty and charm. I am sure that you will ever cherish the memory of such a beautiful little life.[170]

The sadness had barely become bearable when a final blow struck. Raph wrote just seven months later, in December, that their "little boy Burgess" had not been doing well. Dr. Hall had recommended that they take him to America "at once." Symptoms had appeared suddenly, and since children "went down rapidly" in the Philippines, Raph agreed and quickly began to make plans. Norma and Burgess were booked on the President Wilson set to sail the southern route to America with a January 9 departure from Manila. Raph remained in the Philippines, and he honestly was not sure when Norma would return. The only information we have about her return to the Philippines was a letter from Dr. Franklin to Raph dated July 15, 1924, in which he wrote "By the time you receive this notification, Mrs. Thomas will be with you again I expect. I am sure you will be very happy to be reunited again." Separations are not unusual in the lives of missionaries, but one can only imagine Raph's relief in having Norma back after six months of travel and letter-writing by ship. As for Burgess, because of the serious concerns Raph and Norma had about his health if he were to continue to live in the Philippines, Mrs. Peabody agreed to raise him in the absence of his mom and dad.

CHAPTER 16

The Doane Connection

Serve the LORD with gladness: come before his presence with singing.
—Psalm 100:2

Doane Hall and Doane Evangelistic Institute have been mentioned already, but the connection between William Howard Doane and his daughters to the work in the Philippines deserves more explanation.

WILLIAM HOWARD DOANE AND FANNY CROSBY

William Howard Doane was a Connecticut native, born in 1832. From the age of sixteen he worked hard in his father's cotton goods business and became quite successful. Remarkably, it is not for being a wealthy businessman that he has been known by Christians for over a century. Rather, it is because he was a talented singer and writer of hymn tunes. While music was a hobby, and writing poetry was a struggle, he was moved to devote himself more and more to music after suffering a heart attack at age 30. He was convinced that God wanted him to concentrate more on Christian music. He soon compiled three hymnals, but he would not be satisfied until he had a poet who could supply the words for his hymns.

While engaged in prayer for that collaborator, a knock on the door brought him the answer. Fanny Crosby had written a note to the effect that though they had never met, she felt compelled to write him. She sent a poem that he immediately put to music, and the first hymn of their collaboration was born: "More like Jesus would I be." Doane came to New York with Fanny's address in his hand. He was shocked to see the run-down tenement where she lived. He gave her twenty dollars for the poem she had written. That began a friendship and collaboration that lasted for 47 years until Fanny's death and his own soon after. Fanny would frequently visit at the home of William, his wife, also named Fanny, and their two children, Ida and Marguerite. They provided the world with some of the most beautiful, memorable, and moving hymns in the English hymnal. He composed twenty-three hundred hymns. During the same period, Doane patented seventy inventions that revolutionized woodworking machines.[171]

In his philanthropy, William gave large gifts to Dennison University (from which he received an honorary doctorate), Moody Bible Institute, a home for missionary children, various Baptist churches, and other organizations.

MRS. MARGUERITE DOANE (1868–1954)

The daughters of William Howard Doane and Frances Mary "Fanny" Treat Doane (1832–1923) were Marguerite and Ida Doane. Each inherited a fortune from their parents, and they enjoyed using their fortunes to serve others. Ida Frances Doane was born on August 15, 1858, in Plainfield, Connecticut. Marguerite Treat Doane was born on the thirteenth of November 1868, in Cincinnati, Ohio. Ida died at the age of 83 in 1942, in South Orange, New Jersey. Ida remained unmarried, while Marguerite married a cousin, George W. Doane, keeping the Doane family name.

Robert T. Coote, in his history of the Overseas Ministry Study Center, *Renewal for Mission*, describes one of the ministries the sisters co-founded, "Houses of Fellowship" in Ventnor-by-the-Sea.

> Marguerite and Ida Doane, daughters of hymnwriter William Howard Doane (1832-1915), located their complex of missionary houses in the seaside town of

Ventnor, in part for the reputed rejuvenating benefits of seaside living.

The first dwelling was purchased in 1922, and as their very first guest Marguerite and Ida Doane welcomed the family of Alexander C. Hanna, a grandson of Adoniram Judson. The Hannas were to return several times to Ventnor over a period of almost twenty years. In 1940 the minutes of the board report that the residents gathered in the spacious living room of "Sunny Side" (a white stucco, palatial building erected in 1932 that became the social center of the complex) and that Hanna showed slides of his work. The Hannas typified the pattern for those who took advantage of the facilities offered by the Doane sisters:

(I) Families came back year after year. (2) The second generation virtually grew up in Ventnor. "This is the only home we know in the United States," said one teenager in 1939. (3) Socializing and Christian fellowship were central ingredients at the Houses of Fellowship.

Every year on February 3, the date of William Howard Doane's birth, residents gathered in Sunny Side to sing Doane hymns and to recount the story of his life. There were weekly gatherings for prayer and for reports from the overseas fields. There was a formal tea on Thursday afternoons, at which the women were expected to appear in appropriate gowns and the men in suits. Whenever Marguerite was in town (she lived in South Orange, New Jersey), she "received" her guests and visitors at these teas and sometimes placed at their disposal her chauffeured limousine. At the 1940 gathering in Sunny Side, Marguerite was present and shared 8-mm films of the gospel yacht she helped finance for evangelistic tours among the fishing villages of the Philippines.[172]

Marguerite trusted Curtis Lee Laws, the editor of the Watchman-Examiner and she asked Mr. and Mrs. Laws to join the board of trustees of the Society for Foreign Mission Welfare (SFMW), which was the legal organization that operated the Houses of Fellowship. He encouraged Marguerite to keep the Houses on an "open fellowship" footing. Although she was a vital member of the group that would eventually start the Association of Baptists for Evangelization of the Orient (ABEO), Marguerite never formally broke her ties with the Northern Baptist Convention.[173]

Marguerite worked together with Lucy Peabody and Helen Barrett Montgomery in the Woman's Baptist Foreign Missions Society (WBFMS), and in the Central Committee on the United Study of Foreign Missions, publishing books and training women worldwide. Mrs. Peabody referred to Marguerite as "the fairy godmother of the WABFMS because she so frequently brought financial relief to struggling ministries.[174]

There was a special place in Marguerite's heart for the work in the Philippines. This was in part because of her special relationships with Lucy Peabody, Norma, and Raph. She made possible the establishment of several ministry centers mentioned in this biography including Doane Evangelistic Institute (established in 1923), Doane Dormitory for Girls in Manila, the Manila Evangelistic Institute (established in 1930), and the missionary rest home in Baguio. She sent many gifts in response to needs mentioned by Dr. and Mrs. Thomas, including Alberto Franco's ministry among the lepers in Santa Barbara. She helped raise several million dollars "to establish Christian schools of higher learning in Asia."[175]

DOANE REST IN BAGUIO

The back story to Doane Rest is fascinating, and the mention of the bequest above calls for that story to be told. Though the story of the Igorot tribe's village goes back to a time long before westerners ever arrived on the scene, the modern story of the town begins in 1900, when Governor Taft arrived in the hot and humid city of Manila. He immediately deputized a member of his commission, Dean Worcester, to locate a cool place for a retreat. Stanley Karnov tells the story well:

> Worcester dug out an old Spanish medical report that claimed that the climate of mountainous Benguet province "benefited and in many instances cured . . . anemia,

> malaria, chronic catarrhs of the bladder and urinary tracts" as well as "nostalgia and hypochondria."[176]

Immediately an exploration party was formed, and when they had climbed to a beautiful plateau, they discovered the village of Baguio. Along with the Igorots, and a strange German scientist who had adopted the lifestyle of the people, they found a delightful cold breeze – an oasis in a tropical land! An elated Taft ordered that a road be made into Baguio, and plans were laid out for the construction of an American town on that plateau. The cost of the project grew to $3,000,000 – a huge sum at that time – because of everything from typhoon damage to the employment of thousands to make the road. At one point, Governor Taft, though battling with dysentery, made the trip to Baguio on that road by horseback. He cabled Elihu Root, who was the Secretary responsible for much of the Philippine policy, that he had successfully made the trip, and Root – who knew the size of Taft – replied, "How was the horse?"[177]

As investors poured money into the project for gabled houses, a boarding school, and even a country club, missionaries began to join the many who would use Baguio as a retreat and conference site. In 1932, Ida and Marguerite Doane visited the Philippines. After recognizing the need for a retreat center for Protestant missionaries, Marguerite donated the funds to create Doane Rest.

Raph described a visit to Doane Rest and the beauty of Baguio in a 1926 letter to his supporters,

> It is lovely here. How I wish we could transport you to this hill country, with its cold nights (comfortable under 3 or 4 blankets) and its pines. It is almost like home in some ways. Yet one never can forget, it is the Philippines, for on all sides one sees the Igorots or mountain people, with their peculiar dress, or more properly undress, as the men go barelegged with the customary gee string. The women wear brightly colored garments of native weave. The villages are most primitive, I am told. Miss Traber and Miss Hinkley, two of our missionaries, made a trip to Bontoc, several days journey into the hills . . . We have had the good fortune to see a native Igorot dance, and it shows what ferocity must have been the rule when they were head hunters.[178]

IMPACT

It is impossible at this point to adequately measure the impact of the giving hearts of the Doane sisters, particularly Marguerite, on the ministries in the Philippines. They, and those who partnered with them, selflessly, generously supported many aspects of the work of Raph, Norma, and their colleagues in the years before and after the formation of the ABEO.

A final illustration of Marguerite Doane's dedication to the ABEO. can be seen in her last will and testament. Together with the bequeathal of a musical instrument collection (including that of her father) to the Cincinnati Art Museum, and other gifts, Marguerite gave all the properties in the Philippines that were still owned by her to the Association of Baptists for Evangelism in the Orient. She also gave two-ninths of the residue and remainder of her estate to ABEO. This amounted to $53,924.66 (the equivalent of $585,946.56 in 2022).

CHAPTER 17

Serving under ABFMS from 1924

Take therefore no thought for the morrow: for the morrow shall take thought for the things of itself. Sufficient unto the day is the evil thereof.
—Matthew 6:34

The years of 1924 to 1927 in Raph's life and ministry are both spiritually exciting and physically and emotionally exhausting. At the same time, vistas of untapped possibilities are blurred by the arrival of unexpected dark clouds and limitations of visibility that threaten even the most optimistic views of the future. To give a sense of the changing conditions, rather than dividing the areas of service into subsections it will be better to view the whole picture chronologically.

Setting the stage is Lucy Peabody's booklet, "The Philippine Mission. 'Pearl of the Orient'," written about this time. Lucy produced a gem of an account of the Philippines, starting with their discovery by Magellan, describing the various aspects of the Baptist ministries and the missionaries involved, and concluding with the words, "The prayers of the women of our churches are asked for this endeavor to fulfil the promise of God, "The Isles shall wait for His law." A postscript was added entitled "A Word about our 'Pearl of the Orient.'" The following paragraphs are from that postscript, and they help to clarify the relationship of the Woman's Board to the work at that time.

Four provinces of the Philippine Islands, and the island of Samar, furnish a Challenge of Opportunity for Northern Baptists. The Woman's American Baptist Foreign Mission Society has fifteen missionaries in the following stations: Bacolod, Capiz, Iloilo and Pototan. The work is varied and comprehensive; evangelistic work has large emphasis. This includes Bible training, Bible women, evangelistic travel, hospital, dispensary, girls' dormitory, and student work.

The Bible Missionary Training School offers a three year Normal Bible Course, or two years' Kindergarten Teacher Training. Three of the recent graduates are on the faculty and give promise of developing into leaders. An experiment is being tried with Daily Vacation Bible School at the little La Paz chapel.

Student work in all its phases is bearing abundant fruit. A body of consecrated personal workers visit in the neighborhood on Saturdays, seeking to help into the Kingdom all who have intimated their desire to join the followers of Christ.

In Doane Hall, each day is begun with a fifteen minute prayer meeting. Four afternoons a week there is a Bible class at the close of the school day. One midweek prayer meeting each month is made definitely evangelistic. It is not uncommon to see 300 students present with between 75 and 100 taking a stand for Jesus; 89 were baptized from June to October, 1923. The Girls' Dormitory is witnessing for Christ in an unusual manner.

Students' dispensaries are working in connection with prayer meetings at La Paz and Bacolod. District medical work furnishes a great evangelistic opportunity. During the year of 1922 there were reported from the Philippine Island 3,533 church members, 283 baptisms, 1,899 pupils.

The hope of the Philippine Islands is in the new generation which is growing up in the new day of political freedom

> and educational advantages. A far larger number of the people can read and there is a larger demand for Bibles and for our mission papers.[179]

1924

In January of 1924, Raph started a letter to his supporters with an apology:

"I am sorry to be late in reporting for the year, but a trip to Baguio to attend the student conference interfered with my schedule here." If we put this into the context of Chapter 15, it is apparent that after sending Norma and Burgess off to the States, Raph must have gone on to Baguio for the student conference. The following is his summary of the work at that time:

> Hospital going well. Dispensary progressing. Dunwoody Dorm is a hard proposition. Just across the road from the Dormitory and Students' Dispensary, the Catholics have built a church building, mainly for the students and they are working aggressively to defeat our efforts.
>
> My activities in connection with the Women's Board work at Doane Hall have been very satisfactory to me. The women are doing a remarkable work there. I understand that the number of baptisms for the calendar year in the Renfroville student work was 190 or more, and that possibly 30 more were baptized at La Paz Church, which was organized last summer as a result of the work done by the Training School girls here at LaPaz and the students of the Student Church. Since school opened in June 140 have been baptized in Doane Hall.
>
> With the suggested departure of the Presbyterians from Panay Island we may close a chapter of Union work in the Philippines for their opinion is that it has demonstrated both the value and menace of such work. The Presbyterians have held control of Iloilo City, the only Baptist city of real size, in addition to the many large strategic centers throughout the Islands. This seemed an

> unusual distribution of territory. For twenty years and more they have maintained work in the Panayan district far from their other centres in the Eastern Visayas, and in a dialect different from that used in their other work. [180]

At this point, Raph begins an interesting explanation of the kind of changes in translations of the Scriptures that sometimes occur because of the use of the translation by members of a denomination other than that of the first translator. Obviously, the same kind of difficulty can occur in churches influenced by any kind of cooperative effort between denominations. Though the Presbyterians and Baptists had the same evangelistic fervor in the early days of evangelism and church planting in the Philippines, there were doctrinal differences between them. An example would be the mode of baptism.

> Through their influence the Panayan translation of the Scriptures made by Mr. Lund, our Pioneer Baptist missionary, has been changed. Originally the word "baptize" was translated by the word which means to "dip", the basal meaning according to recognized scholarship. Now it is transliterated, and we have to explain why. It might have been, had only Baptists been here, that the Bible Society would not have made the change, a change which might have been difficult since we held the plates. If the Presbyterians leave, we now face the situation of having a transliterated Bible, (even now being revised because of the loss of the plates in the Japanese disaster) to be used in Baptist territory. I wish the return to the "pagtugmaw" edition might be made even now. But the more questionable fact concerning unionism still remains to be settled. Will one Denomination unite with another in union work and then feel no obligation upon them to leave the work in which they participated in such condition that it will "carry on" after their departure. That is the great question of all. Or will they leave under conditions that will largely vitiate the value of progress made during the union? If such should be the outcome, the question of the value of union work must remain to be proved.[181]

The Japanese disaster is apparently a reference to the 1923 Great *Kantō* Earthquake, one of the worst natural disasters to that time in Japanese history, with over 130,000 deaths in the Tokyo-Yokohama area of the main island of Honshu. The benefits of having quality materials printed in Japan were quickly obliterated by this terrible earthquake and its resulting fires.

The relationship of the Presbyterians and Baptists in the hospital ministry in many ways had been a happy one for years, but a crisis was brewing concerning the building in which the hospital was located. The Presbyterian ministry, which had already turned over much of the area to the Baptists, was now looking for a way to move out of the Union Hospital ministry.

In April of 1924, Raph travelled northeast to Samar, a journey of a week to get there, and three and one-half days to return. Samar was said to be the third largest of the islands in the Archipelago, somewhat smaller than Puerto Rico at 5,185 square miles. The population in 1920 was over 380,000.

He remained in the city of Catbalogan for nine days. He spent his time teaching lessons all day for the first two days, and then twice a day for the rest of his time there, in his room. Although more individuals expressed interest, Raph baptized 10 "fine young men." When he wrote about the experience, he added, "I plead for Samar. I mean to do which I can, and to ask for no appropriation, but I pray that Samar may be neglected no longer than is absolutely necessary."

One of the stated purposes of the trip was that "he was searching for the remnant of the little group of baptized believers left from Dr. Sombito's days." Dr. Feliciano Sombito, a graduate of the University of Illinois, was later to become the first President of the Convention of Philippine Baptist Churches. He was critical of the missionaries for a number of reasons, one being that they often failed to treat Filipino believers as equals; and another, that they failed to provide a seminary at the start.[182] The latter is an interesting comment in the context of Raph's work in that he was determined to work with his colleagues to prepare students for ministry, yet was prevented from increasing the training beyond a one-year program.

Dr. Franklin replied to Raph's letter about Samar with a response that is standard in missions, yet sad: there is a need in Samar, but we simply need more missionary personnel. He added, "I feel very strongly that our first responsibility in the Philippines is to strengthen the church life with a view to conserving the results already secured." [183]

Raph presented a very positive view of the work at Doane Hall, and the evangelistic outreaches that flowed from it, in his prayer letters in June and October of 1924. He wrote that the Doane Hall work was prospering. The slogan for its second year was: "The intensive development of the church membership." The Students' Church was blessed with 90 baptisms in seven months, and there was good attendance at the Bible classes for the students. The desire of Raph and his colleagues was for the Student's Church at Doane Hall to be "a normal training school for those who go out to establish churches." They wanted the Institute to send out many self-supporting evangelists to do as William Carey did, make preaching their business and "cobble to pay."

Raph was a regular contributor to the Philippines missionary magazine *Pearl of the Orient*. Here are some examples from the October 1924 issue:

Iloilo:
Union Mission Hospital.

> Patients continue to flock to the wards. The nurses Training School continues to progress. The illness of Miss Fullerton has thrown a heavy burden on Miss Nicolet, but in spite of her added duties she keeps the Hospital esprit de corps in most satisfactory condition. And amid the bustle and rush of hospital routine there is a quiet undercurrent of evangelism that is encouraging. The little nurses have a full Sunday, but are not too tired to have a meeting in their classroom after the regular church services are over. Last Sunday an outsider was present. She gave good attention and later the leader of the meeting was glad to learn that though a Romanist she has become convinced of the truth and wishes baptism. It was also a pleasure to learn that she was the first graduate from the Manila General Hospital. A patient said only today after hearing the Scripture: "That is better than all the medicine".[184]

CHAPTER 17

DOANE EVANGELISTIC INSTITUTE

> One of the helpful features of the Doane Evangelistic Institute curriculum is district evangelism. Not long ago some students were sent to Hinigaran and again to Cadiz to help in evangelistic meetings. In Cadiz alone over seventy expressed their desire to follow the Lord, and quite a company were baptized. . . .
>
> The Institute pins have come and the students are delighted with them. The design is both artistic and significant. The monogram in the centre "DEI" means in Latin "Of God", - as everyone knows, and when coupled with the School motto the complete reading is, - "The Bible Our Message and Everyone a Messenger – of God"....
>
> The Institute reading room and library has become popular. The High School students are patronizing this cozy, quiet rendezvous. Many of the books in their High School reading are to be found on the shelves. . . . One of the most valuable recent acquisitions is the "Cambridge Bible for Schools and Colleges." Among other recent additions we are glad to include works by Mullins, Robertson, Machen, McCartney, William Evans, Torrey, and other evangelistic and conservative thinkers. From this list one might perhaps assume that the Doane Evangelistic Institute has conservative tendencies. And such an assumption would be correct.[185]

In October of 1925, both Raph and Norma submitted articles to *Pearl of the Orient*, along with articles by colleagues E. W. Martien, Bessie Traber, and Helen Hinkley. Raph wrote about the "Theory and Practice" for Doane Hall Evangelistic Institute Students in La Paz.

> The workers of the Doane Hall Evangelistic Institute are learning how to become "Evangelists" by evangelizing. . . . Already a number of well attended meetings have been held in Doane Hall and many have responded to the appeal. But this is not enough. They have launched out to

> La Paz and Iloilo City and even into Negros and Antique. Several drives have been made in Negros, assisting Mr. Valentine and his workers. . . . And in the City of Iloilo open air services have been held. It is suggestive of the atmosphere there that the terms used in the prize fights, "break" (from a clinch) and "fight", are the commonly used terms by the conductors of the buses for "stop" and "start." I could hardly believe my ears when I first heard it and then the fun all oozed out and it became just plain pathos. La Carlota, in Negros, was the home of Pancho Villa, the world famous pugilist. He was just a little cattle boy, until he blossomed out into a full fledged "bruiser." We felt it was worth while to teach some of the fine young men there that it was better to fight as Paul did against "principalities and powers" of evil, than to destroy the features of their fellow men.[186]

In that same issue, Norma wrote some delightful reminiscences of Renfroville. She provides a charming description of their first home there and provides insights into the changes that had taken place.

> It is nearly nine years since I first saw Renfroville, liked the place and decided to live here. We rented one of the little wooden bungalows that surround the concrete tennis court, and at once felt at home. Tall coconut palms and hedges of violetas and hibiscus framed our veranda. A gay little bed of orange cosmos bloomed in the driveway in front, while the great shady acacia trees and restful green grass around the tennis court completed the picture of home for us.
>
> But there were other homes all about us, scattered over the vivid green rice fields. These bamboo shacks, raised high on stilts, sheltered many students, boys and girls, who passed our house daily on their way to the High School. We soon became acquainted with them, for when it rained or in vacant periods, they often gathered in groups on our doorstep. The school was so crowded that the students were not allowed to loiter about the campus, and so they took refuge with us.

> What an opportunity for mission work offered itself among these future leaders of the Philippines! Education alone can never train the kind of leaders needed here.
>
> In nine years great changes have taken place. The bungalows belong to our Woman's Board and Renfroville has become a popular student centre. The small beginning in a single bungalow, which was used as a community house, and where, as the first fruits of this evangelistic venture, seventeen were baptized, all unwittingly on the very day appointed by the women at home for prayer for this student work, has now developed into a full-fledged service for the student population of approximately five thousand that centres here.
>
> The small bungalow used at first was moved in 1923 to make way for Doane Hall, and is now used for class rooms and library. Doane Hall, the Evangelistic Institute, the High School Girls' Dormitories and the Baptist Missionary Training School, together with Dunwoody Dormitory near by, have become a well organized working body. The students' Church has been steadily growing. There have been baptisms at nearly every Sunday morning service since Doane Hall was built, over four hundred and forty in all. The Evangelistic Institute has ten graduates and sixteen enrolled this year.
>
> These reminiscences make us feel that through these years since student work has been begun, God has been leading in a wonderful way.[187]

The compound at Renfroville (which by this time was the former name of the group of houses where the Training School and Doane Evangelistic Institute were located) was in excellent condition. Concrete basements, new bungalows, a better road, and increased accommodations had been built.

Raph added that the Doane Hall Evangelistic Institute had been a tower of strength for the Doane Hall work, involving intensive study and practical work. Some of the students at the Institute were active in what Raph considered "one of the best phases of this work." That was the evangelistic trips of the students to Negros, steaming up the Ileg River. In the Negros work, over the space of nine months, Mr. Valentine reported over a thousand baptisms – a "banner year, and rare." Two young men from the Institute were in Baguio in June, participating in the YMCA student conference.

One highlight of the Negros work was the baptism of Captain Juan Araneta, "the most outstanding personality, in some ways, in Occidental Negros, if not of the whole island." During the anti-American insurgency, Araneta had been a fiery leader, but in "recent days" he had "received Christ as his Lord and was baptized by Mr. Valentine." When he died some relatives wanted to take his body to the Catholic church, but his widow said "No." Mr. Valentine did the service.

It is not unusual for pressure to be put on family members, or to be put on the closest relatives by family members, to undo the effects of the believer's testimony by insisting that the funeral be performed by a religious leader of the prevailing religion of the area, even though the Christian believer had left specific instructions for a Christian funeral to be held. The impact of a Christian memorial service on family and friends can be great.

Raph described the year of 1924 as "one of the richest in my experience in the Philippine Islands. Never in all the yeas that have passed since I came here, over 21 years ago, has my heart been so thrilled by the response to the compelling appeal that always lies in the preached Word." He described some of the blessings to Dr. Franklin and added an important request:

> In every branch of the service, Hospital, dispensaries, dormitory, student, and field work we have aimed to make the evangelistic motive predominant. The various agencies have been made a means to an end and that end is the conversion of souls. And we thank God that many have been won to Him.
>
> May I add, in closing, that my first call is to the ministry. I am glad to be associated in the work at the Union Hospital, but am unwilling to assume full responsibility. I am ready to give such responsibility to a new man, and

> be associated with him as surgeon for the major cases. My evangelistic and student work require this. But its bearing on the present situation should be made clear. If the Presbyterians go, a new man should come at once,- if possible before Dr. Hall leaves. Trusting this may be brought about. Faithfully yours.[188]

Since the unfolding of the next few years will bring to light a very different picture, it is good to stop a moment and highlight a few comments in this letter. Raph's enthusiasm was obvious, and his insistence on reemphasizing the predominance of evangelism plus his concern that he be available for the evangelistic and student work, was an obvious signal as well. He highly valued the medical work he had been doing, but he wanted to turn the full responsibility of the Union Hospital over to someone else so that he could pursue his greater passions. He was not suggesting that he would leave the medical work; only that his work in the hospital would be reduced to that of a surgeon on staff.

As early as June of 1924, Dr. Franklin notified Raph that Dr. Lorenzo Porras, whose tragic death was mentioned briefly in Chapter 14, would be hired to serve in the Philippine mission (at a salary of 3000 pesos!) to help Raph in the absence of Dr. Hall. Dr. Porras did arrive on the field shortly before Dr. Hall's return to the States. Raph was encouraged by his work, and he suggested that with an American Doctor in charge, Dr. Porras could run the hospital quite well.

Raph felt that he needed the additional help due to his commitments to Dunwoody Dorm (LaPaz); the district dispensaries in LaPaz, Santa Barbara, Pototan, Bacolod, and Negros; evangelism; and student work.

The other problem concerning the hospital, the plan of the Presbyterians to sell it, was a major concern on both sides of the Pacific. Toward the end of 1924, it was apparent that the Mission was unable to bear the expense of the full purchase of the hospital if the Presbyterians were to leave. The Presbyterians were looking at dates: perhaps as early as the first of April, 1925. So, Dr. Franklin made it plain in letters to Mr. Valentine and Raph that the Mission was proceeding on the assumption that the Baptists would attempt to continue all the institutions shared up to that time by the Presbyterians and the Baptists. He hoped that the mission would be "led aright."

Dr. Franklin's letter crossed one from Raph in the mail (meaning that they were on ships heading in opposite directions!) in which Raph asked that his letter about this matter be shown to the Board. He felt that it would have been better if the withdrawal and sale had taken place in 1903 when the first plans were made for a cooperative hospital ministry. Since that obviously had not taken place, Raph expressed concern that proposals had been made in the Mission to permit the public sale of the Union interest, which would have put his whole hospital ministry in jeopardy. He also asked why the Board, having already appropriated some 60,000 pesos for building a new hospital building in Iloilo, could not have paid that amount as a down payment to the Presbyterians, setting up a time payment for the remaining 20,000 odd pesos.

1925

In January 1925, a Reference Committee meeting was held with Dr. Hall and Mr. Dawson, a Presbyterian missionary, present. They reported

1) that there was a strong feeling that the hospital should not be sold.
2) that they were willing to do their best to raise what they could to pay the Presbyterians, but that they were probably unable to raise whole amount.
3) that they felt that Dr. Hall should stay to help until the time limit (one year) set by the Presbyterians in their 1907 agreement.
4) a request that an American physician be sent at once to take charge of the Hospital, thus freeing Dr. Hall and relieving Raph.
5) and that a cablegram would be sent.

On February 3, Dr. Franklin wrote Raph to the effect that if Raph's friends (meaning Mrs. Peabody, Mrs. Doane, and others) should not come forward with funds to purchase the hospital, the Presbyterians would have to sell it, and the Mission would have to carry on its medical work in a new hospital as soon as a new property could be found.

In March, Dr. Franklin had some bad news to reveal. Dr. Brown from the Presbyterian Board had written of their decision concerning the sale price of the Union Hospital. The Baptist Board, basing its response on the information they had received from the Philippines, judged the amount asked for to be too high.

On the field, there was a meeting of nine Presbyterian and six Baptist missionaries. Raph reported the following findings. First, the total amount asked for by the Presbyterians on the field was Pesos 55,378.64 as against Pesos 84,957.28 "erroneously" asked for by the Presbyterian Board. Second, the participants in the meeting suggested that ½ of the cost be paid by January, and that the other ½ be paid a year later. Third, Raph personally regarded the sale of the hospital as unethical, and he wished to be relieved of any responsibility for it. Although he did not elaborate on the reason for his question about the ethics, it is probable that he felt that a Christian hospital ministry should remain in the hands of those with a burden for continuing that ministry for the sake of Christ and those served. The fourth point was Raph's sense that Dr. Hall should stay at the hospital since he was just back from a 6-month furlough and Raph was at the end of his 3rd year and not fit. He had not been able to have a vacation for years, and he felt he needed a month or two. He added his hope that another doctor would be provided.

Thankfully, the Lord had been working in the hearts of the "friends" Dr. Franklin had mentioned. Mrs. Peabody met with Dr. Franklin on March 28, 1925, and she gave him the good news that "a group of friends" had agreed to make an offer based upon the estimate made by Dr. Hall. The ABFMS property funds were offered by the Board to meet additional expenses if the amount were no more than $3,500. By April 22, Dr. Franklin was able to report that the purchase was underway. The Presbyterians involved in the Union Hospital work left Iloilo in April, and the hospital was under Baptist supervision from April the first. Miss Fullerton, a Presbyterian nurse agreed to remain with them for a time if the Board was willing, and Miss Nicolet was happy for her help.

'THE GENUS NURSE'

It was about this time that Raph applied his zeal for writing to a subject dear to his heart: 'The Genus Nurse.' He was incredibly grateful for the American nurses who worked with him, but in his brief "autobiography" he frequently mentioned the training, talents, tenderness, and laughable mistakes of the Filipino nurses. "The Genus Nurse" is a testament of praise to women, and, especially, to the Filipino nurses. The article would probably be considered moderately sexist today, but his deep appreciation of these women is obvious.

In the article he takes the reader home with one of the nurses; home to the simplicity of life and upbringing she had received. He wrote of the planting, gathering, and cooking of the family's dietary staple, rice. He learned that the common Tropical disease *beriberi* spread more rapidly because the people ate polished rice with the hull removed. It was found that leaving the hull on the rice would prevent the spread of the disease, so the people began to make a food called *Tiki Tiki* in which the hulled rice was ground up, and they ate red rice rather than polished white rice, to prevent the disease. He described the other foods they would eat, their sources of water (wells and drainage from the roof), and other drinks.

Her home was likely a bamboo shack with a split bamboo floor (convenient for throwing out water and dropping some food for the foraging pigs). There would be a bamboo chair or two, a few pegs for hanging clothes, no books, a tin lamp, an image of a saint, and a bolo (the heavy cleaver that was a "constant companion" of the men). He described how the girls would dress through the stages of their growing up: the bright, beautiful clothes they would sometimes wear in public, and the simple, drab clothes they would wear at home. The mother may have chewed betel nuts, the juice of which leaves a permanent stain on their lips and teeth, and perhaps she even smoked a cigar.

Then he brought the young woman from her home to the hospital, where she would be employed and taught how to be a nurse. She learns to run, not walk, especially when the Head Nurse gives her a job; and she learns that an overdose of medicine is never acceptable.[189]

One of the things the nurse learned quickly was that, unlike any medical source she has ever known, this hospital is a Mission Hospital. "And what do I mean by that?" Raph wrote,

> As I have said, without "pulling my punches," I always have felt that a Mission Hospital should be a center for active evangelism. The ones to do the work are the doctors and the nurses. It is all very well to depend upon imported evangelists for such a ministry, but the patients prefer to

> listen to the ones who treat them. If hearts are softened thereby it is natural for them to look to the ones who soften them, not to others. When the Great Physician (and I say it reverently) healed the sick he also gave the cheering of the saving word. The meant that these little nurses, all of them prejudiced against the Bible as a Book to be read and followed, were unwilling at first even to hear it.[190]

Then, having believed, they went through classes taught by Raph from the Bible on the methods Jesus used. Next, they were given practice in the wards, and they reported what they had done through the week. The results were exciting. The nurses were taught that no one should die in the hospital without having heard of the way of escape. Healing body and soul in the hospital: what an amazing change for a little girl from a little shack in the trees who had never dared to read a book!

Raph wrote that later he encouraged leaders of young people in the United States to teach them to practice Christian Service. But they just continued to fill "heads already overloaded and top heavy" with information they never tried to use. He concluded the account with a story from a Baptist Minister's meeting in Boston. A Chaplain to the hospitals was speaking, outlining various methods of approach for dealing with the gravely ill, but when he finished, a Filipino pastor who had been sitting beside Raph stood up and said: "Would you not raise the matter of personal salvation for a patient about the die?" The Chaplain replied, "Yes, if he raised the question himself." The Filipino answered: "Would you not think a Pastor guilty before God who let a person die without telling him the way of salvation?" Raph continues: "There was no answer. I was proud a Filipino had dared to speak that way in Classic Boston. No doubt I was blamed for this declaration, but I had nothing to do with it. It was a message from a Filipino heart. That is the message they need out there."

FROM REQUESTING A FURLOUGH TO STAYING THE COURSE

As the Fall rolled around, Raph's letters requesting a furlough for health reasons increased. In September he emphasized that while he hoped to return to the U.S. on furlough in the Spring for "family and other reasons," his desire would be to be able to train the new doctor before his departure. He emphasized that Dr. Porras was assuming more responsibilities and that he would soon "know the ropes." In fact, he emphasized that this Filipino doctor, Dr. Porras, "is a man of unusual professional and executive ability . . ." He was concerned, however, that Porras could not long carry the work alone.

On October 9, Dr. Franklin notified Raph that Mr. Munger had been appointed to return to work in the area that was left to ABFMS by the Presbyterians when they left Iloilo. Since Raph had already set his sights on that area, his internal response to this announcement would have been interesting to know. However, he had another matter to deal with first. The Finance Committee of the Board was concerned about the proportion of missionaries on furlough at the same time in comparison to the total number under appointment. As a result, Dr. Franklin asked for a statement of Raph's reasons for wishing to return to the States before his regular furlough.

In his next letter, Raph replied that "Family considerations" were the most important reason. "They have to do with my health. No doctor cares to "take his own medicine" as a rule, but sometimes it is his duty to do so." So, he has written his own "Medical Certificate," like those he had written for other missionaries: "He is not an invalid, and hopes for many more years of active service, but without a furlough it might be too late." He wrote that, for the last three years, he had been under exceptional emotional and mental strain (due to the loss of a child, the double burden he bore during Dr. Hall's absence, and unusual problems "that have taxed me.") He added, "A medical man, as a nurse, is under unusual strain caring for the sick, night service, etc. Ordinarily that wouldn't have caused the present condition, but coupled with other areas it has done so."

He was asking to be relieved for the present. Before his trip to Baguio his pulse rate was 160 to 180 or so after operations. After his rest at Baguio, it was still at 160. He felt that at his age (52) he needed to be especially careful. He recommended that Dr. Franklin check with Mrs. Peabody before cabling him since she might have had further information to share.

Remarkably, though, when the approval for his furlough arrived in December 1925, Raph replied that he felt sufficiently refreshed as to not need an early furlough."

> By planning the work and supervising the workers [I] can cover a large field of service with little expenditure of energy. My vacation in Baguio for the hot summer helped. The recent revival here in Iloilo has stirred my blood and I long to reach out into the district and to a larger work in evangelism.[191]

Raph's desire to stay the course until his regular furlough was fueled by both the revival and by opportunities to serve in a broader way. Little did he know that his decision to stay was to place him in a pressure cooker that would exceed in stress and burdens all that he had experienced in the preceding year.

CHAPTER 18

The Deterioration of the Relationship with the ABFMS

I will be glad and rejoice in thy mercy: for thou hast considered my trouble; thou hast known my soul in adversities. —Psalm 31:7

The distant clouds had begun to form. The relations of the members of the Iloilo missionary staff with those of Jaro and the home office were becoming increasingly strained through the years following the death of little Marguerite. In this conflict, as in any conflict with multiple actors, there were many opposing points of view. It would be the poor historian indeed who would refuse to recognize that there were behaviors, attitudes, and policies on both sides of the argument that resulted in this division.

THE SCHOOL PROBLEM

Raph had sensed a friction between the missionaries at Jaro and the rest of the ABMU missionaries when he first arrived in the Philippines. One of the strands of concern that made up the tapestry of later developments was that of the treatment of Mr. William O. Valentine, the first director of the Industrial School at Jaro. Raph had great respect for Mr. Valentine, and was shocked when, in 1918, "a violent attack" was made against Valentine by his fellow teachers. Raph believed that certain statements made by Dr. Franklin demonstrated that he agreed with those who wanted Mr. Bigelow to replace Valentine. The treatment of Mr. Valentine, even though he had many supporters among the missionaries and staff at the school, was reprehensible to Raph. After having worked with and observed Mr. Valentine for many years, he was saddened this man of God was so mistreated.

On June 15, 1925, Dr. Franklin wrote to the faculty of the Central Philippine College, Iloilo, Panay, and the Doane Evangelistic Institute, following a conference on the eleventh and twelfth of May. The final draft of this letter was also presented to the Boards. The letter states that the two Boards (ABFMS and the Woman's Board) had agreed on a definition of the work of each of the two schools involved. According to those definitions, the theological training for men who have the gospel ministry in view was to be given at the CPC, whose graduates would receive degrees, while the course at Doane Hall was to be for one year only and designed to prepare lay workers for evangelistic service in the churches and Sunday Schools in the localities where their business, profession or other careers may call them, or wherever the Lord may lead them as evangelists or teachers of the Word.

Dunwoody Dorm was to be thrown open for the use of students at DEI as well as for the regular high school students, the donors clearly understanding that the one-year course at DEI was for training of lay workers only.

A "Committee of Conference," regarding the schools, was formed between the two Boards, and a similar Committee of Conference was to be formed at Iloilo to consult with that Home Committee. The members of the Iloilo Committee would include Mr. H. F. Stuart, President of the CPC; Miss Martien, Director of Religious activities at DEI; Dr. R. C. Thomas; and Mr. E. W. Thornton. Dr. Thomas was to be the Chairman. The letter was concluded with the following words "We recognize that a spirit of cooperation in our educational work is more important than any elaborate scheme of coordination of effort."

Dr. Franklin expressing the hope that progress would soon be reported "in the direction approved by the Board."

On February 1, 8, and 15, the Joint Committee in the Philippines on Relations between the Doane Hall Evangelistic Institute and the Central

Philippine College met. Their report expressed agreement with the differing goals of the schools and the points mentioned in the letter of June 15. They unanimously felt that one point, having to do with the eventual reduction of their committee to the two school heads, Martien and Stuart, seemed to suggest an unwillingness on the part of the representatives from Doane Hall to cooperate. They felt that the committee of four should continue, providing a way for cooperation to be without "unfriendly discriminations." Although Raph did have some serious misgivings about some of the faculty of the Jaro school, he was unwilling to let that compromise the opportunity provided by the Committee to support the Doane Hall ministries.

RAPH'S DESIRED EXPANSION OF HIS EVANGELISTIC MINISTRIES

In a "Statement of the Philippine Situation," Raph emphasized that his program from the outset was one that made "medicine a means to the end of evangelism." Even though the "great objective" of the Union Mission Hospital was evangelistic, the medical, training and professional aspects of the hospital were not neglected. The student work gave him great satisfaction in both the number of students who came to Christ and were baptized, and the teams of Evangelistic Institute students who went out into neighboring districts and islands to evangelize.[192]

In May of 1925, Raph wrote the following to Mr. Valentine:

> Although I have more or less to do in connection with my medical and student work, I have an excellent helper in Dr. Porras and also in Mr. Perez. With Alberto Prance to join the force here in June further assistance is assured. I should be willing to undertake the evangelistic supervising of the work the Presbyterians have in Iloilo and Antique, if the Reference Committee approve, for the coming year, at least, and I think I shall have time to do it reasonable justice. [Feeling that he should inherit this from Dr. Hall, anyway, he emphasized that he was "willing to try it."]

> This would not include, however, the supervision of the school work already established. I should wish to do evangelistic work in these schools, but beyond this . . . I am not primarily a school man.[193]

Raph's willingness to undertake "the evangelistic supervising of the work the Presbyterians have in Iloilo and Antique" should be no surprise since it has become apparent that Raph's burden for widespread evangelistic work was vying in his heart more and more with the work in the hospital. He felt that his work there would be more than adequately covered in the future, giving him the needed time to pour himself into a new ministry. Raph requested that the Reference Committee approve this appointment.

Raph's request was refused by the Reference Committee, so he appealed to the Board over their heads. As was already mentioned, in November of 1917 Raph had requested an official separation of his work from that of the other Baptist missionaries in the same territory; he claimed that his work was "quite distinct" from that of his fellow missionaries who were engaged in evangelistic and educational effort. In later correspondence, the Board of ABFMS emphasized that, although formal approval was not given, tacit approval had been given until his request for this new ministry arrived. The Board responded to this request during meetings in January 1926.

Dr. and Mrs. R.C. Thomas were to be advised that the Board would be glad to consider the assignment (with support from Mrs. Henry W. Peabody from the Woman's Board) of a field in Iloilo Province, P.I., for general evangelistic effort in addition to the work to which he is already designated, on several conditions. The conditions were significant! They were, first, that the Thomases agree to be restored to their former status in the Society in the Philippines, a status identical to that of every other missionary there (thus reversing the 1917 request for special status); second, that Dr. Thomas can assure the Board that his health will allow him to "undertake the oversight of an evangelistic field in addition to his duties as superintendent of the hospital at Iloilo, the director of work for students at La Paz, and responsibility for dispensaries in several centers;" and third, that it be understood that the general work they would do would conform with a plan for training of workers in the Philippine Mission agreed upon by the Woman's Board and the General Board on May 12, 1925.[194]

CHAPTER 18

MISSION POLICIES

The Board obviously felt that if Raph were given charge of the Iloilo evangelistic and church work, the reasons for the 1917 request for separation of his work would evaporate. Also, they were concerned that Raph and Mr. Munger would clearly present to the Board the way in which the work in Iloilo Province would be divided among them. With this issue clarified, and the various conditions of the Board met, it would be appropriate for the Thomases to approach the Reference Committee about their readiness for the new assignment. Dr. Franklin wrote,

> In conclusion, please permit me to call special attention to the Board's expression of appreciation of the very useful service you and Mrs. Thomas have rendered in the P.I., and the confidence that your consent to return to your former status in the Philippine Mission would promote greatly the usefulness of the mission as a whole.[195]

In order to understand Raph's response to the Board, it will be necessary to remember that his relationships with some other missionaries not working with him, and especially with the members of the Reference Committee, were not cordial. He could count some of them as friends and willing colleagues, but others resented him and the breadth of ministries he had as a medical doctor. Once the Board required Raph and Norma to return to their pre-1917 status, the Reference Committee began to micromanage things at the hospital, and even to find personnel there who would agree with them that the hospital was being neglected.

Raph's letter of response to the Board is dated March 24, 1926. On March 24, Mr. Munger told Rev. F. H. Rose of the Reference Committee that he was not against dividing the territory along the natural boundary lines of Antique and Southern Iloilo Province, but he privately wrote to Raph that he saw no reason to discuss the issue unless Raph agreed to the provisions the Board.[196] Later (in July), Mr. Munger wrote Raph privately, protesting ministry activities that were going on in Southern Iloilo despite the fact that Raph had not returned "to the fold" as demanded as a condition of such work by the Board. Raph, however, felt that he "was in compliance with" the conditions of the Board, while doubting that the Board was acting to control certain improper behaviors and clandestine activities on the field in the Philippines. One of Raph's concerns about the relationships between the Reference Committee, the Board, and the missionaries was that, on March 30, the Reference Committee had sent a letter to the Board in which they alleged that they had received reports that Dr. Thomas was neglecting the hospital.

Raph believed that two of the missionary nurses at the hospital who had objected to the necessity of working under Dr. Porras were the sources of the reports. He was unhappy about the letter, unhappy about the reports, and unhappy about the lack of support of Dr. Porras by the nurses.

Raph was comfortable with promoting the "Filipinization idea" (turning the work over to the Filipino believers) by supporting and turning responsibilities over to Dr. Porras, especially because of his influence among the people. He felt that Dr. Porras should remain in his position. In fact, this was one of four important issues he had expressed considerable concern about in private correspondence at that time. The other three were: that Doane Hall workers should have the privilege of preaching in Iloilo and Antique under the proper supervision of missionaries; that the interests of Doane Hall should not be interfered with by Jaro; and that the hospital and Dunwoody Dormitory should be under conservatives. The last point is significant because, though, as we shall see, Raph did not emphasize theological conservativism or liberalism as primary reasons for his determination to resign, it was obviously on his mind.

Raph's letter to the Board reflected these concerns, plus concerns about past and present actions and innuendos of the Reference Committee members and others. The following is the response in full:

> We shall be happy to accept the responsibility of becoming field missionaries for this part of Iloilo on the conditions laid down in the action of the Board . . . But we would expect the Board to accept the following conditions, which we believe it will be quite willing to do, before our final acceptance of the conditions laid down for us:
>
> (1) That frankness and forbearance henceforth be encouraged on both sides
> (2) That the rule of submitting any statement touching work, character, or methods of a missionary

to the missionary involved, before transmission to the Secretary of the Board, either by official or private correspondence, be observed.

(3) That personal correspondence concerning mission policies, between individual missionaries and the Secretary of the Board, be referred to the Reference Committee before being accepted by the Board as valid evidence

(4) that the same measure of freedom be allotted to all missionaries in their field work

(5) That any action, or proposed action, of the Board, involving a missionary or his work, be transmitted to the missionary involved and to the Reference Committee simultaneously, and his views be awaited and with due regard for his technical knowledge of his department of service, especially if he is not too recent an arrival.

(6) That correspondence between the Reference Committee officers and the Secretary of the Board be open to all missionaries.

(7) That the Reference Committee refrain from negotiations for the sale or long lease of property in any field, without first consulting the missionary in charge; from altering the field designation of a missionary during his absence or furlough, without first consulting the missionary in charge; from permitting a missionary in temporary charge of a field missionary's territory, during the latter's absence on furlough, from radically changing the known policies of the absentee without due correspondence with him; and from permitting any missionary to overrule the advice of a fellow missionary to his workers concerning his ordination of candidates for the ministry in his own field, or in any other way of influencing his workers against his policies.

(8) That without mutual consent and agreement no missionary shall work in the field of another missionary.[197]

Raph obviously knew that he was presuming a lot when he suggested that the Board would be willing to accept his conditions. Though he was dealing with Christian gentlemen, they were still human . . . and they were in charge. Their expectation was that Raph would accept their conditions and move on. His expectation was that they would listen to the concerns of a veteran missionary doctor and accept them for the benefit of all of the missionaries – not merely for his own benefit. With the on-field context in mind, Raph's conditions would have been clear; but without the specific details that led to his conditions, some of them would have been difficult to interpret. Though his communication was based upon grievances, the statement that he believed the Board would be "quite willing" to accept his conditions, seems to imply Raph's confidence that the Board would understand the foundation of the grievances and respond favorably to his conditions.

On May 11, the Board of Managers acted in response to Raph's letter. They stated that for the Philippine Mission, they considered it "inexpedient" to adopt further rules or understandings on the matters mentioned in addition to the "recognized principles governing the work on all the fields of the society."[198]

In defense of the Board, adding new rules or policies, or even revisiting policies already in place, based upon the recommendation of any one missionary would be most extraordinary! Perhaps, if Raph had worded his letter differently, he would have accomplished more. If his letter had consisted of a list of concerns about the moral, ethical, procedural, and behavioral actions of various missionaries; the actions of the Reference Committee; the Board's acceptance of information not previously submitted to Raph as the subject of the complaints; and things decided (without his knowledge) about areas under his responsibility; the discussion might have gone differently. However, Raph was old school, and he felt that things should be handled by principle above personal grievances.

The Board claimed that they had received charges concerning the hospital, but they refused to deal with them until Raph received an opportunity to respond. They did, however, table the idea of granting permission for the broader responsibilities Raph and Norma had requested until the issue of the hospital was dealt with.

Concerning this reversal, Raph wrote:

> Recognizing the attitude of the Reference Committee as hostile to my cherished program for medical mission work, whereby I was committed both to practice and preach, I saw no way of escape but resignation. . . . I felt that my happy experience of baptizing over a thousand Filipinos in a period of four years and a half was worth considering, even had the medical work suffered. As it did not suffer my feeling was even stronger that student work and field work and hospital evangelism that brought such results should have been encouraged in a medical missionary program and not so completely discountenanced.[199]

In a private letter to Mrs. Peabody, Raph wrote the following regarding the charge of his neglecting the medical work:

> As to neglect of patients etc. you need not be alarmed. I have had standing orders that no private patient is to be kept waiting long without notifying me. I know that Miss Nicolet has cririced [*sic*] me for such things, but I believe she has made a mistake in doing so. I make regular ward visits and feel that I have done justice to the medical work, though I also maintain that medical missionary has other obligations in an evangelistic way that are as much a part of his duty as medicine and have tried to give this side proper attention. But, as I say, I do not care to discuss with Dr. M. or anyone else my medical practice.[200]

Since the information communicated within America is as important as that communicated to America from the field to provide a context to all that was going on, it is interesting that a meeting of Dr. Franklin, Mrs. Peabody, and members of the Woman's Board was held on May 13, 1926. Dr. Franklin wrote to Raph about the assurances given at that meeting. The Board recognized that the student work at La Paz was strategic, and good work had been done at Doane Hall and Doane Evangelistic Institute ("as a school offering a one-year course for lay workers only"). Dr. Franklin told the ladies that as far as he was aware, none of the missionaries in the

Philippines objected to the work on that basis. Furthermore, since the generous friends of Dr. Thomas who enabled the Mission to purchase the Presbyterian interest in the Dormitory were interested in the student work, the Board felt it appropriate to designate half of the space in the dorm to be used to house lay workers in the one-year course.

Also, remarkably, Raph's request for another doctor was answered in this same period. Dr. Dwight Johnson of Manitoba was appointed to serve as Raph's colleague at the Iloilo hospital. He was expected to sail in August, and the Board requested assurances from Raph that he would remain on the field long enough to train Dr. Johnson.

RESIGNATION SUBMITTED

However, despite these good reports, Raph's mind was fully occupied by the Board's response to the information received from the Reference Committee. He felt that resignation was the only course he could take. His response was clearly spelled out in a July letter to the ABFMS Board:

> To my surprise I learned that a letter had been sent home accusing me of neglect of my work in the hospital. I did not see the letter before it was sent and had no opportunity to refute the charges and determined to wait and see whether the Board would, contrary to its rules, consider such charges before hearing from me. I have since learned from Dr. Franklin that I am, on the strength of that letter, prohibited from any work in the field . . . until I have accepted the orders of the Reference Committee and answered those charges.
>
> I will not go into any defense of myself or attack on my brethren. Their attack on me is unfounded and can easily be disproved by my record. Their letter was irregular, and the decision of the Board based on this letter notifying me that I am prohibited from preaching in this field is also irregular.

> In order that I may be faithful to the donors who have so generously furnished the means, at my request, to give this field to the Baptists, I will continue until December 1st.
>
> I hereby present my resignation to take effect at that time, since I feel the compulsion which I have always felt and clearly stated to the Board, that I must preach the Gospel as well as practice medicine in my work as a foreign missionary and to do this I must be allowed a field and the ordinary liberty of a Baptist.[201]

Two actions of the Reference Committee in the Philippines are worthy of mention. One was a report made to the Reference Committee that Iloilo students were being denied opportunity to evangelize in the Antique field, but the Committee claimed that they had not accepted this report. The other, an action by the Reference Committee was based upon several of the members of the Committee having heard that Dr. Thomas had negotiations underway to purchase land near the University of the Philippines in Manila. He and Mr. Wolfe, a former member of the "Christian Missionary force" in the Philippines, were reputedly seeking land to launch a Theological Seminary in Manila. Since they had been approached by members of the staff of the Union Seminary of Manila with the question of whether ABFMS was behind this activity, the Reference Committee acted to declare themselves to be uninvolved in the rumored activity. Copies of this resolution were sent to the President of Union Seminary and to the Foreign Secretary, Dr. Franklin.

About that time, Raph wrote a brief comment in a letter to "Mother" about the possibility of future ministry in Manila if she (Mrs. Peabody) and Mrs. Doane did not want him to resign.[202] It is apparent that Mr. Wolfe, a theological conservative, had been seeking a property in Manila. A letter written to Mrs. Doane in 1926 was a confidential revelation that Raph, Norma, and Miss Martien were impressed with the wisdom of purchasing a lot of land next to the Dormitory in Manila which had already been purchased by Mrs. Doane. They were thinking that it might be useful in the future.

Several points of interest stand out in this letter. First, Raph quotes Mr. Wolfe's data concerning a possible piece of land. Second, Raph encourages Mrs. Doane to think of the possibilities of starting a work in Manila like

Doane Hall in Iloilo, and beginning "the First Baptist Church of Manila." Third, Raph mentions his concern that the policies of the General Board were such that it was unlikely that they would ever go into Manila in the way he was envisioning the work. Fourth, he suggests that if Dr. Pemberton were to come, Raph might be free to go the Manila after his furlough. Fifth, he admits that the plan of starting a work like Doane Hall in Manila might seem premature to Mrs. Doane and Mrs. Peabody, and that they could well feel that he was trying "to cover too much territory." His response to that thought in the letter is that he feels that this is the way he can do the best work. He explained,

> Supervision and generalship is the proper work for a missionary, and if we can train the natives and supervise ... we can cover a big field. Masa will help in the Iloilo field, and Franco in Doane Hall and Porras in the medical work. This means I should supervise rather than attend to too much detail. I know Franco is dubious but we must hope and pray he will improve. He may grow into the work in time. It might be that Mrs. Munger would help temporarily at Doane Hall, though this is not at all sure, and if she does that will leave me even freer this year.[203]

Raph concludes by emphasizing that if all of this seems to be too Utopian at present, hopefully the thoughts concerning a larger work will help with the future planning for the Dormitory work.

So, to sum up, it appears that as early as April of 1926, Raph's fertile mind was considering the possibility of developing a full-fledged ministry in Manila. He and Mr. Wolfe had no fears of comity violation in such a move. In other words, they did not feel that it violated the division of ministry locations agreed upon by the various denomination. But, Raph felt that ABFMS would not seek to develop the kinds of ministries he had in mind for Manila – especially starting a school since it would be a conservative alternative to the Union Seminary. While the Reference Committee in the Philippines was still considering Raph to be a missionary with the ABFMS (which he was since Raph did not formally send a letter of resignation until July) and was developing a case against him, he was already contemplating future ministry possibilities in April.

In September of 1926, Mrs. Peabody appeared before the Board with a statement about the resignation of Dr. and Mrs. Thomas. She was apparently unable to remain in the meeting long enough to discuss her statement, but she promised to provide a copy of her statement to the Board. Perhaps because she felt that some of the information in the statement needed to be clarified by Raph himself, she never sent the copy to the Board. In notifying Raph of this meeting, Dr. Franklin expressed his hope that a happy solution could be found, and that Raph would withdraw his resignation. The matter of Raph's resignation was referred to the Board of Managers for review and recommendation to the Board.

THE COMMISSION

Based upon Raph's resignation letter and Mrs. Peabody's appearance before the Board, it was obvious to Dr. Franklin and to the Board that there were misunderstandings to be discussed before formal action could be taken. Doctor Franklin emphasized to Raph that the Board did not desire to accept his resignation, hoping that a satisfactory solution could be found.

As a result of this decision, and other needs in Asia, the Board appointed a Commission Board of Managers. The scope of their responsibilities was wide in that they were a deputation to the Far East, intended to meet serious problems and unusual opportunities in person in China, Japan, and the Philippines. The members of the Commission included two well-known denominational leaders, Rev. J. F. Watson, Secretary of the West Washington Baptist State Convention; and Rev. D. B. MacQueen, Pastor of First Baptist Church of Rochester, New York. Also included were Miss Mabel R. McVeigh, Foreign Secretary of the Woman's Board; ABFMS Foreign Secretary J. H. Franklin; Dr. And Mrs. A. W. Beaven, members respectively of the General Board and the Woman's Board; and George B. Huntington, the Treasurer of the Society, who would be joining them in South China.

One issue to be investigated by the delegation was whether the Doane Evangelistic Institute interfered with and rivaled the theological school at the Central Philippines College in Jaro. As Raph explained many times, he believed that the Institute was meeting a need not being met by the theological school in Jaro, in that through the Institute evangelists and Christian workers burdened for their people were being prepared and sent out to serve. He was also concerned that the inclusive policy of the ABFMS was allowing an admixture of modernistic teaching in the school at Jaro. Raph was asked to remain longer in Iloilo, until March of 1927, in order that he might complete his regular term of service, help Dr. Johnson to become better acquainted with the work of the hospital, and meet with the delegation. Raph was assured that if he was satisfied with his meeting with the Commission in the Philippines, he could meet with the Board of Managers of the Mission after his return to America.

Raph's frustration with the Reference Committee was further enhanced by a letter sent by the Reference Committee to Doctor Porras. He was informed that his position as Director of the hospital would be ceasing since the emergency for which he was hired had ceased to exist. He was told that he could remain in the hospital as Dr. Johnson's assistant for a short period if funds for his continuing there should be available. Raph called the action "ridiculous," and told Porras to forget the letter since only the Board should be able to take such an action. Raph reported this to the Board of Managers in November.

The stage was now set for the formal parting of the ways of Raph and Norma and the Board under which they had served so long. Yet, as is often the case in periods of personal turmoil, God continued to work. In December of 1926, Raph and Norma sent a nicely printed report to supporters in which December activities in Renfroville, a religious awakening at Doane Hall, and some incidents in a recent evangelistic campaign at Renfroville were all reported.

Raph was busy but so excited about the revival! All of those involved in the ministry were rejoicing. He helped with the follow up work for two hundred and twenty students who said they were ready to receive Christ during the 50 or so meetings held between Monday and Friday, but fewer came to the examination. Parental opposition, doubts, and misunderstanding held some back, but some students came. Eleven came to receive Christ at the Friendly Corner alone.

In his final report to Dr. Franklin about the work at Doane Hall, Dunwoody Dorm, Union Mission Hospital, and the Student and dispensary work, Raph expressed his gratitude to God that progress could be reported in both medical and evangelistic service. He emphasized that it had been a source of satisfaction to him that in the past the Board had allowed him free play to accomplish his openly avowed objective of ministerial and medical service. He suggested that student work and field evangelism provided good opportunities for medical missionary work as an adjunct to evangelism. This kind of ministry had been a happy experience for him; more so than a strictly localized service at a hospital or a single dispensary. He felt that he was an asset in the process of nationalizing the work after so many years of this kind of ministry. Dr. Porras was praised in the report for his abilities and the ways in which he assumed responsibility in the hospital. Despite being a church of transients, from the time of the opening of the school at Doane Hall, over 140 baptisms had taken place in the student church. Lastly, Raph expressed sorrow at the death of Pedro E. Mosa, the Pastor of the student church. His messages had been powerful, and he manifested all the qualities needed to lead the Doane Hall ministry.

The last letter Raph and Norma sent to their "Dear Friends," in January, from Iloilo was focused on their furlough ministry and the message they hoped to have after returning to the States:

> It is hard to humanize bald statements like this, but when we see you face to face, we would like to try to persuade you that the great objective for medicine, education, and the other agencies in the foreign file is the saving of souls not only by education or medicine, valuable as they are, but by reasonable time spent by all the agents in DIRECT EVANGELISM itself, whether it be in the field, church, or student work.
>
> "Hasta Luego," as we say over here, which means we hope to meet another time; and then we can make it all clearer. Meanwhile, pray for the evangelization of the Filipino. He needs that more than politics – or even education and medicine.
>
> Faithfully yours, R. C. Thomas[204]

CHAPTER 19

The Parting of the Ways

And the contention was so sharp between them, that they departed asunder one from the other ——Acts 15:39

In December of 1926, while Dr. Franklin was enroute to the Philippines as a member of the Commission, he received a telegram from Raph. In it, Raph stated that he did not see what was to be gained by the Commission. He expressed his "entire disapproval." Since Miss Martien was in the States, Raph felt that it would be far more profitable for a meeting of the Board with Martien, Bigelow, and Thomas in America.

Dr. Franklin answered that the Commission and the Board were disappointed, and he expressed hope that Raph and Norma would change their minds about sailing on January 6. He and Miss McVeigh had telegraphed all the members of the Philippine mission to make themselves available for the Commission from January 24 to February 8.

Raph was sorry to disappoint the members of the Commission, but he felt that "under conditions prevailing on the field, an investigation in this time and place would not be the part of wisdom." With the absence of the principal of the Institute, Miss Martien, and with his understanding of the attitude of the Reference Committee, he felt it unwise to stay. He suggested that the gathering of evidence apart from many interviews would probably help the Commission to do its job.

Fueling Raph's frustration with the current "conditions" was a refusal on the part of the Reference Committee to forward to him a copy of the letter they had sent to the Board concerning him, and the names of people who had made accusations or complaints about him; they replied that they were holding them for the Commission. When Raph expressed his disappointment, Harland Stuart of the Reference Committee emphasized that it was the desire of the Reference Committee to keep "personalities" out of the affairs of the Mission. He reminded Raph of the need for Raph and Norma to request a special meeting of the Reference Committee to receive approval of their furlough.

Though Raph had expressed regret about their missing "the social side" of the visit of the "kind friends" from America who had come to the Philippines as members of the Committee, he had assured Dr. Franklin that he hoped to meet them in America, after their return, to express his regrets personally. As for their fellow missionaries in the Philippines, in early February, Raph, writing for him and his "Senora," wished his "Fellow Missionaries" success.

As it turned out, Norma became ill, and their departure was delayed. The delay resulted in Raph and Norma being in Manila at the same time as the arrival of the Commission! Dr. Franklin invited them to meet with the Commission members at the Luneta Hotel, where the delegation was staying. Raph accepted the invitation and suggested that they meet on the morning of the 5th. He concluded his brief note with the words: "Trusting, then, to see you tomorrow, and assuming that the hour is convenient unless we hear from you to the contrary, I am, Faithfully yours, R.C.T." Whether that meeting took place, and what was discussed, we do not know.

The deputation asked all the missionaries to the Philippine Baptist Mission to meet with them at the Central Philippine College on Monday morning, February 14, 1927, for a conference for "inspirational purposes" and the hearing of reports from the missionaries. They desired to obtain full information with reference to "the present conditions and urgent needs on the several fields, and the adjustment of problems" confronting the Boards and missionaries.

MEETING WITH THE BOARD

At the conclusion of the Commission's work in the Philippines, and before appearing at the Board of Manager's meeting in the States, Raph requested that he be furnished with a copy of the Commission's report on its findings in the Philippines. He was told that the Board of Managers would be meeting on May 19, and that his resignation would be a topic of discussion. He was invited to come at the Board's expense to make any statement on his mind. The date of the Board's discussion of the resignation was changed to the thirtieth of May, and Raph was told that the Philippine report of the Commission would not be available until that date. No doubt this was very disturbing to Raph, since he would be entering the meeting without proper preparation to discuss the contents of the Commission's report.

After the meeting with the Board of Managers, Raph and Norma waited for the final action of the Board. It arrived in the form of a June 4 letter from Dr. Franklin. The letter read as follows:

> At a meeting of the Board of Managers this a.m., further consideration was given to resignation resulting in the following action:
>
> Vote: "That although the Board takes decided exception to certain statements in the letter of resignation of Dr. R. C. Thomas, dated July 7, 1926, which statements the Board regards as inconsistent with the facts, yet because he has repeatedly declared his resignation to be final, and because of his declared inability longer to support the Board's methods of administration," and "loyally to support the administration in the Philippines," and also because he is unable to be able to accept for himself the conditions under which every other missionary of the Society is serving,
>
> Therefore, the Board feels compelled, after prolonged and most serious consideration including conference with Dr. Thomas, to accept, and does now regretfully accept, the resignation of Dr. R. C. Thomas as a missionary of the American Baptist Foreign Missionary Society, to take effect on July 1, 1927.
>
> The Board is mindful of your devoted services as a missionary and deeply regrets the apparent necessity for the

> acceptance of your resignation. We had hoped, as indicated to you in letters, that you could see you way to accept a status identical with that of other missionaries of the Society. Now that your resignation has been presented and accepted, I will merely add, on behalf of the entire Board, the assurance of our hope that you and Mrs. Thomas will enjoy the highest measure of usefulness and happiness in such service as you may undertake in the future.[205]

The mention of "certain statements" In Raph's letter of resignation that the Board regarded as "inconsistent with the facts" fueled both Raph's curiosity and indignation. He answered on the first of June with a request for a description of those inconsistencies. The response from Dr. Franklin was that this phrase meant no more than such inconsistencies "as might arise from misunderstanding," and that this phrase was only communicated to Raph. The Board of Managers later granted permission for the Philippine section of the Special Deputation report to be sent to Raph, and they repeated the statement that there was no suggestion in the correspondence from the Board of Raph's dishonesty, just misunderstanding.

The Philippine report included positive information about the evangelistic work done, with emphasis on the need to be careful that evangelistic work would result in the establishment of churches. The Field was said to suffer from a lack of coordination, cooperation, and wholesome leadership. There was seen to be a need for a Mission Conference, for better reporting procedures, and for work on title, property, and legal issues, especially relating to transfer of property to indigenous religious bodies. One of the concerns Raph expressed in response to the report was that it included a suggestion that there was a problem with the finances of the Hospital. He insisted that up to the time that he had turned over responsibility for those finances, there was a surplus of funds.

From this point on, correspondence to and from the Board, whether from Raph, Dr. Franklin, Mrs. Peabody, or other members of the ABFMS or the Woman's Board were attempts to clarify statements and positions, demand further information, or discuss various unresolved financial issues. Instead of emphasizing further details from this period, as sad and important as they were, it would be better to summarize the perspectives of the Board and of Raph.

CHAPTER 19

THE BOARD'S STATEMENT

In response to statements published by friends and supporters of Dr. and Mrs. Thomas and their colleagues, and by such publications as *The Sunday School Times* and the *Watchman Examiner* (Dr. Law's publication), the Board of Managers of the ABFMS published a statement on "The Resignation of Dr. Raphael C. Thomas." The following is a summary of the response.

1. The Board of Managers denied that Dr. Thomas' theology was not congenial to the home authorities, and that he was forced out of the mission because of his loyalty to evangelicalism. At no time during the nine hours of meetings with the Board after his return to America, nor in his correspondence with the Board, was the issue of theological difference mentioned.
2. The Board understood his resignation to be based upon differences between Dr. Thomas, the Board, and the Philippine administration related to administrative measures. Dr. Thomas expressed his inability to loyally support the administration in the Philippines.
3. In November of 1917, "following the adoption of certain administrative measures by the Board, after very careful investigation," Dr. Thomas requested an official separation of his work from that of the other Baptist missionaries in the area because, he stated, his hospital, dispensary, and dormitory work was "quite distinct from that of our fellow missionaries who are engaged in evangelistic and educational service." While the Board did not formally consent to this request, it "tacitly acquiesced for the time" to the desire of Dr. Thomas for a separation. The Board emphasized in this statement that this gave Dr. Thomas a status not enjoyed by any other member of the mission Society.
4. In 1926, Dr. Thomas requested designation to an evangelistic field in addition to his other responsibilities. This was in spite of the fact that he had reported just a few months before that an additional doctor was required immediately at the hospital to work with him. The Board voted that it would be glad to consider designating Dr. and Mrs. Thomas to a field for evangelistic efforts in addition to their other

responsibilities if (a) they would agree to being "restored to their former status in the Philippine Mission," a collaborative status identical to that of all other missionaries in the Philippine Islands; (b) the health of Dr. Thomas had been restored sufficiently to allow such additional responsibilities; and, (c) if such general work assigned to them would be "conducted in harmony with the plan unanimously approved on May 12, 1925, by both the Woman's Board and the General Board with reference to the training of workers in the Philippine Mission and reported to the field on June 15, 1925."

5. About the same time, word was received by the Board through official channels that the missionaries serving as nurses under Dr. Thomas' supervision, were dissatisfied with the conditions at the hospital. "Questions were raised as to whether Dr. Thomas was giving sufficient time to the hospital." While the Board was unwilling to take the reports seriously without giving Dr. Thomas an opportunity to answer the charges, the conditions in the hospital "might have a bearing on the Board's willingness to place heavier responsibilities on the Superintendent of the hospital." The Board therefore decided to postpone further consideration of Dr. Thomas' request until he would "have opportunity to reply to the statements received concerning the hospital. Upon receiving this word Dr. Thomas tendered his resignation."
6. The Board promptly cabled Dr. Thomas with news of the "commission about to sail for the Orient" including the Philippines, and with a request that he wait for their arrival for a conference on the field "regarding questions involving his work." He replied that he did not approve of the conference on the field but preferred a conference with the Board in America. He was urged again to remain in the Philippines, but he declined to do so, though he was still present in the Philippines when the Commission arrived. Upon his return nine hours were given in two sessions of the Board "to a discussion of his resignation and the reasons for it." Dr. Thomas was present for, and participated in the discussion, at the end of which he asked permission to add a sentence summarizing his reasons for resignation. After hearing the discussion, the Board voted unanimously to accept his resignation.

7. The statement included two paragraphs that will, because of their importance, be quoted below:

> The Board denies again that Dr. Thomas "was forced out on account of his evangelical loyalty." Theological differences were not mentioned in connection with his resignation. His statement, "I resign because of my inability loyally to support the administration in the Philippines" is supported by the facts.
>
> The Board of Managers of the Foreign Mission Society has never sought to prevent the return of Dr. Thomas or others to the Philippine Islands as missionaries, although the hope was entertained that they would enter some of the unoccupied areas in the Philippine Islands rather than go back to fields where missionaries of our Philippine Baptist Mission were already at work.[206]

RAPH'S RESPONSE

Although Mrs. Peabody replied in Raph's defense, he felt obligated to make his own statement to "his friends" who were expecting him to respond. The following is a summary of his reply. He wanted to emphasize that "there really is another side." The statement that was released as his formal reason for resigning: "I resign because I cannot loyally support the policies of the Board in the Philippines" was coined during the Chicago interview when the Board was looking for a technical resignation statement that could be responded to unanimously. Raph afterwards felt that unless the reasons that led up to that statement were given, it would leave "the false impression that I was refractory and disloyal to the Board. This is untrue."

He continued with the statement that his spirit had been friendly to the Board but became out of harmony with its policies in later years. He had been sorrowfully trying to carry on a conservative work in a modernistic atmosphere but was "driven to the wall" despite his efforts to keep the peace in the bonds of love. His semi-isolation was not permitted. He realized that he was required to do his work as a medical missionary in ways approved by the Reference Committee. Since the Foreign Secretary and the Board supported the Reference Committee, he felt he could not submit to the limitations imposed upon him. This led to his resignation.

Raph did not, in his appearance before the Board, nor did he in his reply to them, make "definite heresy charges" against the Secretary, Board or Reference Committee. However, he felt that an underlying cause of the pressure put on him could be characterized as "the fruit of modernistic thought" the world over. His desire to combine medicine and evangelism in the "old fashioned way" was hindered and finally forbidden. He felt that the demands were clear: he must either be a doctor, or an evangelist, but not both.

As to the question of whether he was "forced to resign," he claimed that he was not "told" to resign, but the conditions were arranged in such a way that he felt that it was impossible not to resign and, at the same time, to maintain his self-respect and a clear conscience. About the question of whether there were theological issues at play in his resignation, Raph mentioned that his silence in that regard did not mean that this was not an issue. In this response, Raph broke his silence (which he claimed to have maintained to prevent the Board from losing financial support) regarding that matter for the first time publicly and stated his opinion that in the Philippines, the program of the Board "is now and has been for years in the interest of modernism." He had considered resigning before but decided to remain and do his bit to give the Filipinos, whom he loved, a conservative message.

Since the Reference Committee had demands concerning how the work was to be done, he had desired to work independently without "modernistic interference." Since that was not allowed, he resigned with a clear conscience. He felt that suggestions that he was unwilling to cooperate with his fellow missionaries were completely misguided. He only desired to be free from service on committees and voting. Raph desired not to become officially involved in measures he could not endorse, or perpetually be a minority voice in deliberations. Otherwise, he wanted to be treated like all the rest of the missionaries. He attended conferences and conferred freely, desiring to have a friendly attitude toward his fellows.

Though the Board had tacitly permitted him to have this unique status, pressure from the Reference Committee continued. As we have seen, when he requested the field of Southern Iloilo, the Board expressed willingness to allow it based on his fulfilling certain requirements. One of them was returning to his former status with the Reference Committee. In addition, certain issues were raised that had been reported to the Board by the Reference Committee. Because of his concerns about the behavior and insinuations of the Reference Committee, he wrote the response to the Board in which he and Norma had agreed to return to normal voting status if the Board would accept certain conditions, primarily concerning submission by the Reference Committee, or any field missionary, of any correspondence related to a member or his work before that correspondence is forwarded to the Board. He considered this to be an overture to reconciliation, but the Board did not receive it as such. The Board refused to adopt further rules. He was willing to acquiesce and return to the demanded status, but the matter was closed.

Raph felt that the mission had changed in policies and personnel, so that his "old fashioned faith and methods" brought a different reaction than it had when he had first arrived on the field in 1904. Then, he had been given the freedom to serve as both a doctor and an evangelistic missionary. The Reference Committee had emphasized the need for a full-time doctor unless "Dr. Thomas gives practically all of his time and attention to the medical work, which he has not expressed a willingness to do." In 1905, Dr. Thomas was given a district of about 50,000 people for his own evangelistic field. Recently, the Reference Committee had tried to cut him off from student evangelism, and from opening the new territory which he and the Institute students wished to evangelize. While the old Board never interfered with his medico-evangelistic program, the Reference Committee and Board were distrusting his twenty-three years of experience. They were willing to accept unsubstantiated evidence, some of it gathered through calling individuals to testify in his absence, that had been sent to the Board without an opportunity for rebuttal.

As a final illustration of the changes that had taken place, he cited an issue that had deeply grieved him for decades. Mr. W. O. Valentine had established the Jaro Industrial School in 1905, and it was thought to be a model of its kind. The Bible School, which had its beginning in the Valentine home in 1905, was "entirely conservative in doctrine and method." Valentine Hall on the Campus of Central Philippine University is dedicated to him. Shortly after Dr. Franklin's visit to the field, Mr. Valentine was put out of the school, and even though many who had assisted him wanted to have him reinstated, he never was. Raph believed that the school had changed, that it had been made the center of attention of the work in the Philippines, and that the reduced emphasis on field evangelism was a change from the old days. Mr. Valentine went on to serve with great success in Negros Occidental, and he remained a close friend of Raph until his death of complications from malaria in 1928.

Raph further clarified the inference that his health would not warrant his taking on the challenge of the new evangelistic field and had precipitated his request for Dr. Porras to take on further responsibilities in the hospital. Raph felt that Dr. Porras was needed in the work, and he had worked tirelessly to teach him many of the details of hospital administration in order that Raph might be released from more of his hospital responsibilities and freed for more important service.

Knowing what he now knew of the Commission sent to the Philippines and its methods, he felt that his decision to return to America "would have been made with even greater dispatch."

In his final response, Raph dealt with the hope expressed by the Board that, if he and Norma should return to the Philippines, they would enter some of the unoccupied areas of the Philippines rather than return to the fields where the ABFMS Philippine Baptist missionaries were already at work. He replied that this was an unreasonable hope. The Association of Baptists for Evangelism in the Orient, the new board of which he was by this time a member, did go to Manila, an open territory not allotted to any one denomination, but they also felt that they had to return to Iloilo to carry on the strictly conservative work of the Doane Evangelistic Institute.

Articles, books, pamphlets, and statements about the multiplicity of attitudes, opinions, decisions, and actions of the people involved in this sad parting of the ways made their appearance over the next few years. Even this account, as long as it is, does not include some of the details revealed in documents presented to the Board for their eyes only, and letters and accounts written by Raph, Mrs. Peabody and others in support of the resignations. No story with as many players as this can be simply told, but this should be enough to clarify that no account presented by anyone in the Philippines or in America could tell the story adequately.

From the perspective of the Board, the usual complaints included Raph's not being a team player; his determination to focus on the expansion of his own ministries and territory; his overcommitment to ministries (including evangelistic and educational) apart from his responsibilities as a doctor and administrator of the hospital; his negative attitudes toward the school at Jaro, the Reference Committee, the Board, and its representatives; his perception of the theological status of the Mission; and his lack of support of the policies of the Mission.

From Raph's perspective, his attempts to nationalize the hospital; to develop training schools for men and women to prepare them from the ministry; to work with the students in evangelizing ever expanding areas of the islands; to keep away from the politics and policies of the Reference Committee, especially because of what he felt was their increasing desire to damage his reputation; and to work toward the steady growth of all of the ministries with which he was involved; were not truly appreciated. From his conservative theological position, he did view with concern what he feared to be inroads of a more liberal theology on the part of school and missionary, yet he emphasized his inability to support some of the policies and actions of the Board as his primary reason for resigning, striving not to denigrate the integrity of the Board. Always a man of high principles, old-fashioned honor, and deep conviction, Raph continually argued for the right as he saw the right.

That there were substantial concerns on both sides is obvious. Motives and emotions behind the actions of the Reference Committee, field missionaries, members of the Board, hospital personnel, educators, Raph, Norma, and others were seldom recorded. Those things are rarely recorded, even though discussed with others. They remained, but the end had come. Twenty-three years after arriving in the Philippines, Dr. Raphael Thomas left the Philippines and the ABFMS.

Dr. Jesse B. Thomas

Raphael Thomas in 1904

Winifred Cheney Thomas (1908)

Bird's-Eye View of Iloilo (Early 1900's)

Union Mission Hospital (1908)

Norma Thomas (1916)

Filipino Boy with Carabao,
[Original of Photo taken by Norma and used in "Jack and Janet in the Philippines"]

Jesse and Marguerite (1921)

Mrs. Lucy Peabody

Marguerite Doane

Doan Hall Evangelistic Institute (ca. 1927)

Doane Rest

Rev. Alberto Franco (center) and Other Ministry Leaders

The First A.B.E.O. Missionaries

From left to right: Bessie Traber, Helen Hinkley, Mrs. Darby (a guest); Ellen Martien; Dr. Thomas; Norma Thomas.

Manila Carnival Stand (Late 1920's)

First Baptist Church, Manila

Left to Right: Simon Meeks, Leland Wang, and Harold Commons
At the Keswick Camp near Manila

Raphael, Jesse, and Norma Thomas

Raph and His Daughter "Winky"

Miss Martien, Pastor Alejandro Caspe, and his daughter: "Three Generations."

The Gospel Ship

Dr. Thomas in the 1950's

CHAPTER 20

The Parent-Child Relationship and Missionary Service

And, ye fathers, provoke not your children to wrath: but bring them up in the nurture and admonition of the Lord. —Ephesians 6:4

One of the important subjects that is difficult to unveil is that of the personal lives of Raph's children. Raph rarely commented on family life and his children in his writings and correspondence.

Raph and his wife Winifred had only a short time together in raising their daughter Winifred ("Winky") before her mother died. The young girl was precious to him, but he felt the need to discover the best possible living situation for his daughter. He prayerfully decided to accept the invitation of her grandparents, on her mother's side, Edward and Sarah Chessey, to raise Winky in America.

Though in later years, correspondence between father and daughter was lamentably scarce, in the earlier years they wrote each other frequently. Through this pair of letters, written in September of 1927, a flood of light is thrown on the heart attitudes of both the daughter and her father, and the principles upon which Raph made his decisions about the raising of both Winky and her half-brother Burgess are revealed. The first letter was written by Winifred:[207]

> But, Daddy, I have had a fatherless home, too. It is hard to have a father living that you don't know. It wasn't in my power as much as it was in yours to remedy the family side of it. I just couldn't have my daddy and that's all there was to it, because I was only a mere child. Couldn't you take a church or work in the hospital? Please do not let my brother grow up without having a father. You'll regret it if you do. Maybe I am too hard on you, Father, but you will be sorry if you do not live with Burgess. Am I wrong in saying that you owe it to your child? A child needs his/her own daddy to talk over troubles to & feel the companionship. Please do not misunderstand me; that is the disadvantage in writing letters.
>
> In reference to my home—I have certainly had a most wonderful home, thanks to my mother's dear people. They have been wonderful to me. Uncle Guy & Grandma have given me all my musical education. It is often hard for Grandma, too, as she is not a young woman. I often tell her that it wasn't fair for her having to raise me, because I think after a woman has raised four children, she should have a complete rest from child raising. Isn't that true? She should be having a good time now instead of devoting herself to me. Grandma & Grandpa are wonderful people.

The following is her father's reply:[208]

> And, of course, now that you are growing up, our letters will become more and more dear to us. We can really talk now on the big things of life. I love you, my dear, though you may think my love is a little cold because I have seen so little of you. And that brings me to the very heart of your letter. You cannot fool Papa. I could see that under all the kind things you said there was an undercurrent of dissatisfaction because I absented myself from you in the past. Let us speak of that.
>
> The question you raise is one that is familiar to every missionary. People who are unwilling to go to the foreign

field themselves feel quite competent to judge for those who do go. Some go so far as to say that missionaries ought not to have children if they do not stay with them at home to look after them. But such talk as that is not only absurd, but also heartless and based largely on ignorance.

The only way to judge such a question is on its own merits. Has it been true that missionaries' children have turned out badly? Certainly not! I have known many of them and found them unusually intelligent and happy in many cases. Many have returned to the fields where their parents have labored and so, for generations, carried on the work (Scudders, Vintons, Adams, etc.). Many have had to go to children's homes and this is not so pleasant as home life, I think. But even, they have made good. But when they have homes such as you and Burgess have, it is almost the same as being with their parents. In that case, it is far better for them, for they have a better climate, better schools, and less dangerous associations (as young people in heathen lands often are not good companions).

In the case of Burgess, we had no choice. Your little sister Marguerite died and he was rapidly going downhill. I feel we got him away just in time. Do you honestly think that anyone could criticize me for sending him home when he was dying? Would you advocate that? Or would Home Boards agree to a policy that brought their missionaries home in two years, after the Boards had paid their way out, neglecting the fields they had promised the Boards to care for just because some people thought that a boy like Burgess in a home like that of Mrs. Peabody could be better cared for by me? He has every comfort and attention and all the love a grandmother can bestow, and you ought to know what that is. Being cared for by one's own flesh and blood is, after all, a good deal, isn't it? Certainly in the case of Burgess, it would have been the height of folly to let him remain or to let him go back now. He is a blonde and he cannot stand the Tropics.

He is happy and contented and under the best possible surroundings. What more can he wish?

"Oh," you say, "he has not a father's love to watch over him." Yes, that is true, but he has a grandmother's love, and that is tender and true. No, my dear, I do not know where you get such ideas, but Burgess will do very well with his grandmother, and it is I who will suffer, not he, for I know perfectly well that child will not have the same feeling for a father who stays away. That is almost inevitable. Later, parent and child will resume a relationship, but a father who does not have his children in his home when they are young misses something dear to him. I know that as well as anyone. BUT I have been glad to give up these Joys for the service of the Lord who said, "he that loves children more than me is not worthy of me." I have seen the need of the millions of children in the Philippines and have tried to minister to them. Do not forget, my dear, that when Jesus was on the cross He had one word for his mother and John, and the rest for of His words were for the world. I do not love you any less because I love the Lord more. In fact, I think that is why I can love you as I do: because I love Him so.

This is all unintelligible jargon to those who do not have a simple trust in Christ and a simple obedience to His commands. Many put the state or the family ahead of Him. This is wrong and unbiblical. We must put Him first. If He calls us, we must obey, wherever He sends us. He called me to the Philippines, and I cannot allow anything to turn me back, however dear the ties may be, with His sanction. You remember when He asked one to follow Him and the man said, "I must first go and bury my father"? Jesus said, "Let the dead bury their dead." He will tolerate no other call when He calls. And this is what the average lukewarm Christian never will understand.

It would have been a joy to me to have stayed with you, but what about the thousand or more whom God gave me to baptize just during this last term of service? Would

> you have preferred to have had me here doing work in hospital or church that an abundance of workers are already doing, or doing that neglected work out there? These are sheep "for whom Christ died also." If you were suffering hardship or without loving and tender care of your own blood relations and without the best of church and school privileges, it would be different. But as it is, I think you are a very lucky girl. You not only have had the best climate and school, but even music. And your home has been the one your mother was brought up in. I could ask no better.
>
> In conclusion, I will say that my conscience is perfectly clear in your case as well as in that of Burgess. You never will know all the circumstances, but what I have said will show you a little of what I feel myself. Now I think it is a very natural thing for you, as my own daughter and a little girl yet, to allow me to judge what is right for you and for myself. If you are dissatisfied with the way in which I have seen fit to look after you, I am sorry, for it will mean that you are unwilling to trust my judgement. If anybody else ever tries to persuade you that you have been abused and that I am a careless and neglectful father to leave you as I have done, I think that you had better just forget it, unless you think they have an argument. You will always find plenty of people who are ready to "knock" missionaries. It is quite the custom among non-church members, and even among many nominal church members. They do not approve of missionaries, and naturally find fault with what missionaries do. But I long have ceased to pay any attention to them. I advise you to do the same.

In another 1927 letter to Mrs. Chessy, Raph explained his situation (of leaving his ministry in the Philippines with ABFMS) and expressed concern about Winky's traveling to the East to see them while his and Norma's situation and plans for the future were unclear. He offered to pay for her to attend the Convention that year – which she desired to do – but Sarah felt that it would not be wise for her to travel alone at her age. At that point, Raph did not know whether they would be staying in the United States or not, and he raised the possibility of his remaining and having Winky stay with them, but – despite some financial difficulties – Sarah and Edward were comfortable with the idea of having her remain with them until the Thomases' situation should become clear. Winky and her dad did have that visit, in early 1928, but the "childless" return of Raph and Norma to the Philippines ended their brief time of reunion.

In 1937, back in the States for good, Raph wrote Mrs. Peabody with a gleam in his eye, describing the progress Burgess was making at Newton, especially in Greek, and the hope he and Norma had, though they were not at all sure, that Burgess would enter Harvard the following year. He did enter Harvard and graduated with a degree in languages. He was later in the merchant marines, served as a naval historian, and drove a cab!

Raph wrote both Winky and Burge (Jesse) frequently. He even wrote Burge after it became difficult to find his peripatetic son, always asking Winky to let him know the latest. In one of his later letters, Raph reminded Burge that he was always welcome to come home but warned him not to come for a visit too soon, because Norma was in the hospital for a procedure, and Burge would have had to eat his dad's cooking! He really hoped that Burge would come soon so that they could "talk shop and politics and things in general." He even encouraged his son to settle down near him rather than "careering around in the Orient, a "hot spot" now."

These letters are hard to read. For hundreds of years, missionaries have struggled with the question of whether to raise children in the difficult areas where they served, or to send them off to relatives, schools, or "safer countries." To many, there was no question: where God was sending the parents, he was also sending their children; eventually the parents would be alone on the field, but they wanted to have their children with them as long as possible. To others, the children should be left where they could receive the best education and enculturation in the land of their parents. Whether one agrees with the "how" of Raph's raising of his children, or not, he leaves no question as to the "why" in his explanation to his beloved daughter.

CHAPTER 21

A New Mission Board is Born

For we cannot but speak the things which we
have seen and heard. —Acts 4:20

FORMATION OF THE ASSOCIATION OF BAPTISTS FOR EVANGELISM IN THE ORIENT

When the Thomases and Miss Ellen Martien returned to the United States in June 1927 due to their resignations, Miss Bessie Traber and Miss Alice Drake, both independent and self-supporting missionaries, remained in the Philippines. Miss Traber remained in charge at Doane Evangelistic Institute.

After the flurry of letters and meetings that had surrounded the resignations had quieted a bit, a historic meeting was held in August at the home of Mrs. Doane in Watch Hill, Rhode Island. As we have already seen, she had been a generous supporter of the Woman's American Baptist Foreign Missionary Society and was especially close to the work in the Philippines. She had maintained a very close relationship with Dr. and Mrs. Thomas through the years and was sympathetic with the need to provide a way for their work in the Philippines to continue.

Dr. and Mrs. Thomas, Mrs. Peabody, Dr. Curtis Lee Laws, and several other influential Baptist friends, prayed together concerning the future of ministry in the Philippines, and their prayers were answered with a plan. Support would be provided by members of the group to enable the Thomases, Miss Martien, and those who would be willing to join them, to serve the Lord in the Philippines independently. This was the beginning of the informal association of friends and supporters that was to become the Association of Baptists for Evangelism in the Orient (ABEO). Miss Traber and Miss Drake quickly joined the group, as did Miss Helen Hinkley, who resigned from the WBFMS to cover the work for Miss Traber when she had to return to America because of illness. The group soon numbered fifteen.

In later years, Dr. Harold Commons liked to tell new missionaries the stories of Miss Traber and Miss Drake. Miss Traber was supported by her family as she served alongside Raph, Norma, and other missionaries with ABFMS. Because she was not officially a missionary with the Board, she felt free to affiliate herself with Miss Martien and Miss Hinkley. Miss Drake, a graduate of Moody Bible Institute, was on a tour of the world at the time the resignations were taking place. When she arrived in the Philippines, Miss Drake befriended Miss Traber. She told Miss Traber that if a new work should begin, "let me know and maybe I'll come back and help you." She continued her round-the-world trip as far as Egypt, where she received a message from Miss Traber in Iloilo which basically said, "Come on back and help!" She left her companions on the tour, flew back to the Philippines, and joined in the new work of the ABEO!

As ABEO began to take shape, Mrs. Doane had been convinced that Doane Evangelistic Institute (DEI) should move to another location, but the Woman's Board objected to this action, and desired that all the ministries of DEI remain at its present location. When Miss Traber was approached about her thoughts, she cabled back that she was concerned that the conservative cause would be weakened if the DEI should remain under the Reference Committee, and if that should be the final decision, Miss Drake and Miss Traber "must resign." One of their fears was that the work would be controlled by Jaro and that it would finally be abandoned in favor of the seminary there. While the Woman's Board retained the property, with Mrs. Doane's blessing Miss Martien, with the help of Miss Drake, continued the full work of the Institute at a rented location in Iloilo. The name of Doane Evangelistic Institute was removed from the old location and given to the new one, on Ledesma Street in Iloilo. In 1932, DEI was moved to 45 Bonifacio Drive.

CHAPTER 21

INCREASING THE ORGANIZATION OF THE ABEO

The first meeting of the new mission board for incorporation under the laws of the Commonwealth of Massachusetts was held in the office of Fred E. Crawford in Boston on December 17, 1928. Present were Lucy W. Peabody, Hilda L. Olson, Fred E. Crawford, Nita M. Crawford, Caroline Atwater Mason, Margaret C. Tatro, and Ward S. Crawford. The purposes for which the corporation was formed were the following:

> To give aid, financial or otherwise, to such agencies as now exist or may hereafter exist, which are engaged in propagating the Christian religion in the Orient according to the accepted belief and practice of the Conservative Baptist Faith with especial emphasis upon evangelism, religious education and church life; to appoint, send, and maintain missionaries and teachers to the Orient; and to acquire property, real and personal, necessary or convenient, to be used in connection with these objects.

An executive meeting of the corporation was held at the same place that day after the incorporation meeting. Lucy W. Peabody was elected president of the corporation by ballot, and Fred E. Crawford was elected vice-president in the same way.

The first Annual Meeting of the ABEO, on April 25, 1930, was an exciting affair. Lucy Peabody and Fred Crawford were once again elected as President and Vice-President of the Corporation, and Bessie M. Traber was elected Secretary of the Executive Committee. Marguerite Doane, Alice Drake, Bessie Traber, Sarah Ropes, Alice Hudson, William Ayer, Mattie C. Crawford, and Thomas Gladding were elected members of the new mission board. The names of M. W. Castrodale, Bernice Hahn, Helen Hinkley, and Alberto Franco were all mentioned in the minutes for support, acceptance, or ministry-related employment. Concerning the latter, Dr. Thomas was encouraged to secure the services of Alberto Franco, whom we have already met, for Doane Evangelistic Institute for the school year.

In that same meeting, an action taken March 15, 1930, relating to the location of work in the Philippines was ratified. The motion had been that,

> because there were many fine workers ready to go into the field, the Association approves that our workers go into any town in Antique, Negros, Iloilo or other provinces where no organized work is being done by the American Baptist Foreign Mission Society and without aiding any organized church.[209]

FIRST TERM IN THE PHILIPPINES UNDER ABEO

Raphael and Norma, together with Miss Martien, arrived in the Philippines as representatives of their fledgling association in March of 1928. Even while they were traveling to the Philippines – and grew very tired of ship life on the way - they were wondering whether to set up housekeeping in Iloilo or in Manila. They finally decided that it would be best to make their headquarters in Manila. They realized that occasional "quiet trips" (under the radar) to Iloilo would be preferable to establishing themselves there, especially because there was already considerable controversy related to ABEO's positioning themselves in ministries and locations in close proximity to those of the ABFMS.

Raph later included a statement about the return to the Visayas in a "Policies of the Mission" statement that concluded a history he wrote to explain to new missionaries the background of the formation of ABEO. The three policies were the following:

> First - We believe our return to the Visayas wholly justified, because the Doane Evan. Inst. was being dropped. We were obliged to continue this great work and in conjunction with it the Doane Hall and district work as an outlet for our student workers. To abandon the Visayas now would be unthinkable.
>
> Second - Our mission policy is in accord with the Asso. slogan, "the apostolic message and method". This we understand to be a proclamation of the gospel wherever it is needed, with special attention to unoccupied and neglected districts. We also understand that it advocates evangelism rather than education, medicine or institutional work.

> Third - Our attitude toward other missionaries of our own Board, as well as other Boards, is meant to be friendly. We desire to pursue our own course permitting them to pursue theirs, which should be a constructive program. Our separation from groups that are modernistic in tendencies, is wholly due to conscientious scruples, and not to personal antagonism or animosity. The fact that we, perforce, are separatists is supported by our great objective of a sound gospel message. We seek quietness and unobtrusive service, keeping our own counsel, with prayer and humility.[210]

Onboard ship it was exciting to plan things in his head. Raph was thinking about a variety of scenarios related to the staffing of the works in Iloilo and Manila. He expected to spend a good amount of time in Iloilo, planning the whole program in consultation with others. He imagined himself helping with the teaching, the medical work, and the district work. He knew that he was biting off a big piece of work but hoped that with God's help and that of the colleagues He was providing, the work would lessen in time.

The planting of the First Baptist Church of Manila began shortly after they arrived. Raph described the planting of that work in an article in the Report of the ABEO in 1932.

> Our first task was the establishment of a Baptist Church in this metropolis of over 300,000. In a few weeks a sufficiently large group of Baptists was assembled, and the First Baptist Church of Manila was organized and incorporated. During four years several hundred members have been received, the large majority being new converts; and seven preaching centers have been established in strategic districts in the city. At two or three of these, outdoor preaching services have been held daily. At most of them kindergartens have been carried on by our three, and later five, trained kindergartners, and at several of them medical clinics have been conducted by Dr. Culley and myself, with the assistance of trained nurses. Resident workers have been in charge.

Many of the members of that "large group of Baptists" came from their Visayan students who had moved to Manila to study at the University. God's blessing on the Church was obvious as several hundred members were added to the church in the first four years.

The work began with the Dormitory near the University of the Philippines and the "little center across the river at San Rafael" (the big High School opportunity). Mrs. Doane had purchased property a short distance from where the First Baptist Church and the Institute would be located, and there the Doane Dormitory for Girls was founded in 1928. Miss Martien, who was at this time in Manila though she eventually returned to Iloilo, served as Director of the Dormitory.

Early on, a Bible Students' Bulletin was started to advertise meetings in this city of over 300,000, but it was obvious that some addition preaching centers were needed. The first of the seven preaching centers Raph mentioned was in a neighboring district of Manila called Pandacan. There a "young man of great consecration" was willing to work for a tiny salary. He soon led over a dozen to Christ, and they were baptized at the Student Center (on San Rafael Street). This ministry was presented in the Tagalog dialect. The second center, called "The Friendly Center" was established near Rizal Avenue in the Business Section of Manila on a busy corner. Open air evangelistic meetings were held there, and they attracted many intelligent young businessmen.

The positive experience with Doane Evangelistic Institute in Iloilo was such that it was decided to establish a new institution in Manila. It was to be called the Manila Evangelistic Institute. Raph was planning this step while traveling to the Philippines. His presentation of the idea to Mrs. Peabody was almost apologetic, asking her not to think that he was "plunging" because he mentioned it at that early date. His concern was to prevent the student workers, either in Iloilo or Manila, from being sent to non-conservative schools like Jaro or Manila Union Theological Seminary, and he desired that ABEO provide alternatives in both places. Raph envisioned a conservative Baptist school for preachers, one that would be open to students from denominations of similar faith. The school was established in 1930 in Manila, but eventually moved to Rizal, north of Manila, with the name Baptist Bible Seminary and Institute.

Because of the death of Mr. Valentine in 1928, Raph was also concerned that the work in Negros, the neighboring island to the east of Panay, be supported. Valentine and his pastors had been experiencing great growth, and the provision of financial support for the pastors and additional workers from DEI was imperative.

The Lord's provision of missionary workers, American and Filipino, was a great matter of thanksgiving. It was the theme of the report of the ABEO for 1928-29, printed in booklet form. Miss Bessie Traber, a Vassar and Biblical Seminary of New York graduate, was instrumental in moving the students of DEI from the old building to a rented building in another part of Iloilo to prevent any break in the work of DEI during the transition of that ministry to ABEO. The world-traveler, Alice Drake, has already been mentioned. She was a graduate of Moody Bible Institute. Miss Drake remained in Iloilo as a vital member of the DEI staff. Miss Helen Hinkley, a graduate of Gordon Bible College, had finished her term of service under the WBFMS and was preparing to return home on furlough when she learned that Miss Traber was very ill. She had no promise of support but stepped out in faith and remained to take her place. Together with Mr. and Mrs. Castrodale, she helped to make sure that the school was fully staffed.

Rev. and Mrs. Milford W. Castrodale met Dr. Thomas while he was taking some graduate work at the Prince Medical Clinic in Chicago. Mr. Castrodale was the organist and Assistant Director of Moody Bible Institute. When Raph learned that he was a Baptist, that he had served as acting pastor of a church, and that he was praying about going to the foreign mission field, Raph began to recruit this couple for the Philippines. They sailed for the field in May of 1928. Also recruited for the work in Iloilo was Rev. Percy Pemberton, who was an educator in China and the Philippines, and who served well the students at Doane Hall. In July, Miss Edith Webster, a graduate of Eastern Theological Seminary, Philadelphia, arrived in Iloilo. She had served under an independent board in South America and spoke Spanish which gave her an edge in settling into the ministry in the Philippines.

Of course, the fledgling, but rapidly growing, work in Manila needed additional workers, too. In addition to Miss Ellen Martien, who is already well known to us, Miss Bernice Hahn, who had completed the three-year course at North Western Bible School, was welcomed into the mission.

Miss Martien was particularly thrilled, because Miss Hahn's knowledge of bookkeeping and treasury would enable her to give those responsibilities to Bernice. She was also musical, a blessing to any ministry, but especially among people who love music as much as the Filipinos.

Dr. Paul Cully, a graduate of Cornell University and Johns Hopkins Medical School, was burdened to become a medical missionary. He declined to go with the Northern Baptist board, and the Southern Baptist board was not able to send him, but he met with Dr. Thomas before Raph left for the Philippines and caught a vision for what he could do in serving there. He was informed that he was provisionally appointed by the Association as he was on his way with Dr. Melvin Grove Kyle's expedition to the Holy Land. Kyle's account of his exploratory and archaeological work done near the Dead Sea, published in 1927, was called *Explorations at Sodom*. After Cully's time in Palestine, he and his mother, Lillian, continued to travel eastward toward the Philippines. They arrived in August 1928. Dr. Cully passed the examination required by the Medical Board of the Philippines with flying colors, and he set up a dispensary near the University of the Philippines. Lillian made "a home for him," and was involved in ministry to the people in a variety of ways.

In 1930, Dr. Culley wrote a piece for the new 'magazine' of the ABEO (consisting at that point of only four pages and called "A Message From the Association of Baptists for Evangelism in the Orient, Inc.") entitled "Touring in the Iloilo District." He mentioned that in "14 towns and barrios" they visited in Iloilo, 168 patients were given medical treatment and at least 1200 people heard the gospel preached. He mentioned a new station in Alimodian and old stations where churches had been established. For example, in Salvacion, Buenavista, there was a church of over forty members pastored by Mr. Alvior; and the church of East Valencia was "carrying on vigorously" under the leadership of Mr. and Mrs. Gaitano.

Then Dr. Culley went back in his mind to his arrival in Manila. He wrote,

> I was soon lost in a maze of sights as Dr. Thomas drove through beautiful wide streets or narrow congested ones, from the better residential sections with lovely Spanish type houses surrounded with luxuriant tropical foliage to the crowded smelly business section where all seemed to me so disordered, so dirty and so different.

> What an eye-opener these days have been. Little did I dream of the growth of the work in Manila and the possibilities of phenomenal growth in the near future. Evangelistic work of this sort is so new to the inhabitants of this city and is so sorely needed. In its growth by leaps and bounds, the work seems to have the direct seal of approval from God. And the opportunities are legion.
>
> Since this is an educational center with an immense student body, there is such a call to train these English speaking students in the Word, and through them rapidly to spread the Gospel out in the Islands among those who speak only the dialects. . . The work with the students has been an especial thrill to me. I am amazed at how well established is the new Manila Evangelistic Institute only about six weeks old. As I visited some of the classes, I felt right at home, having been so recently in classes at Moody. . . I know you would be just as thrilled as I am to watch the crowds gather at the street meetings and listen eagerly to a talk either in English or Tagolog and then fill the mission center for the after meeting where they can ask questions of those coming in. And there are many keen questions asked. Those who come in seem to be mostly keen business men or students who are deep in the study of secular things, and to whom the open Bible is often a new thing.

Dr. Paul next described his first visit to the new center in Manila. It began with an invitation from Miss Martien to see the work and stay for supper.

> At 5 P. M. Dr. Thomas began the street meeting after which he invited those who had questions to come over to the mission. There he stayed but a short time before he had to go on another meeting and so turned the questions over to Miss Martien. She in turn entertained us in what she called "true Tom Sawyer fashion" by passing the work over to Miss Hahn and me. I had to s-o-s Him for help! But it is impossible to describe the thrill.[211]

He went on to describe the Student Church, Doane Dormitory for girls, and the kindergartens. What an introduction to those exciting early days of God's work through ABEO.

Though his energy was not as great as it had been decades before, Raph's enthusiasm was unbounded, and he poured himself into every opportunity to present the gospel, to teach, to baptize, and to provide direction in the development of stations, centers, churches, and schools in Manila and the south in those heady early years.

Paid Filipino leaders were needed, too, to support and grow the various ministries. Along with Alberto Franco, Patricio Confessor and Mr. Illustre were mentioned in the report. Mr. Confessor was a graduate of Gordon Bible College and had also studied a year at Newton Seminary. He helped to direct the fieldwork of the students at DEI. Mr. Illustre was with the YMCA in Manila, but having stepped down from his position was looking for another way to work with students. He and his wife were able to open the work in a small way that was eventually built up through collaboration with Dr. Thomas and the rest of the Manila team.

From 1930 to 1934, the years in which Raph and Norma were most directly involved with the work of ABEO in the Philippines, dozens of Filipino workers were added, many of them graduates of the Doane Evangelistic Institute in Iloilo. Missionary additions included Ellis and Ruth Skolfield, Edna Hotchkiss, Alexander Sutherland, Mr. and Mrs. Russell Jones, Bethel France, Stella Mower, Esther Yerger, and Ruth Woodworth.

PALAWAN

Under the comity agreement, the Presbyterian Philippine Mission had been responsible for the Province of Palawan, consisting of many islands near Borneo. They offered it to ABEO in 1930,[212] so Dr. and Mrs. Thomas decided to take a trip to Palawan to "spy out the land." The following is his account of that experience.

> As we landed from the steamer at Brookes Point, named after Rajah Brooke so famous in Northern Borneo, we met the Filipino doctor, deathly sick with malignant

malaria, being carried away to the hospital farther north. We wished to find a house while we tarried in this village, but none was vacant but the one the doctor had left. That proposition was not attractive, but we had no choice so settled there and began housekeeping at once.

It was just an ordinary bamboo house with nipa roof, such as I have already described. It had only one occupant, a little Ilocano maidservant of the doctors. Evidently she regarded us as intruders. It came to a climax when she discovered we liked eggs, fresh ones. (The Filipino prefers old ones as they are richer). But we liked the fresh ones better, and when the hens cackled we ran for the eggs. The doctor had quite a brood of hens, and their eggs were not bad. But the Ilocano girl understood their language better than we did, and when they cackled she beat us to it. Alas, our eggs were few. Then the hens took pity on us. We saw an old biddy stalking into our boudoir, and she went behind the door. Then another followed. We became suspicious and looked behind the door and the secret was out. There was a large sack of rice with a hole in it. Biddy knew that, but she was also wise to our necessity and soon we found eggs lying about the room. FINE. But we were hard up for water. It was extra dry down there. No rain. The wells were dangerous. However, the town official let us have half a tin full of rain water from his cistern. (The Standard Oil tins are used for pails down there. They knock the top out, insert a wooden handle, and there you are: a real pail). This water was carefully boiled and set to cool in the corner of the room. Unfortunately, there was also a cat, a great big cat, on the premises. He loved to climb the walls and perambulate on the sheet that was stretched overhead to keep the nipa dust from the roof from falling on us. That was all right with us until one time he ventured too far, in the corner where the water was cooling, and the rattan that held the sheet broke and everything, dust of ages and all, yes all but the cat, fell into the water. What was to be done? We strained it, reboiled it and drank it!

Being in a hastily fumigated home, with a lack of available food and water, did not stop the intrepid missionaries from preparing interesting meals while they were there. There were also unique opportunities to heal their neighbors.

> The cooking arrangements were just ordinary Filipino: a table for a stove and pigs below eager for dishwater. We also had a small canned heat tin as a luxury. Rice and bananas and canned goods for food. It was all very primitive. But, again, tragedy was close at hand for a medico. A native came rushing in with a plea for help. His friend had been sitting at the window of his home when a Tagbanwa or Palawano, as the mountaineers are called down here, had sent a dart from a blowpipe into his side. These blowpipes are eight feet, more or less, in length and a native can blow one right through the trunk of a banana palm. (I saw one do it). Worse than that, they poison the point, shaped with a flange like a fish hook, and when it enters it breaks away from the shaft, which is nicked for that purpose, and the nasty little poisonous point is anchored firmly inside, out of sight. When I arrived I found the patient suffering severe pain. The wound was in the side of the chest where the dart had become embedded deep between the ribs. I had no nurse with me and no general anesthetic or anyone to administer it if I had, so resorted to Novocain, a poor substitute. But the Filipino stands pain well, and I inserted a pointed forceps into the tiny opening left by the dart and felt it grate against something. I hoped and prayed it might be the dart and not a broken rib. To make a mistake down there might be embarrassing to say the least: but it did prove to be the dart point and when I drew it out you may imagine the relief of the patient and his gratitude. He had chewed the leaf of a tree that was supposed to be an antidote, but I doubt if he had much confidence in it. He felt I had saved his life, I feel sure, and "all a man hath will he give for his life". This is when a Medical Missionary feels glad he heard the "call" and went!

CHAPTER 21

I wished to tour the surrounding country and when Mr. Edwards, an ex-American school teacher, and the only white man in the village, asked me to hike with him into the hills I was glad to accept the invitation. We started off on our shaggy little ponies. Nearby the grassy land soon turned into forest: and just at the edge of the woods we saw a group of naked, or nearly naked, Tagbanwas lurking, bearing blowpipes and other weapons. That was not so encouraging, after I had seen what a blowpipe could do: but Edwards was apparently acquainted with the savages, and they talked with him in the lingo they use. He kept the store at Brookes Point, where they brought the gum from the trees that was used for making varnish. Evidently they were on good terms. We left them, quite willingly, and pressed on into the forest, and crossed numerous river beds now dry as tinder, but evidently freshets in the rainy season. In one village we met a headman with whiskers. That is strange for a Filipino. They pluck their beards with two clam shells. I often have seen them doing it in the doors of their shacks: just as we often see the women and children, three deep, carefully examining each other's scalps for the little wanderers that make life miserable for them. This old man was shaking with malaria. We gave him some quinine and were his friends for life. Chinese overcharge for it. When we gave it to them for nothing, or rather for love, it carried its own lesson. It softened hearts for the "Good Seed."

We left this village and passed through others, some of which were deserted, as they are likely to leave a village when death occurs. Soon we came to a village where the headman had lined up huge jars in his bamboo meeting place, filled with intoxicating beverage. No doubt these jars were antiques. They were of Chinese make and for aught we knew may have been there for centuries. Edwards imagined they were very old. The custom was for the headman to call his men together, insert tubes into these jars, and drink themselves drunk. What a strange orgy. These natives do have a semblance of religion. They worship a Supreme

> Being they call AMPO(?) [Apo?], and sacrifice a chicken over running water, set a small boat sailing downstream and in other ways seem to be groping in the dark for a higher life in ways that would interest an anthropologist. How badly they need the true religion, Christianity!

The practice of sending boats downstream with offerings to the gods or spirits is not unusual in a variety of Asian systems of belief. Quite common, too, is the practice of going to a place where hot springs abound for healing of the body. Raph learned this after enjoying the benefits of hot springs for a tired body.

> We left this village for a hike. My friend took me to the river to wash and I discovered a hot spring bubbling up. They say some of these hot springs will cook an egg. In Negros I found similar springs, and a hollow in a rock where one could bathe. I lolled there and enjoyed it until someone told me that sick people come to bathe there: then I quit. LEPERS at once came to mind: no more such baths for me.
>
> After we had washed our faces and hands we started on the short hike to a nearby hilltop. Our guide went ahead, and we carried canes. I did not know why until we were forced to climb a cliff like the side of a house. On reaching the top, after a hard scramble using the canes as props, we lay down for much needed rest. Imagine our surprise on returning by a gentle and easy path to the village whence we had come. We asked why we did not go that way and were informed that the guide wished to take a bath in the river where we clambered up the cliff. A real Filipino argument!
>
> We started on our return journey, after spending the night in a half –built shack, where the wind tossed our nets about, exposing us to the deadly mosquitoes, and plunged into the forest where the bamboos have to be cut thru with bolos for the trail. Once I remember my toe in a tennis shoe caught on a bamboo spike and I was in danger of losing my shoe, if not my foot, as the stubborn little pony insisted on forging ahead. But we eventually broke

> loose and came to rivers that were said to be infested with crocodiles. One of our preachers reported one of his men caught by a crocodile, but he said "God closed the mouths of the lions for Daniel, and he will close the mouths of the crocodiles for us." He kept right on crossing that river. But these here are really dangerous. As dusk approached I noticed that Edwards seemed a little nervous, as crossing these rivers at night is not the custom. We had hoped to return by the beach, but found the tide too high, so were forced to take chances. These submerged with their ugly snouts scarcely visible and they have snapped many a luckless victim. I did not realize all this, but Edwards did, and his wife did as well. When we arrived they were anxiously awaiting us. I learned a Moro had been snapped up on the nearby beach not long before as he squatted on his heels, the customary way of resting for a Filipino.

Within a year, three Filipino pastors, two from DEI, and one from Manila Evangelistic Institute had been established in strategic locations on the main island, and the neighboring small island of Cuyo.

ON A WALK IN ILOILO

Raph's colorful description of Palawan provides a good opportunity to compare that rural area with the conditions around Doane Evangelistic Institute in Iloilo at that time. Miss Edna Hotchkiss, a missionary teacher at Doane, wrote the following account of her walk to prayer meeting under a brilliant blue sky after a rainy night, in which she "realized afresh that this was indeed the Orient."

> Everything seemed so clean in our garden and the Provincial park across the street and even a gander was taking a bath in the puddles out in the middle of the asphalt street, fussing at the passing cars and calesas. But in five minutes of walking, what a change! It is true the sand and gravel roads did not leave their usual coat on the high polish our little boot-black had given my shoes,

but the squalor and filth around was a sharp contrast to the cleanliness above. There were many green scummed ponds, sometimes even under the stilted nipa houses. Most of the houses are made from the nipa palm and bamboo. Here and there were the inevitable petroleum cans half submerged, rusted almost beyond recognition. Several of the houses were on their last legs, literally so, built upon stilts as they are.

Walking along I noticed on the opposite corner of the road, across the lower part of a house, a large sign, "Cafeteria Con Tuba." (It was only this past week that I first saw them climbing the coconut palms where they were tapping for the sap which when fermented makes the native "strong drink.") My stomach turned over as I thought of the whiffs of that disgusting odor I had smelled passing natives carrying by heavy keg at each end of their shoulder sticks. And, just then, assailed by a worse odor, my nose warned me in time for me to turn out for a dead dog in the gutter. As to odors, I am sure a Filipino can stand far more than the average American!

Opposite the Catholic hospital I saw a sight that was appalling. It was near the spot where several days before I saw a pitiful specimen of humanity, a blind man being led along, clothed with filthy rags which did not hide the open sores on his body. (The blindness out here which is so prevalent is caused no doubt by uncleanliness and carelessness, not only the physical, but also the spiritual blindness!) This time it was not until I was very close that I could make out the object being wheeled along in a low wooden cart. For the woman had her head mostly covered with a dirty rag. But from below here ragged faded skirt protruded two gaunt diseased legs that looked decidedly leprous to me.

Yes, these people need your prayers. And so do the workers, who are meeting the same tests and difficulties that all meet when trespassing on Satan's territory.[213]

CHAPTER 21

THE ABRUPT CONCLUSION OF THEIR TERM OF MINISTRY

In May of 1931, at the Second Conference of the Philippine Mission, held at Baguio, Raph was elected permanent chairman for the year. However, after Dr. and Mrs. Thomas returned from their pioneering trip to Palawan, they were struck by a speeding automobile in Manila. Norma was hospitalized for a time. After she was released, they went to Baguio for a time of rest because Raph was not well. Raph was eventually diagnosed with an illness not related to the accident. He was told that he had pernicious anemia. Pernicious anemia is a rare condition in which the body is not able to produce the substance that enables the small intestine to absorb vitamin B_{12} which is essential for red-blood cell production. He had several of the risk factors including heritage and his age.

It is helpful to put Raph's diagnosis in its place in the history of our knowledge of this disease and its treatment. In the nineteenth century, hookworm was suggested as a cause of pernicious anemia by Joseph Leidy. Because Raph's diet for years had included at least the possibility of ingesting a fish tapeworm, he could have had competition for the vitamin B_{12} that was in his body. In 1925, Whipple and Robscheit-Robbins presented evidence of benefit derived from raw beef liver for the regeneration of red blood cells in anemia patients, and this also became a treatment for those suffering from pernicious anemia. This could well have been recommended to Raph. But it was not known that vitamin B_{12} is an effective treatment (as shown by Randolph West) until 1948, long after Raph was diagnosed.[214]

Apart from fatigue, there is no direct evidence of the symptoms Raph had. They could have included headache, pale skin, muscle weakness, and perhaps even peripheral neuropathy. The doctors told him that another trip to Palawan would be extremely dangerous in his current state of health. By the end of the year, they were on their way back to America, with Raph's health as one of the reasons for their return.

However, Raph's and Norma's enthusiasm for the fledgling field of Palawan and the Sulu Sea turned into a flood of interest in the young mission. They began to pray about two seemingly impossible needs: a ship that could sail the seas between the islands, and an available missionary with a burden to reach those people. In answer to those prayers, the Lord provided both the ship and the missionary in some truly remarkable ways! In fact, as is often the case, the provision of those answers had begun long before the asking.

CHAPTER 22

God's Ship in the Sulu Sea

> The voice of the LORD is upon the waters: the God of glory thundereth: the LORD is upon many waters. —Psalm 29:3

When the *Report of Association of Baptists for Evangelism in the Orient, Inc.*, 1932-1933 appeared, it included some valuable information about the growth of the organization and the development of the work in the Philippines. The growth of the missionary team in the Philippines together with the locations of their ministries, was highlighted on page 2 with the section entitled Our Missionaries:

> **Manila:** Dr. and Mrs. R. C. Thomas, Miss Ellen Martien, Dr. Paul Culley, Mr. Illustre, Miss Bernice Hahn, Miss Bethel France, Rev. Russell Bradley Jones, Mrs. Jones.
> **Associate at Manila:** Miss Margaret Scheirich;
> **Iloilo:** Miss Bessie Traber (in U.S.), Miss Alice Drake (in U.S.), Miss Helen Hinkley, Miss Edith Webster, Miss Stella Mower, Rev. Alberto Franco, Miss Edna Hotchkiss.
> **Palawan:** Capt. Ellis Skolfield, Mrs. Ellis Skolfield

This chapter will highlight the last couple mentioned and the unique ministry they had on the Gospel Ship, a ministry Raph delighted in, though he had reservations at first:

> I will confess that at the outset I was something of a "doubting Thomas," but the evidences of Providential guidance were too great to be denied, and I firmly believe that this whole transaction was of the Lord.

For 25 years, Presbyterians had held – according to the division of ministry labor mentioned above – a group of nearly a hundred islands. These were the Palawan Islands to the west of Panay in the Sulu Sea. They decided to offer this field to ABEO. This was a great opportunity for evangelism, but with the gift came a number of problems. The Presbyterians had not been able to do extensive work in the islands for lack of resources, and the ABEO would face some of the same difficulties. There were no missionaries to spare and Filipino personnel would not be available for a while in sufficient numbers to reach out to so many islands. The Committee of leaders of the ABEO prayed fervently about the offer, and the Lord gave them a firm conviction that they should take the islands, even without a clear picture of how these needs would be met. They believed that the needs of this ministry could only be met by the provision of missionaries and a boat to sail the sea in itinerant ministry to the islands. The Lord had a wonderful surprise for them. Here is a portion of the description of God's amazing provision from the Association's *Report*:

> Heavenly wireless is not slow! The following day three members of the Committee met Captain and Mrs. Ellis Skolfield in Philadelphia, where he is attending Eastern Theological Seminary, not expecting, however, to graduate. . . . Captain Skolfield will be of the greatest help to Dr. Thomas in the field work, while Mrs. Skolfield will give more of her time to the Manila Bible School. All felt that a year on the field with Dr. Thomas, in preparation for the work when he must leave, would be of greater value than to finish his course at Eastern Theological Seminary, which he can easily complete during his first furlough. He is continuing until the last moment his evangelistic work under Dr. Livingston, in preparation for his work in the Islands.[215]

God's provision of the ship was equally remarkable. There was, in Japan, the perfect ship, one that had been constructed for missionary work. It was called the *Fukuin Maru* (the Japanese word *Fukuin* means "gospel;"and *Maru* is the suffix given to the name of a ship).

THE *FUKUIN MARU*

The story of the *Fukuin Maru* and its first Captain is a story worth telling in its similarity to that just told about the provision of the Gospel Ship to ABEO.

In Glasgow there was a gracious Christian woman from a wealthy family with a long history in the business of shipping. Mrs. Allan had a great burden for the people of the Inland Sea in Japan. The Inland Sea (*Seto Naikai*) is a body of water located between the main island of *Honshu* (on the north and east), the large island of *Shikoku* (on the south), and *Kyūshu* (on the west). It consists of over 1,000 islands and smaller islets. Mrs. Allan had visited the city of Kobe, near Osaka, and had seen the need of the island people to hear the Good News of Jesus. After her death, her son Robert decided to help to provide the answer to his mother's prayers for the islanders. In her memory, through missionary Dr. Robert Thomson, Robert offered the ABFMS the means of building a ship suitable for ministry to the islanders of the Inland Sea.[216]

Some members of the ABFMS traveled to the Publishing House operated by a certain Dr. Philipp Bickel in Hamburg. Dr. Bickel, an American citizen, had moved to his native country of Germany to provide Christian literature. Their purpose was to present to him the exciting proposal of the ship, and to ask him whether he felt that his son, Luke, would be the right person to approach about becoming the Captain of the new ship. Dr. Bickel had hoped that his son would become a doctor, but Luke loved the sea, and he begged that he might have the opportunity to learn all he could about being a sailor. He had travelled extensively in Asia, and had become a Master Mariner, before settling down for a time in London, England, as a married man. He was at the time actively involved in the business of London Baptist Publication House and was devoted to the children of London and to Sunday School work among them. Feeling that it was not appropriate for him to answer for his son, Dr. Bickel encouraged the deputation to go to London and ask his son. They did make the trip to London and approached Captain Bickel about the possibility of becoming a missionary mariner, ministering to the people of the Inland Sea on a ship of his design. "Love and duty" prevailed with Mrs. Bickel, as well, and made her willing to accompany her husband on the future ship.

> Their proposal that he should become missionary to the Japanese Islanders at first amazed him, he never having taken a course in theology, but finally he recognized in their request the voice of Him who appeared to Isaiah in the temple: "Whom shall we send? And who will go for us? "and humbly replied, "Here am I, send me."
>
> His love for the sea, and a long cherished feeling that some day he might become a missionary, made this response an easier one to him, though always when duty called he had ears only for her voice.[217]

In, May, 1898, Captain Bickel, his wife, and their son Philip, arrived in Kobe, Japan. He began superintending the building of the ship while studying the Japanese language. He had a great facility in language, speaking German, Dutch, French, Spanish, and English, so the Lord had prepared his mind for the task of learning the language he would be using to minister to the islanders of the Inland Sea. Knowing the challenge involved in learning Japanese with years of intensive study, it is remarkable to this writer that Captain Bickel was able to learn enough Japanese in a year to be able to work with a Japanese crew and to personally minister to people in their own dialect (which is not the Tokyo dialect learned by Japanese students today).

So, in a shipyard on the outskirts of Yokohama, the Little White Ship was built, the perfect craft for missionary work, including even a dispensary and a chapel. The cost of her building was $42,000. On September 13, a service of dedication was held, and the name given her was suggested by a Yokohama missionary, who was the brother of Captain Bickel's biographer. The Fukuin Maru began a long and fruitful ministry under Captain Bickel. In April 1917, a meeting of the Fukuin Maru church took place with dozens of those who had come to Christ in attendance. Shortly after that, Captain Bickel died. He was replaced for a time as Captain by his son Philip, and later the evangelistic responsibilities were given to Mr. and Mrs. Fred Steadman, but in time the Mission decided that the funds to operate the ship should be used elsewhere.

THE GOSPEL SHIP

The ship was to be sold to fishermen, but God intended it to change fields, not purposes. It remained in the Kobe harbor for three years. At the end of that time, at the suggestion of missionaries in Japan, the Association began to prayerfully consider the possibility of using the Fukuin Maru in the Philippines. By faith, the leadership of the ABEO took a 3 months' option on the ship while negotiating on price. A lady who had heard about the ship wrote to the Committee and in the letter was a check for $10,000; just what was needed to purchase the ship. Shortly after that, another check, this time for $5,000 was received, and this took care of the overhauling, transfer from Kobe to Manila, and the maintenance of the ship for the first few months.[218]

In the ABEO Report article, an encouraging summary was given of the first year of the Gospel ship's ministry:

> During this past year, this wonderful little Gospel Ship has been sailing in and out that long chain of islands in a work of pioneer evangelism that seems just like a modern replica of the Book of Acts. Equipped with a native crew made up of boys from the Bible Institute, everybody on board a Christian, the ship would put in at a harbor, all would go ashore and hold meetings, distribute gospels and tracts, give medical attention to the bodies, and seek the multitudes with the Bread of Life for their souls.
>
> In November the Gospel Ship, finding itself at the southern tip of the island archipelago, and only 60 miles from Northern Borneo, sailed over and touched at Sandakan, Borneo, establishing first contact with that

> vast unevangelized field which presents one of the greatest missionary challenges in the world today. Who knows but that the Lord may enable this Association to establish a real work in Borneo in the years that lie ahead, should the Lord tarry?

This story would not be complete if Raph's accounts of his knowledge of, and experiences with the Gospel Ship were not included. For instance, there is his description of the adventures of Master Mariner Captain Skolfield piloting the *Fukuin Maru* from Kobe to the Philippines:

> On the way to Manila he was caught in a typhoon and barely escaped wreck on a lee shore, by hoisting the small auxiliary sails (the boat had semi diesel engines, none too powerful) and rounding a point, though another Master Mariner accompanying him advised against it. Again his oil tank sprung a leak. What should he do? He discovered a tiny island in the deep seas and on arrival there found [Japanese] inhabited it. They arrested him on suspicion as he was an American Captain on a ship with a Japanese name. They cabled to Kobe, learned the facts, and he was released. But this was characteristic of the hazards he ran throughout his career in Palawan, where he took the ship.

Here are some of the experiences Raph had when he went on ministry trips with Captain Skolfield:

> My experiences on this ship were full of incident. We were accustomed to go ashore, hold clinics and meetings and prepare the way for churches later. They have been established since then, with a corps of missionaries to care for them.
>
> Another time when I was with him on a voyage, we glimpsed the top of a huge rock that was just breaking the surface of the water, a rock not charted by the Geodetic and Coast survey: a narrow escape for our ship.

> My experiences on this ship were thrilling. We went to islands bypassed by the ordinary steamers: wandered about among the coral reefs, where the sunshine turns the shallows to a bright green and the depths of the limpid seas reveal all the wonder of tropical beauty. Memories of it linger!

There are far too many adventures experienced by the missionaries in the Gospel Ship than can be recounted here, but Raph did describe the kind of enthusiastic response the missionaries had to new lands and peoples in his account of the exciting news that new tribes had been discovered in New Guinea:

> When the report reached us, just before the war, that new tribes had been discovered in Dutch New Guinea by airplane prospectors, it stirred our blood. Volunteer missionaries offered their services. Dr. Paul Culley, a Phi Beta Kappa graduate from Cornell, and also a graduate from Johns Hopkins Medical School, went with Captain Skolfield to investigate. He had a thrilling tour inland toward the Wissel Lakes, but had to return as the war threatened. His carriers were a rough lot. I heard some of them were cannibals. But he secured some very interesting technicolor motion pictures of the weirdest looking assortment of humans imaginable. The Association now is trying to enter: missionaries are ready: as soon as the Dutch Government permits the work will begin.

Early in the occupation of Manila by the Japanese, Captain Skolfield had another interesting transportation-related ministry in behalf of his former ABEO colleagues in the Philippines. In December of 1941, the Japanese began to attack airfields and cities in the Philippines, and by January 2, 1942, Japanese troops were entering the city of Manila. On Sunday, January 4, a major Filipino-owned newspaper carried the word that the Sovereignty of the United States was gone, and that the Japanese were planning to totally emancipate the islands of the Philippines for the Filipinos as a part of their Co-Prosperity Sphere.

The Japanese soon began to encourage all the Protestant and Catholic pastors and religious leaders to work cooperatively with them. Some of the Protestant leaders were willing to make a Pledge of Cooperation with the Japanese, but the ABEO (by then, ABWE) missionaries, and a few others, refused to sign the Pledge.

Sunday morning, February 15, cars came for Mr. Bomm, considered to be the "head" of the ABWE missionaries, and some other dissenting leaders, and they were imprisoned at the Santo Tomas internment camp, but without their wives. Mr. Bomm and his wife Marion were separated for two years. It soon became apparent that the Japanese intended to round up all the missionaries and put them into internment camps. Only those who received advance warning and were hidden by the Filipinos in the hills were able to escape imprisonment. The missionaries were kept in three different internment camps in the Manila area: Santo Tomas, Bilibad prison, and Los Baños.

Captain Skolfield, now an officer in the U. S. Navy, was tasked with burning down of the naval base at Cavite. While he was still in Manila, he did all he could to check on the status of the missionaries he could reach. Since the American troops were to be withdrawn, and there would be a great need for food in the future, he set aside a 2-ton truckload of canned goods and delivered it to Miss Woodworth. Some of the food remained to be smuggled into her internment camp, Los Baños.[219] Early in February, Santo Tomas and Bilibid were both liberated. Three weeks later, the daring raid of the Eleventh Airborne freed the prisoners of the Los Baños camp. They found out the next day that the Japanese were planning on killing the prisoners that day. But these stories are from a decade in the future; long after Raph experienced the wind, the waves, and the evangelistic opportunities of the Gospel Ship.

In his 1948 autobiographical piece, in the post-war language of his day, Raph gave a colorful account of Captain Skolfield's exploits and the eventual fate of the Gospel Ship:

> But the ultimate fate of the ship was dismal. When the war broke Captain Skolfield re-enlisted. One morning I saw headlines in the Boston Globe that startled me. It reported that five naval officers had escaped from Cebu to Australia and Skolfield was the pilot. It happened in

> this way. Skolfield was at Cavite when it fell. Then he was at Corregidor, and finally, with four officers, was at Cebu when the [Japanese] invaded. They embarked in an open sailboat, a *parao*, and journeyed for six weeks in the open sea, living on limpits [sic] and whatever they could pick up. The Captain was reported to have had "a broken alarm clock, a page of maps from a Geography", and a lot of horse sense, of course could be assumed. They did reach Australia safely, but only after a hair-raising pursuit by fuzzy wuzzies [apparently aboriginals], who on catching up with them proved to be friendly. The ship alas was never again heard from. The Association had offered her to the Government when the war broke, but before the transaction was settled, the [Japanese] struck.

Throughout history, many unique methods of bearing testimony concerning Jesus Christ have been developed. The Apostle Paul bore witness of his faith in Christ on a commercial ship that was shipwrecked, providing one of the most dramatic scenes in the book of Acts. But what dramatic, heart-warming, and glorious stories have come since then from ships dedicated to the purposes of meeting the spiritual and physical needs of people otherwise difficult to reach!

CHAPTER 23

Further Organization of ABEO, and The Problem of Imminence

With all lowliness and meekness, with longsuffering,
forbearing one another in love
—Ephesians 4:2

Although there were no slots open on the 12-member ABEO Board, in 1931 Mrs. Peabody asked Pastor Harold T. Commons if he would be willing to serve through regular attendance and taking the minutes for the Executive Committee. He was, at that time, pastor of the First Baptist Church of Atlantic City, New Jersey, and a friend of Board Member and Pastor David Otis Fuller.

In the early years of the ABEO, much of the business of the young mission was discussed in frequently exchanged letters between Raph and "Mother," Mrs. Peabody. In one of those letters, dated March 24, 1932, Raph sent some sketches of his views on matters to be considered at the annual meeting, which both would soon attend. In item 19 [!] of his list, Thomas expressed the following:

> Policies for DEI and M.E.I. may need to be re-enforced. I understand we stress evangelism and conservativism, but do not include pre-millennialism in our advertised

> school curriculum. (Think it will be unwise to make too much of this at present, however, as I have a notion that nearly all those on the field are vigorous pre-millennialists. Miss Martien will be the exception. It does not seem worth while to make it an issue, but on the other hand, I believe the stand we have taken here is more e[xpe]dient and less likely to estrange conservatives at home, some of whom feel that pre-millennialism is likely to develop extremists).[220]

On April 7, 1932, the annual meeting of the Association of Baptists for Evangelism in the Orient, Inc., was held at the Hotel Robert Morris and the Schaff Building in downtown Philadelphia. After Miss Hudson's treasurer's report, the question was asked, "What shall be our Policy in the future?" In answer to this question, three committees were appointed by the "Chairman," Mrs. Henry W. Peabody, to "crystallize the sentiment expressed in the meeting relative to organization, doctrinal statement and the policy of procedure." To the second of those committees, responsible for the doctrinal statement, Mrs. Peabody appointed Dr. Raphael Thomas, Mrs. Peabody, Dr. Ayer, and Dr. (David Otis) Fuller.[221]

On the following day, Dr. Ayer presented the report of the Doctrinal Committee with the following statement:

> WE BELIEVE in the Bible as the Plenary Inspired Word of God and the ONLY RECORD of His Son, our Lord and Saviour, Jesus Christ.
> WE BELIEVE He was born of a Virgin, lived a sinless life, wrought miracles, preached an Everlasting, Unchanging Gospel.
> WE BELIEVE in the Absolute Deity of the Lord Jesus Christ, that He is Very God and Very Man.
> WE BELIEVE in the Blood Atonement of Jesus Christ, that he "died for our sins" and rose bodily the third day from the dead.
> WE BELIEVE in the Personal, imminent Return of our Lord Jesus Christ.
> WE BELIEVE in Salvation by Regeneration, being Born Again by the Holy Spirit.

> WE BELIEVE the Holy Spirit abides with us to lead us into all truth and to give us power to go into all the world and preach, baptize, and teach as our Risen Lord commanded.
> WE BELIEVE in baptism of believers on profession of faith through immersion, the symbol of death to sin and rising to newness of life.
> WE BELIEVE we are called to be His witnesses by word and deed.[222]

The record indicates that the motion "To accept the Doctrinal Statement as read, looking forward to a more complete statement in the future" was carried.[223]

THE MYSTERY

At this point, leaving the chronological narrative of Raph's life for a time, it is time to introduce an interesting historical and doctrinal mystery. Included in the doctrinal statement was the phrase "the imminent return of the Lord Jesus Christ," and it was with this simple phrase that all the "trouble" began. Raph's dissatisfaction with this phrase continued to the end of his life. It was also a contributing factor to some discontent among the missionaries in the Philippines, to his eventual permanent return from the Philippines, and to his unique relationship to the Board through the years.

As will be further explored and explained below, in the doctrine of last things (eschatology), as understood by premillennialists, the return of Christ will appear in two phases. Before the Tribulation Period, when the wrath of God will be visited on the earth, He will come in the clouds and take up the saints (the believers in Christ), dead and alive, to be with Him. At the second appearance, at the end of the Tribulation and just before the millennium, He will return to earth to establish His Kingdom. This view of the future includes the concept that, since all other prerequisites for the return of Christ have been fulfilled, Christ could return at any time. The phrase usually used to describe that "any time" return is "the imminent return of Christ." In Chapter Two, we learned that Raph was taught a different system of eschatology – a different view of when and how Christ will return.

On page forty-seven of the earliest public report of the Association of Baptists for Evangelism in the Orient, for 1928-1929, a preliminary doctrinal statement was given in the following language:

> *We believe in the Divine inspiration and authority of the Bible, as the Word of God and the ONLY RECORD of His Son, our Lord and Saviour, Jesus Christ. We believe He was born of a Virgin, lived a sinless life, wrought miracles, preached an everlasting unchanging Gospel. We believe He died for our sins and rose again with the promise of return for which we wait. We believe the Holy Spirit abides with us to lead us into all truth and to give us power to go into all the world and preach, baptize, and teach as our risen Lord commanded. We believe in baptism of believers on profession of faith through immersion, the symbol of death to sin and rising to newness of life. We believe we are called to be His witnesses by word and deed.* [Emphasis added][224]

It is apparent that the author of that statement felt no need to include the "imminent return," choosing instead to merely refer to the promise of His return.

The mystery appears here. Why did doctrinal committee members Raph and Lucy Peabody accept a doctrinal statement affirming belief in the imminent return of the Lord, when that language was not used earlier, and both would later object to the use of that language in the statement?

The only available answers to this mystery, in the absence of committee notes, are found in the wording of Raph's earlier letter and the language of the official record. In his letter, Raph had suggested that it might not be "wise" or "worthwhile" to make too much of the pre-millennial issue because of the number of premillennialists on the field. With that in mind, and perhaps not wanting to make an issue of the wording of what was received as a preliminary, less than complete, doctrinal statement, it appears that Mrs. Peabody and Raph went along with the language of the doctrinal statement. As will be seen later, Mrs. Peabody apparently objected, but refrained from voting against it because she was chairing the meeting. In later correspondence, Raph seems to have forgotten that he was present.

In this chapter, we will attempt to answer the questions of when, how, and why this simple phrase became a problem to Raph. Was he confused about the pre-millennial significance of the term "imminent?" Was Raph a post-millennialist (believing that Christ would only return at the end of a period of church growth for a thousand years)? Or was he simply a man deeply concerned about the practice of date-setting: about excess in an area where he felt caution was needed; and about the influence of those who espoused premillennialism possibly to the hurt of evangelism and the mission?

Raph's sentiments regarding the "imminent return" portion of the Statement of Faith are spelled out in a letter he wrote, soon after the April 1932 meeting, to the missionaries in the Philippines as their new Executive Representative. In this letter, dated May 28, he wrote seven suggestions to his fellow missionaries, with a "word or two of explanation." [In many of the following letters and documents, the words premillennial and premillennialism are usually misspelled. Rather than interrupting the flow of the sentences, the reader is asked to simply remember that the words are misspelled.] The fifth item on his list read:

> 5. The training of evangelists always has been the primary objective of the Evangelistic Institutes, as the name implies. Pastoral care of churches must also be considered, of course, in the training of students in these Institutes, but the primary emphasis, so far has been to provide evangelists. As a corollary to this policy the stress has been laid on evangelism rather than pre-millenialism.
>
> The Statement of Faith accepted by the Association, when presented to it at the Annual Meeting in Philadelphia April 7th by the Committee specially appointed for the purpose of formulating it, frankly affirms the acceptance of the "Imminent Return" of our Lord. This is understood. But it has been equally clear that the policy has been and is for the present anyway to stress evangelism. Perhaps the happiest expression of this situation is the word that Mr. Jeffrey uttered in Manila, at the meeting held on Pennsylvania Ave. He said if I recall the words

> correctly, - that we must not forget that "Many have not heard He has come even once." This policy chiefly concerns the curriculum at the Institutes, or of any other schools for religious instruction that may be established while this policy remains unchanged. The students under the care of the Association are to be trained to evangelism. The methods advised and the message to be delivered are explained in the Bulletins of the Institutes. **This does not mean at all that missionaries are to be limited in their appreciation of this doctrine of pre-millenialism or to be hampered in their preaching of it, if they feel called to do so. The only limitations in the latter direction would be if stressing this theme interfered with greater stress on the greater theme of evangelism. No student, however, who attends any school of the Association, until this policy is changed, will be obliged to subscribe to this doctrine to be admitted, nor will the teaching of it be expected to interfere in any way with the stressing of evangelism.**[225]

While it was "understood" that the language of the Statement of Faith handed down by the committee (of which he was a member) affirms the "Imminent Return" of Christ, Raph was clearly suggesting that missionaries who appreciated that "doctrine of pre-millenialism" should not allow their stressing of this theme to interfere with their stressing of the greater theme of evangelism. He was particularly concerned that no student should be obliged to subscribe to the imminent return to be admitted to the schools in the Philippines. As if to underline his concern, Raph emphasized that the teaching of the imminent return should in no way interfere with the proper emphasis on evangelism in the school. As will become clear later, Raph, Mrs. Peabody, and others had several reasons for wanting to reduce the emphasis on the doctrine of pre-millennialism and the imminent return of Christ, but Raph's ultimate concern was evangelism. He clearly felt that whatever the convictions of individual missionaries might be concerning the return of Christ, those convictions should not be considered as important in preaching and teaching as the gospel and evangelism.

CHAPTER 23

Raph's letter to the Philippines lit the fuse of an explosive response from one of the pre-millennialists on the field, Rev. A. M. Sutherland. After receiving Raph's letter at Puerto Princessa, Palawan, in July of 1932, Sutherland, who was from a Plymouth Brethren background, wrote the following indignant response:

> The matter of premillennialism opened by you, while it does not alarm me, it provokes to much thought. I am sorry this matter is covered by a policy. You say, in effect, that missionaries are free to hold this doctrine, that they are not limited in their appreciation of it, nor at all hampered in their preaching of it; and yet a limitation is imposed when, as when you say, 'If the stressing this theme interfered with greater stress on the greater theme of evangelism.' I do not know, of course, what are the terms of the limitation, you do not say what they are, but, dear brother, I accept NO LIMITATION as to the place I shall give or the manner in which I shall preach any of the fundamental doctrines of the Word of God. Mine is a highly-prized liberty as a bondman of Christ. I must stand ABSOLUTELY FREE in declaring all the counsel of God. To me premillennialism is the highest type of evangelism. I give a large place in my preaching to this precious truth, and the Gospel is incomplete without it. I fear a very serious issue of this matter, and if any limitation is imposed I shall not feel satisfied until I am acquainted with its terms.[226]

In November of 1932, this same A.M. Sutherland, in a letter to the Association written in care of Raph, announced his resignation from the Mission. Concerning his reasons, he wrote that there were many, but he listed two. Only the first is germane to this biography, and it read:

> [1] The desire on the part of the Mission to interfere with the personal liberty of the Missionaries; as in the attempt to suppress the teaching of the doctrine of the near return of our beloved Lord Jesus, and [2] the unauthorized interference with the Missionaries' connection with

> the new testimony in the Islands – 'The Philippine Evangelist."[227]

After receiving Sutherland's letter, Harold Commons, Secretary to the Executive Committee, sent a gracious response in February. Sutherland, in his reply, dated April 10, 1933, offered the following remarks about the doctrinal statement and the official communication that had started this round of correspondence:

> The doctrinal statement of the Association is as clear and uncompromising as any similar declaration I have seen. I find no fault with the doctrinal basis. I still maintain, however, that the attitude of the Association, expressed in official communications, tends to discourage the emphatic preaching of the imminent return of our Lord Jesus. An official letter from the Executive Representative [Dr. Thomas] – dated 28th.May, 1932 – states at some length the place given this blessed truth in the Mission's programme of teaching and preaching. I grant you it is said that the missionaries are free to preach this truth as they feel led, but that privilege is practically denied and a limitation imposed, as you may read in that letter. I look upon the very suggestion of a restriction on the preaching of this or any other truth as an interference with my personal liberty as a bondman of Christ. I cannot understand why this doctrine was singled out for special mention if there was no feeling against its free proclamation.[228]

In conclusion, Mr. Southerland reiterated his request that his resignation be accepted and acted upon.

Considering his previous experiences in the Philippines, Raph was concerned that problems be prevented by his providing a comprehensive set of rules, words of wisdom, advice and policies. Unwittingly, he had, in his first official letter to the field, set in motion a polarization of missionaries who held the imminent return of the Savior to be a vital part of their message, and those who saw eschatological issues to be controversial and of dubious importance compared to the evangelism of the lost.

CHAPTER 23

RAPH BECOMES MORE OUTSPOKEN ABOUT HIS CONCERNS

Mrs. Doane was one concerned supporter of the Association with whom Raph had corresponded for decades. In the following early letter about methods used in the Manila work, dated October 28, 1933, Raph revealed several of his concerns about "hyper pre-millenialism."

> Miss Martien, Mrs. Thomas and I were used of God to open the Manila work. We did so on exactly the same lines as the work in Renfroville[229] and with equal blessing. Manila was a hard field and the response to the frank evangelistic methods was almost miraculous. Our own workers from Iloilo, who admitted the success there was unprecedented, were free to admit that they were skeptical about such methods in sophisticated hardened Manila, but now they admit their error. The methods were triumphant.
>
> What were these methods? They were fundamental but not extreme. From the first hyper pre-millenialism was avoided and the lessons learned here at home by Dr. Goodchild, leader of the Fundamentalist Movement and others was profited by. You see I knew something of the inside workings here. I am certain that this middle course was wise. There are those associated with the work of our Assn. who would stress pre-millenialism unduly and I am certain it would be a mistake. Miss Martien and I have always stood for <u>moderation</u>. I feel certain that a good deal of the unrest on the field comes from this source. I could name five at least on the field or six who make much of this doctrine and are inclined to make it divisive. Any here who sympathize with such a stand would be inclined to favor those who advocated it, even though they might not approve all the methods used. Miss Martien has suffered from this attitude I am sure, and I am equally sure that Mrs. Thomas and I are more or less under fire on the same charge. Our stand has been a deliberate and

> conscientious one, however, and we do not feel inclined to be overpersuaded by newcomers, who do not realize that we are standing as we do from conscientious motives and not because of ignorance or stubbornness. To make this doctrine of equal importance in evangelism as the cross and resurrection I believe wrong. To require our students to over emphasize the doctrine in their preaching I believe will make them unbalanced. To advertise our work on this basis here at home, I believe will estrange honest conservatives, who are not hyper pre-millenialists, and will weaken our hold. If the Assn. adheres to its statement on this subject, accepted after long conference at Philadelphia, I feel it will be dangerous. I honestly believe this already has been done to a certain extent, and the tendency should be checked. I feel it to be an important factor in the estimate of Miss Martien by certain ones there. I feel that you should know of it.[230]

The key to understanding Raph's gradually unfolding position is to note his vocabulary in letters like this (including his disregard for the proper spelling of millennialism). Raph saw his and Miss Martien's position as being "fundamental but not extreme;" a "middle course;" emphasizing "moderation;" and held not in ignorance of the issues but with "conscientious motives." On the other hand, he feared the influence of those in the Association who espoused "hyper pre-millenialism;" stressing "pre-millenialism unduly;" who were "hyper-millenialists;" mistakenly making their eschatological doctrine "of equal importance" with other foundational doctrines and through this "over" emphasis proving to be "divisive;" estranging many supporters of the Association who do not hold their position. Sadly, a whole book could be written on the use of "hyper" by those who are seeking to declare a doctrinal position to be 'excessive.'

Raph referred to Dr. F. M. Goodchild, Pastor of Central Baptist Church in New York City and, at one time, a leader in the Fundamentalist Fellowship. A Confession of Faith named after him was prepared for presentation at the Northern Baptist Convention (NBC) in 1921, but not presented. This was one example of the frustrations of a man who continually struggled to recapture the NBC from the liberals yet failed. It may be that the "lessons learned" were learned in the process of the fundamentalists moving away in the 1930's from the more accommodating position of the fundamentalist Baptist Bible Union, to take a modified stand on prophecy that accepted all Baptists regardless of their interpretation of the millennial position providing that they believed in the personal bodily return of Christ.[231]

It is apparent from the next letter sent to Mrs. Peabody that Raph had two primary concerns about the direction of the mission, both of them rooted in his own broad educational background and his desire to embrace a broader constituency in the cause of world missions. The first concern was his attitude toward the specific interpretation of the circumstances of the coming of Christ that was more and more widely held in the mission. The second was his response to the separation issue among fundamentalists within the NBC. Not that Raph condoned the liberalism in the NBC. As we have seen, one of his reasons for leaving the American Baptist Foreign Mission Board was the liberalism he detected in the organization. He simply wanted to remain open to the good men who were fighting liberalism within the NBC, and whose Baptist money could support Baptist missions. He was aware of the positions of the new seminaries that stood opposed to Eastern and other old-line seminaries where dispensationalism had not yet made much headway. His was not a cry to be part of an "ecumenical movement." He merely wanted to keep the support of, or garner new support from, the fundamentalists within the NBC who were not dispensationalists or pre-millennialists.

TEMPORARY RETURN TO THE FIELD

In 1932, Raph was appointed Executive Representative by the Executive Board of ABEO. Because of several concerns they were best qualified to address, Raph and Norma were authorized by the Board to travel to the Philippines, to see how things were progressing, and to do anything they could to advance the work in each area of ministry, for a limited time, with the approval of Raph's doctor.[232] He was accompanied by Norma, Burgess, Dr. Russel Bradley Jones and his family, and Miss Bethel France. They departed the States in September 1932 and arrived in the Philippines on the twentieth of October 1932.

In October, Raph wrote to Mrs. Doane, describing some of the blessings and financial hardships they had experienced on the field. Here again, the financial difficulties he describes are directly related to the Great Depression in the United States. Raph wrote,

> There is a fast mail going tomorrow and as I go to Iloilo next Wednesday and shall be farther from mail boats I'll send a word tonight. All looks prosperous here in the work. Today we went about with Dr. Jones and Miss France and Dr. Culley to the various centers and saw them in action. There was an air of permanence about them that was gratifying. Evidently our two main centers at San Rafael and over here by the U. P. [University of the Philippines, in Manila] are well established. Dr. Jones preached at the morning service over here, after we returned from our tour of the centers. I judge there were a hundred or more out, and at each service the appeal is given and nearly always it meets with response. This work assuredly is evangelistic. This afternoon at the evangelistic service at San Rafael there were baptisms (were also baptisms last Sunday, and many are waiting, receiving instruction in inquirer's class) and after that Dr. Jones gave a talk and on the appeal several came forward. It is amazing to see how the same program that was so successful in Iloilo at Doane Hall is successful here, though at the outset when the work first began students said it would not work. It is working, and the same power is making it successful, the power of the Spirit. How grateful we all should be to see how God protects such work.
>
> The two girls in Iloilo are overburdened, and as there seems to be no logical candidate to help them out I am going next Wednesday and probably I shall remain until after Miss Mower comes. We are so happy that she is coming. That need truly was an emergency.
>
> Now the Mission resources are so low that they have asked me if Mr. Ilustre can cut on his salary. It was a painful task. He is praying over it. Also, fear I shall have to tell

> Franco same. It hurts but if it has to be done, I suppose I am the one to do it. Poor Alberto. We must pray for him. "Once a leper always a leper" seems all too likely. I'll write soon from Iloilo.
>
> With love from the "Trio", Faithfully yours, Raphael C. Thomas.

Mrs. Doane and her friends were among those whose financial assistance helped to provide for these ministries through this difficult period. Their experience was certainly that of all who give sacrificially to the Lord's work, an experience described beautifully by the Apostle Paul in 2 Corinthians 9:10-15:

> Now He who supplies seed to the sower and bread for food will supply and multiply your seed for sowing and increase the harvest of your righteousness; you will be enriched in everything for all liberality, which through us is producing thanksgiving to God. For the ministry of this service is not only fully supplying the needs of the saints but is also overflowing through many thanksgivings to God. Because of the proof given by this ministry, they will glorify God for *your* obedience to your confession of the gospel of Christ and for the liberality of your contribution to them and to all, while they also, by prayer on your behalf, yearn for you because of the surpassing grace of God in you. Thanks be to God for His indescribable gift!

God enriched them bountifully to enable them to bountifully bless others, who in turn bountifully thanked and glorified God for the meeting of their needs, the generosity of the givers, and the grace of God who provided it all!

In addition to the ministries Raph mentioned in his letter, Captain and Mrs. Skolfield were ministering through the islands on the Gospel Ship, and Alexander Sutherland was experiencing great blessings as he collaborated with Pastors Negosa, Gebala, Alvior, and Caspe in evangelism and the establishment of preaching stations in Palawan.

In the January and February 1933 issue of *The Message*, mention was made of the necessity of the return of Dr. Thomas and family to the United States in April. Though this was not mentioned in the article, this was to be the final return of the Raph and Norma from the Philippines to America. Also mentioned in the same issue was the Lord's goodness to Norma and Burgess in keeping them safe when a fire swept through Doane Rest while they were asleep. Doane Rest had to be completely rebuilt. Before their return, Raph had experienced a five weeks' cruise on the Gospel Ship, and the fire evidently took place during his absence.

Before leaving for the States in May, Raph wrote a letter to the Philippine team. It was a letter intended to serve as "preventative medicine," fending off possible infections of bad behavior and relationships among the ABEO missionaries in the Philippines. He did not complete the writing of the letter until he had an opportunity to show it to Mrs. Peabody, so the date of the letter was May 28, 1928. He had seven suggestions for the missionaries:

1. Avoidance of criticism or controversy amongst ourselves or our neighbors.
2. Understand and support established mission policies.
3. Make no changes of established policies without Association sanction.
4. Fulfill completely and exactly all official Association requests.
5. Cultivate complete solidarity of whole mission field without rivalry.
6. Lay supreme emphasis on doctrines of salvation, giving first place to evangelism and establishment of Baptist churches, in accordance with (the) "apostolic method and message".
7. Maintain whole-hearted loyalty to the Association as an agency providentially adapted to the service of our Lord and Master, Jesus Christ.[233]

With all of the struggles he had experienced through the years with policy and Board-issues with ABFMS, it is interesting that Raph was as insistent as he was concerning the necessity of support of the Association and its policies. This is probably not inconsistency; rather it is Raph's way of encouraging the missionaries to trust their leadership and one another.

The October–November 1933 issue of the ABEO magazine *The Message* asked for thanksgiving for the safe return of Miss Webster, Miss Hotchkiss, and Dr. and Mrs. Thomas. In that same issue, the first invitation was given to contact Dr. Thomas in Ventnor, NJ, who was "ready to go with the moving pictures to the churches that are interested in this work of evangelism." Mrs. Doane had paid for the "moving picture outfits", and Dr. Paul Culley had "secured the fine sets of films."

As late as the May 1935 issue of *The Message*, Dr. and Mrs. R. C. Thomas are still listed in the "Our Missionaries" section as serving in Manila, along with Dr. and Mrs. Paul Culley, Mrs. Lilliam G. Culley, Miss Bernice Hahn, Dr. and Mrs. Russell Bradley Jones, and Miss Bethel France. This was in keeping with their continuing correspondence with and counsel to those who were serving there. In the meantime, though no longer field missionaries, they continued to make themselves available to speak on behalf of missions, the ABEO, and the work in the Philippines.

CHAPTER 24

Change of Mission Leadership, and Signing on the Dotted Line

Now he that planteth and he that watereth are one: and every man shall receive his own reward according to his own labour. —1 Corinthians 3:8

MRS. PEABODY'S RESIGNATIONS

In the May 1935 edition of *The Message*, Mrs. Peabody wrote of her resignation from the position of President of the Association of Baptists for Evangelism in the Orient, Inc.

> After seven years of service as President of the Association of Baptists for Evangelism in the Orient, I have felt it imperative that my resignation be accepted.
>
> My major reasons for resigning are the propriety and wisdom of electing a man to fill this important office since it deals with churches and pastors, as well as with questions which properly belong to masculine leadership in the Church.

> Since the position has also involved to a large extent the work of a corresponding secretary, it seemed necessary, as the work grows, to maintain an office where the President or Secretary, could give full time to the many lines of work which are developing. These include a large correspondence, with many sections of the country. There are various important committees, executive, finance, and candidate committees, requiring arrangement and attendance. It is important that the deputation work which has rapidly increased should be systematized and guided. The publication and editing of the monthly paper The Message, and the Annual Report, with important leaflet literature, call for time and attention. An inexpensive office centrally located, under the direction of an officer of the Association, who can give full time to this work seem to me essential.
>
> It will be a privilege to accept election to the Board of the Association, and to serve a little longer as Editor and Publisher of The Message. So in transferring responsibility for leadership to the incoming president, I am not saying farewell to the many friends with whom I have been associated during these years.[234]

There are unstated issues in Mrs. Peabody's statement that have direct links to both Raph's ministries and the trouble with imminence that deserve further treatment. Initially, the Board did not want to let her go. In 1933, Mrs. Peabody submitted her resignation as President/Chairwoman of ABEO for the first time. The Executive Committee of the Association rejected her letter of resignation during their January 1933 meeting. In April of 1935, she sent another letter of resignation from the office of President, and this was accepted at the Annual Meeting of the ABEO in April of that year. As a result, though she was listed in the April 1935, issue as "Chairman" and Editor of *The Message*, the official newsletter of the ABEO, Mr. Commons was introduced in the September issue as President and Editor of "The Message." Mrs. Peabody also requested that she be excused from serving on both the Executive and Finance Committees, but because she had been elected to those positions in April, the Executive

Committee voted to ask her to continue to serve on those committees whenever she was able to attend. For reason of accountability for certain funds, she agreed to remain on the Board. A special fund was established, called the Peabody Special Gift, into which some generous special gifts would be placed, and from which some of the expenses of the work on the field, including passage funds for Raph and Norma.

On November 2, 1936, and January 7, 1937, Mrs. Peabody again expressed her desire to resign. However, during a special meeting of the Voting Board on the 27 of April, her request was again rejected, even though on that same day, several issues that had been brought up in Mrs. Peabody's communications were discussed with concern. Action was taken concerning her list of suggestions for changing procedures and policies of the Board. After a day of prayer and discussion, the Board decided not to accept the recommendations made by Mrs. Peabody, except her advice that it was inadvisable for ABEO to cooperate with J. Frank Norris or his program.

Though, there is no need to repeat all of Mrs. Peabody's comments and recommendations, there is value in learning what she had to say about Raph. This was her comment:

> When the association sent Dr. Thomas as Executive Representative to Manila he encountered opposition at the first meeting. It was voiced by Mrs. Culley and worked out by her and Dr. Culley. They refused to accept Dr. Thomas's appointment as Executive Representative, and demanded that all control be on the Field. The Mission and the Board agreed to their demands, and failed to support Dr. Thomas. Dr. Jones and Mr. Sutherland joined Dr. Cully in statements regarding Dr. Thomas which he did not see and which were entirely unfounded. The Executive Committee yielded to the threats of these members that they would split the Association.
>
> Dr. Thomas made no reply and no defense, depending upon the Board in the office to which they had appointed him… .

The unfairness of the response to Raph when he and Norma returned to the field, and the apparent support by the Board of the demands of the field missionaries (and not of Dr. Thomas), hurt Mrs. Peabody deeply. Though the degree of self-governance on the field was always a controversial issue, it was obvious in this case that the reasons for the desire to control things on the field included a reluctance to be under the leadership of Dr. Thomas, an "old guard" missionary statesman.

In the sixth of the suggestions provided to the Board, entitled "Confession of Faith," Mrs. Peabody asked that "the word "Imanent" [imminent] be changed, as the Imanence [imminence] theory is not a cardinal doctrine of the Baptist Faith." She mentioned that some of the Board, and most of the large givers, prefer the "Clear teaching of the New Testament" regarding the time of the return of Christ, rather than certain forms of "Prophetical Interpretation." Mrs. Peabody, though a faithful student of the Word of God, was not a theologian, and she made no effort to clarify what she and others considered to be the "clear teaching of the New Testament" in regard to the return of the Lord. Her letter continued with this explanation:

> By this change each group is left to its own leading on the matter of interpretation. While I do not hold the view of some of the Board and on the Field, I have not allowed this to work against appointment of candidates who seemed otherwise qualified to hold a position under the Baptist Board, nor should a contrary view lead members of the Executive Committee or Board to discard candidates not committed to their ideas of Prophetical interpretation. As Baptists, where there may be differences on minor matters, we have the privilege of individual interpretation and conviction; but in a Corporation, chartered as an Association of Baptists, we have no right to make compulsory teaching that is not entirely within the Baptist Confession of Faith.[235]

We should not be surprised to learn that one of the recommendations is that a change to the Confession of Faith be made eliminating the word imminent in that it was, in her way of thinking, not a cardinal doctrine of the faith. In the body of her letter, Mrs. Peabody emphasized her belief that "Some people are so carried away by the peculiar interpretations of Prophecy that they ignore the weightier matters of the law."[236]

She objected to this Baptist organization making this one interpretation the standard, especially since the Association was taking large gifts from people who did not believe in the imminent, pre-millennial return of Christ. Mrs. Peabody felt that if that interpretation were to be made so large an issue, she would feel obliged to return the gifts of those who do not believe it. Concerning those who hold to the imminence position, Mrs. Peabody wrote

> As I have watched the people who carry this to an extreme, I have noted their utter lack of Christian sentiment and attitude on some very important matters. In fact, some of these people are responsible for the present situation in the Association. I have no objection to their holding personal views which I may not hold, if they stand by Baptist teaching and the spirit of the New Testament which is the spirit of the Lord.[237]

The Board's response to Mrs. Peabody's letter was stated in the minutes of a Special Meeting of the Voting Board, held at the Hotel Pennsylvania, New York City, April 27th, 1937. After a day of prayer and careful discussion, it was determined that "we do not see our way clear to concur in the recommendations for reorganization, change in wording of faith, etc." The vote regarding reorganization "stood 2 Yes and 7 No." The vote regarding a change of the statement on the premillennial position "stood 2 Yes, 5 No, 1 not voting."[238]

THE NEW PRESIDENT

The Board elected Harold T. Commons as its first fulltime president. Since Dr. Commons appears frequently in this account, some of his story deserves to be told. He was born in 1906. As a boy, Harold had attended a Quaker (Religious Society of Friends) meeting house in Brooklyn, New York, and his father became a Quaker minister in New York State, then a congregationalist minister in Massachusetts. He was received into membership in the Congregationalist church with no idea as to what he should believe other than believing in God, having a high moral code, and following the teachings of Jesus as best one can. He confessed in an interview that his personal theology was most consistent with Unitarianism, not believing in the deity of Jesus, nor accepting such things as heaven, hell, miracles, creation or the vicarious atonement of Christ.

He was schooled at the Moses Brown School, a Quaker boarding school, in Rhode Island, and Williams College (majoring in English literature). Neither of these schools provided any kind of positive spiritual influence; in fact, the faculty at Williams did their best to strip students of any kind of belief.

His life was transformed in the year 1924 through two experiences. The first was to go with eight fellow-students to an Oxford Group Movement week. They presented four absolutes (honesty, absolute purity, absolute truthfulness, and absolute unselfishness), and encouraged the participants to examine their lives in the light of these absolutes. For the first time, Harold was confronted with the truth of the absolute holiness of God, and his own sinfulness. The second came just a month later when Harold visited a dear uncle during Spring vacation from college. His uncle listened to Harold's description of the moral conviction he was under, then began to question him. He opened his Bible and showed him the necessity for a personal faith in Jesus Christ, and for the first time helped him to know "how to study the Bible and to understand what it teaches and how important it is to know what we believe and why we believe it. Suddenly everything took on new meaning and life has been different for me ever since." He said, "Now life is wonderful and full of meaning, and the Lord Jesus Christ is very real to me." He then knew that when he prayed, he was not going through a religious exercise, but he was talking with a personal God who hears and answers prayers.

From Williams he went to two different Presbyterian Theological Seminaries, Princeton and Westminster. During his studies, he became convinced that baptism by immersion was biblical, and that the "fundamental doctrines and distinctives" of the Baptists were clearly taught in the Scriptures. The progression of his thought was such that he was raised a Quaker and Congregationalist Unitarian, attended two Presbyterian seminaries, married Miss Corinth E. Tracy in an Episcopalian ceremony, and "wound up" a Baptist. During his last year at Westminster, he was rebaptized by immersion, joined a Baptist church, and was called to pastor First Baptist Church in Atlantic City. He made it known early in his ministry that he did not approve of the Northern Baptist Convention's mission agencies.

In 1933, Harold moved from Atlantic City to Johnson City, New York, where he became Pastor of First Baptist Church and the President of Baptist Bible Seminary. He was 27. In his continuing relationship with the Association, in 1934 he was elected to the position of Vice President. In April of 1935, Harold was elected President. This necessitated his leaving his church and the presidency of the Seminary. He was president of ABEO/ABWE until 1971, and the size and scope of the Association was blessed by God with a great increase. In an interview with Dr. Commons a few years before his death at 101 years of age, he reiterated to me that which he had said many times before, "Doctor Thomas was like a father to me."

SIGNING ON THE DOTTED LINE: AN ILLUMINATING EXCHANGE

In 1935, Raph wrote to Mrs. Peabody about a copy of a letter he had received from Harold Commons concerning the Baptist Bible Union. He used it as an opportunity to express his opinions on that issue and to restate his concerns about an unhealthy "emphasis" on pre-millennialism and its results.

> The letter from Commons (of which he sent me a copy) was about what I expected. Evidently this movement is making headway and it may be all right, provided Norris keeps in the background PERMANENTLY. But of that I do not feel so sure. Also, you can readily see that PRE-MILENNIALISM is conspicuously displayed in the statement. It would seem to me that they are putting the EMPHASIS THERE rather than on EVANGELISM. That is what I object to: THE EMPHASIS. The Laymen put it on EDUCATION AND SOCIAL SERVICE and the Fundamentalists on PRE-MIL. In either case, I do not see that EVANGELISM is the GREAT objective. I

> can see danger in this. I should not wonder if it was not at the bottom of our trouble. It was the plank Sutherland and Culley and Traber went off on. If it leads to such methods as he used and she is using now, I can see where it is dangerous. Certainly Barnhouse is not the man to follow if all I heard about him is true. Anyway, we are BAPTIST and many of these PRE-MIL people make that more important than the BAPTIST idea of exact obedience to the Bible. I stand for that.[239]

Here Raph compares the emphasis placed on premillennialism by "Fundamentalists" with the emphasis on education and social service of the "Laymen" in their manifesto on missions. His references to missionaries in the Philippines reflect both his hurt at the treatment he had received from their hands, his dissatisfaction with some of the methods they used, and his concern about the "plank" of premillennialism they stood on and "made more important than" evangelism and "exact" obedience to the Bible. Raph's language, while intended for sympathetic eyes and undoubtedly induced by painful experience, is uncharacteristically unbalanced by the inference that those who are premillennialists cannot balance their eschatology with evangelism and obedience to the text of Scripture. His reference here to what he had heard about Donald Grey Barnhouse is not explained in the context of the letter.

Most of Raph's comments related to the issue of that word 'imminent' are to be found in many letters he wrote to Harold Commons, by then president of the Association, and to Mrs. Peabody. Since it had become a policy of the mission that missionaries should subscribe to the principles, policies, and doctrinal statement of the Board, the arrival of the paperwork at the home of Raph and Norma Thomas always caused a stir. The following flurry of letters written between May 31st and the middle of July in 1937, is illustrative of the seriousness of the whole matter to all concerned, the semantic basis of some of the arguments, and the unnecessary confusion brought into the picture through time.

The debate began with Raph's refusal to sign on the dotted line.

> The other matter concerns myself. Strange as it may seem to you I hardly feel than [that] I can sign on the dotted line if that word "imminent" remains in the policies that

> all related to the Assn. are expected to approve. It has too much of the "date" setting connotation that so many object to. I am looking for His return, but do not feel it necessary to speak dogmatically in any way or to require others to do so. When we began the Assn. evangelism was the one big objective as it is with me now. If that is not enough I hope that the Committee will inform me. I have no quarrel with anyone who wishes to use this word himself, but do not feel that I should be required to subscribe to it now, since I did not when we began. It may seem a small matter, but I feel that it will do our cause no good if we expect to interest co-operating men, for many of them do not favor it I am sure: and some of them vary sane theologians. I speak of this privately for I do not imagine that the Committee will go so far as to insist that we all must approve, even if the Committee itself does. But I wished to be frank and to let you know in advance to avoid complications later.[240]

Raph stated only one reason for his unwillingness to sign, and that remains fairly standard throughout the correspondence. The presence of the word "imminent" in the doctrinal statement is the hitch, and in most of these letters he gives a number of reasons for his objection to its use. In this letter, the following reasons are given: 1) it has the connotation of date-setting "that so many object to;" 2) although he is looking for the coming of the Lord, he does not want to be dogmatic, or force others to be, about the circumstances of His coming; 3) he hints at his concern about over-emphasis; 4) he did not have to subscribe to the use of the word when he began; 5) he feels that co-operating men (presumably in the N.B.C.) will not give to ABEO if a specific eschatological position is taken; and, 6) many of those who would object to the pre-millennial imminent coming of Christ are good theologians. Raph wrote these things to Harold Commons hoping that the Board would not make an issue of forcing people to sign.

President Commons responded to Raph's concerns in the following letter:

> I note your reference to your personal situation with regard to signing our present doctrinal statement. It seems a bit strange that after ten years without any question

being raised whatever, and with the whole Association committed to that doctrinal statement including a plain reference to our belief in the personal, imminent return of our Lord there should arise this strong desire to change our statement. If it came as opposition to something new which was being added, it would be understandable, but to attempt to change it after ten years seems to me quite anomalous. There has never been any question from our supporters about our doctrinal basis. Is it any wonder that the Association refused to consider a change which would immediately arouse a storm of criticism and question and protest from our present supporters?

I believe that you have a wrong connotation attached to the word imminent. I disagree with you very decidedly that it has any tendency whatever to the "date-setting" business which is an abomination. The term has never meant nor has it been intended to mean that the coming of Christ must take place within any given period of time. All it has ever meant is that it might take place at any time. It has never meant "immediate". You spoke of not wishing to subscribe to it now since you did not when the Association began. Why then did you not protest the adoption of the doctrinal statement which had it very clearly in it? The time to have made such a protest was when it was first adopted, not nine or ten years after it has stood as the official doctrinal basis of the Association to which all are supposed to agree. You speak of our not being able to interest cooperating men (many of them) if we have this word in our doctrinal statement, as if this was any new thing which is just being added and which will hinder our appeal. I can't see the logic, for we have had it for ten years, and there has never been a question raised, as far as I know, from any of these cooperating men regarding the issue of the coming of Christ. The only question that has arisen, to my knowledge, was when Dr. Taylor (I think that is his name) at Eastern Seminary wrote me a letter asking what our official position was on the subject, and that only came about as a result of

> our rejection of Mr. Baker, when I believe it was Mrs. Peabody herself, one of our own members who started the discussion and raised the question in the minds of some of the folks at Eastern.
>
> Personally I believe this whole matter is a tempest in a teapot, and if we allow ourselves to get into a doctrinal discussion on this subject, such as the Presbyterians have just had between themselves resulting in a split in the new church and two independent mission boards now existing, then we shall be as guilty of foolishness and unwise statesmanship as they were. The devil loves to split the camp and divide the brethren, and if he can't do it one way, he will another. We just can't allow it. If we will stop raising these issues and be content to go along on the same platform and doctrinal basis on which we have always operated, then everything will be all right. I hope this appeals to you as being sensible, for it does to me.[241]

Several things should be noted here. First, the 10-year period Mr. Commons alluded to takes the discussion back to the very beginning of ABEO, about five years before the "imminent return" was included in any formal document of ABEO. This misstatement would come back to plague him. He further wondered why Raph had not made an issue of the use of the phrase at the time of its being introduced: an issue discussed above as "the mystery."

Rather than create a problem for potential supporters, President Commons, continued, a change in the doctrinal statement in 1937 would likely cause the present supporters to raise a storm of protest. Later in his letter, he expressed doubt that a statement that had been the position of the mission for ten years should surprise or keep any of the cooperating men from supporting ABEO, as though it were a new thing.

The semantic debate begun here with Raph was to continue for decades. Mr. Commons disagreed with Raph's understanding of the term "imminent," claiming that it had no concept of "immediate," nor was there any necessity of stating that Christ's coming must take place at a given time, which would smack of date-setting. Commons made it quite clear that he, too, considered date-setting to be an abomination. Finally, Mr. Commons expressed his heart-felt belief that this debate was a "tempest in a teapot" (a phrase Raph obviously did not appreciate), likely to be used of the devil to divide the brethren just as the Presbyterians had recently been divided in their churches and mission. To prevent such poor statesmanship, there should be no more disputes over a "platform and doctrinal basis" which had long been upheld.

That the discussion was not over is clearly seen in the next letter Raph wrote to Mrs. Peabody:

> Just had a letter from Commons, after a long wait. I wrote him a month ago . . . He alludes to the matter of "imminent" and takes the stand that it has nothing to do with "immediacy". He also seems to think that this Pre-Mil. Idea has been with us from the first, alleging that for ten years it has been understood to be our position and that if I decided to object I should have done so before. My reply is that what I now object to is signing, as we evidently will be expected to do, to a statement that I do not accept. I am not convinced that "imminent" has no connotation of immediacy; therefore I still am unwilling to sign. That we from the first (when we began in 1918 [1928]) had any such attitude of over emphasis on Pre.Mil. ideas I deny. But I do not mean to argue with him. Nor do I mean to sign as I feel now. So that's that. We can let it rest.[242]

But let it rest, he could not, as he was still troubled over the connotation of immediacy in the word imminent, and the apparent belittling of his concern by President Commons in his use of the phrase "tempest in a teapot." In addition, the surprise over the "ten years," on the part of Commons, was now matched by Raph's own confusion as reflected in this next letter. As was seen earlier, the meeting at which 'imminent' was discussed was in 1932, not 1931, and Raph was not only present, but he was also on the committee.

The one who was like a father to Commons was a bit upset at being lectured by the son. Still, his approach was not to attack, but to leave the matter in the Lord's hands, as a godly gentleman would.

Of the two millennial positions, Raph chose to identify himself as 'pre-mil' because he was looking for the Lord's return, wanted to be ready, and was leaving the exact timing up to the Lord. In a letter to Mrs. Doane, Raph explained his position:

> Our mission will become known as DEFINITELY PRE-MIL, which to most minds mean extreme emphasis on the doctrine, making it of equal importance with the other great cardinal doctrines such as the deity of our Lord, Atonement, Resurrection and Bible as final authority. Of course I am pre-millenial, as against post-millenial, which means I am looking for His return and wish to be ready when He comes. But I am not ready to refuse fellowship with one who does not stand for all the dispensational teaching and dogmatic interpretation of prophecy. I do not think you would either. And were it so small a matter (a "tempest in a teapot" as Bro. Commons called it in a letter to me in speaking of IMMINENT), I'd not care so much. But I see it to be DIVISIVE. It was so in our Mission, has been so in the Machen controversy, and is so now among those in the East and those in the Middle West, who are more extreme.

Although his attitude had at times seemed combative, Raph seemed generally to write and to say things "quietly," so as not to stir up trouble. At times, Raph gave expression to his fear concerning the potential effect of dogmatism on the part of the mission toward candidates and supporters. He was concerned about candidates being told that the schools in the Philippines were definitely pre-millennial and dispensational, unless they were; if so, neither he nor his colleagues were responsible for that. They had left the Filipinos believing that Christ is coming again and that we "are to be ready to meet him," but that they are not to be dogmatic on interpretation of prophecy or dogmatic as to "times and seasons".

In one of his letters, Raph mentions the disposition of the cases of some missionaries who had come to ABWE with positions on eschatology that differed from that of the mission. For reasons of the various views of eschatology in fundamentalist/evangelical circles, many came to the mission through the years with perspectives on eschatology not in agreement with the position adopted by ABEO and ABWE. In some cases, the differing position was rock solid; in others, the candidate had never seriously developed a position on issues in eschatology.

Raph was not interested in this issue in a passive way, as his letters have revealed. He sought the help of theologians to see if others were having the same trouble with the word imminent, and its connotations.

> Now again let me repeat that I feel even a small issue like this might make a disturbance: knowing how "close communion", "single cup" etc. have been something of a disturbance already. The Advent Christian stand also now is coming up, as the letters indicate, and "annihilation" etc. cut out Hell, as the Universalists and Modernists do; very convenient but serious! So even a "fly", small as it is, is out of place in the "ointment". I asked, out of curiosity what [John] Walvoord might think of it, and was not satisfied with his answer, when at the Prophecy Conference in Newton, and also [Merrill C.] Tenney (and felt he was not so sure of the accepted idea that it meant ONLY "at any time.") Well, here I am running on like Tennyson's "Brook", when I said I'd consume a small amount of stationary and incidentally of your VALUABLE TIME! IF you feel I should return this slip SIGNED on the dotted line, please let me know. [243]

> However, I am not trying to start anything, and tell you this only because I do not wish to be harboring any "reservations of conscience whatsoever." I've asked leaders such as Dr. Tenney and others, and find they do not seem inclined to <u>rule out</u> those who feel the word does not primarily mean "at any time," without the idea of "<u>immediacy</u>." (Honestly, though Hal, I have more and more been inclined to feel the end of the age is NOT far off.)[244]

Like all of us, he seemed to gather and report mostly opinions that agreed with him, but his investigations make for interesting reading for those to whom the names he mentioned are those of theologians who are now with the Lord, but who were young men when he talked with them.

The rest of the correspondence concerning this matter is interesting, but too long and involved for this narrative of Raph's life. Suffice it to say that the correspondence – particularly that of Raph with Dr. Commons – continued annually almost to his death.

How did Raph's views change in his later years? In a letter to Mrs. Doane, written in 1953, he wrote:

> A week ago I attended a Conference on Prophecy, and it was most informative. "The times are in His hand" but we are told to "watch", and surely there are significant signs to be "watched" at this critical period in the world's history. If only the nations would serve the Lord as some of them serve their country, we would be free from the horrors of war; and the Lord might hasten His return![245]

This brief note is Raph's response to a letter from Harold Commons:

> Thanks for the nice letter just in concerning that little nuisance of a word "imminent." Personally I prefer, at my time of life (on 'borrowed time') to emphasize the other word 'immanent". I hope to meet Him before long & whether through the gateway of death or by being "caught up" is less important to me than to "WATCH my step" & realize He is <u>here</u> to keep me from slipping before we meet "over there."
>
> I did not know Miss Martien felt the same for I felt it wiser not to broadcast my own views just over the connotation of a word! But realize that we both date back to a time before this word was included in our articles.
>
> Greatly appreciate the Comm's. willingness to deal so gently with us. It was good of you all. I'll enclose my preference here (as I've returned the slip to you) as "believing in the Imminent return of our Lord if the word means only 'at any time', but feeling it primarily means <u>immediacy</u>, prefer to say "at any time of His own choosing. Hope it may be soon![246]

Signing on the dotted line was no longer required in regard to the Doctrinal Statement. Although occasional slip-ups occurred and Raph received a Declaration to Sign, the privilege to sign a declaration qualified with a statement about the one reservation they held, had long before been extended to Raph, Norma, and Miss Martien. The following letter from Dr. Commons deals with that privilege:

> Many thanks for your letter of April 9th with reference to the pledge of allegiance to our Doctrinal Statement and Principles and Practices.
>
> The notice that was sent to you was purely of a routine nature and each notice did not receive my personal attention. … I should have written you a personal accompanying note saying that we really ought to have something in our file each year by way of a signed Declaration of Allegiance but that in your case and also in that of Miss Martien's, the privilege was granted some time ago of signing qualified declarations stating the one point of reservation which each of you holds.
>
> We fully understand one another on this matter and it is not something which is done in a corner but is an open matter of record. I am sure that you can see, however, that it is wiser for us to have your qualified Declaration of Allegiance in our files than nothing at all.[247]

The following is the last letter Raph wrote to Dr. Commons about the "Allegiance" blank:

> Dear "Hal":
>
> No answer please: unless you disagree with what I may have said on the "Allegiance" blank, as not telling the whole story. My whole disagreement with using the word "imminent", as I have said before, is one of "connotation." The Dictionary distinctly says it means "impending"! That suggests immediacy. I prefer to leave all timing to the Lord and "WATCH" and "WORK" to win souls

> before we all are "caught up". I am sending this to you and you can state it in the blank, if you think it necessary. I honestly feel that the signs of the times indicate the end of the age may be drawing near, but prefer to leave all that to God's decision. IMMANENCE to me is vastly more important, and for one living on borrowed time I feel sure the time for me to meet Him is not for long! That is for me the time to prepare for, whether before I go, or after! All this you knew before. Am I too fussy over a word? Maybe so, but guess I'm built that way![248]

As is apparent from the note, his mind was still sharp, and his position had not changed. He still felt that the dictionary definition of "impending" was the one to follow, and that "suggests immediacy." His burden for souls was unabated, desiring to reach the lost before "we all are 'caught up.'" As one living "on borrowed time," certain of his soon departure, Raph was thinking more about the immanence of God and his preparedness to meet Him. What better theme could occupy one's mind?

Many of these letters, with their dissertations on the meaning of the word "imminent," the lack of triviality of the subject, the significance of little things like words, and the importance of taking a stand, illustrate both Raph's great store of humor and of good will, since he was finally willing to be told to sign "on the dotted line" by his beloved Brother Commons.

It has become clear from a careful examination of Raph's writings that the concerns he had about the use of the term "imminent" in the official doctrinal statement of the ABEO and, later, ABWE were numerous, complex, and diverse.

He was convinced that there was a relationship between the concept of the imminent coming of Christ and the practice of date setting. He felt the need to shun dogmatism about times and seasons, leaving those matters with the Lord. His training and reading were in an environment, and at a time, in which little emphasis was put on the return of Christ except that His return was coming, and that the believer should be prepared for it. Though Raph appears not to have been a postmillennialist by conviction, he was also not a dispensationalist, and his training left him in an eschatologically ambiguous state. The theology of his teachers and texts, and much of the missiological hymnology of the age, was either postmillennial, opposed to premillennialism, or otherwise ambiguous. Few of his arguments were Biblical or theological in nature, and in the one place where he classifies himself as anything other than "moderate" in his views, he identifies himself as pre-millennial as to his hope and expectation of Christ's return.

He was concerned about the dispensationalists who arrived on the field primarily because of what he saw to be their insistence upon placing issues of eschatology on par with teachings concerning Christ and salvation, but secondarily because he feared that the mission's emphasis on premillennialism would alienate them from the evangelical Northern Baptists and their support.

Finally, as we have seen, Raph was preeminently concerned about evangelism. Throughout his ministry, he placed everything – including his medical work – below the great priority of his life and ministry: evangelism. He expected others to agree with him about this priority, and worried that an emphasis on pre-millennialism and the imminent return of Christ would somehow exist as a higher priority in the mission.

What better way is there to conclude this chapter than to quote the last words Raph wrote on the subject: "Am I too fussy over a word? Maybe so, but guess I'm built that way."

CHAPTER 25

Transition to Ministry in America

For I long to see you, that I may impart unto you some spiritual gift, to the end ye may be established; That is, that I may be comforted together with you by the mutual faith both of you and me. —Romans 1:11-12

REPRESENTATIVE

Raph's responsibilities in the early years of the ministry of ABEO, and the responses to his leadership reveal that his status, experience, and position in the Philippines and the new mission were not adequate to create awe and acceptance of his leadership in the hearts of some of the new missionaries. With all their appreciation for their mission agency, missionaries have often resented any interference from "the top," preferring to have the freedom to operate as a peer-to-peer group on the field. They feel that they best understand the people, and the needs of the work. Although the older missionaries who had worked together in earlier years were accepting and appreciative of the leadership of the new board, and Raph, their long-time colleague, the newer missionaries were cautious.

Another characteristic of missionaries is that they are often smart, talented, capable, and thus confident that with the help of the Lord they can do the work and make things better. They come with a set of skills and a lot of ideas about what can and should be done. They do, however, need both humility and direction, especially because of their lack of knowledge of the people they serve.

Finally, missionaries, like anyone who is consciously or unconsciously protective of his or her "turf," tend to resist assignments or outside influences that they feel threaten or undermine their personal areas of ministry.

As missions has changed, with a greater emphasis now on supporting rather than pioneering, these problems have declined, but – Christian missionaries being human – they still exist.

Raph summarized his seven month trip to the Philippines in a report submitted to the Board. On September 9, 1933, at Watch Hill, Rhode Island, Raph was asked to oversee Deputation Contacts; to open the way for invitations to churches for representatives of the Association to present the work of the mission.[249]

On April 3, 1934, the Executive Committee voted

> that we hereby elect Dr. Thomas Association Representative to make known the work of the Association in Churches, conferences, assemblies, and meetings all over the land, and that he have the privilege of attending the Executive Committee meetings.[250]

His attendance at the meetings would be permitted and encouraged, but voluntary since there were no funds available to pay his way to the meetings except when an appropriation of funds should bring him to a meeting for a special purpose.

AN ANNUAL MEETING

The Annual Meetings of the young board were reflective of the deeply felt significance of missions in the Fundamental churches of that era. The following is an example, just one of the early meetings in which Raph was a participant.

The 1934 Annual Meeting, on April 23 and 24, at The Belmont Avenue Baptist Church, Philadelphia, Pennsylvania. Everyone came in their finest: men in suits and hats, and the ladies in long coats and hats.

The preliminary schedule for the two days began with a "Preliminary Fundamentalist Conference for Pastors and Laymen, Open to the Public."

The first session began Monday at 7:30 in the evening. Rev. H. T. Commons was presiding. The Committee of Fifteen report was given by Dr. Carey Thomas. Rev. Norman S. McPherson, pastor of Calvary Baptist Church, Norwich, New York, spoke concerning "The Present Relationship of the Northern Baptist Convention to the Baptist Church." Dr. Raphael C. Thomas, Missionary to the Philippines, then spoke on "The Laymen's Missionary Inquiry and Program Going into Effect in the Philippines." The next speaker was an outstanding teacher and Bible scholar, Dr. J. Gresham Machen, DD, LL.D. At that time, Dr. Machen was Chairman of the Westminster Theological Seminary, which was founded in 1929 under his leadership. He spoke on the subject, "Why Independent Missionary Organizations are Needed." Dr. David Otis Fuller, a heavily committed board member of the ABEO, who was then pastor of Chelsea Baptist Church, Atlantic City, New Jersey, spoke next on "Why the Association of Baptists?" During Monday's presentations, questions were written out and handed in to be read and discussed.

Tuesday's afternoon program began at 2:30 with Rev. David Otis Fuller presiding. The opening devotional was given by Coulson Shepherd, Pastor of First Baptist Church, Atlantic City. Rev. George Moaba, Pastor of Belmont Avenue Baptist Church, greeted those in attendance. Miss Bernice M. Hahn spoke on "The Power of the Word." She was followed by Miss Edna R. Hotchkiss, who spoke about "The Training of Leaders in the Philippine Islands." Miss Bessie M. Traber spoke of "The Lord's Leading through the Year." The earlier portion of the day's meeting ended at 2:30 P.M. Raph was the last speaker, and he introduced the listeners to "The Great Field for Evangelism in Manila."

Tuesday evening's final session, with Mrs. Henry W. Peabody presiding, included activities and addresses. Pastor Moaba provided the devotional message, and following that, the new ABEO missionaries were presented to the attendees. Mrs. Peabody gave the opening with a timely topic: "The Dangers of Communism in Church and State." Rev. Commons told "The Story of The Association of Baptists." "Evangelism in the Iloilo District" was the subject of Miss Edith M. Webster's talk. Then, finally, Raph spoke on "The Gospel Ship, Palawan and the Regions Beyond." Following his talk, "moving pictures" of the Gospel Ship at work were shown. Through the years, the Annual Meeting took on different forms, but it was always an opportunity to review the great things God had done.

FINANCES

The financial situation of the mission and the country was still difficult at that time. Although the levels of annual support for missionaries in the 1920's and 30's were very low, the costs associated with such things as land and building purchases, operation of existing and new ministries, and travel continued. During the Great Depression, funds were scarce, and many generous givers of the past were no longer able to give. Thankfully, Mrs. Peabody, Mrs. Doane, and other supporters of the mission had been blessed with fortunes that made their travel and donations possible, but missionaries and others in the ministry had to squeeze their pennies until they shouted "ouch!" Long after the Depression had ended, people associated with missions often carried the "Depression mindset" into the distribution of funds. Transmission of funds from America to other fields was often held up to gain a few cents in the transaction. In some fields, banks would do the same thing, sitting on transmitted funds for a day or two to lose less money based on the exchange rate.

CHANGE OF LOCATION AND TYPE OF MINISTRY

As his monthly reports will attest, during the later months of 1934, Raph was busy speaking at churches, meeting various Baptist leaders, and attending Ministers' meetings throughout the East and Midwest.

At the Executive Committee meeting in June 1935, Raph informed the members of the committee that he was doubtful that it was the Lord's will for him to return to the Philippine Islands at that time.[251] Two important factors in his decision were his health, and the question in his mind about signing the Statement of Allegiance to the Principles and Practices of the Association of Baptists for World Evangelism due to the presence of the word imminent. The Committee later agreed with Raph that they should wait upon the Lord for His definite leading of the couple in the future.[252]

On November 9 of that same year, John J. Bryson, widower, with John F. Bryson and his wife Edith, sold a lot and house in Georgetown, Essex County, Massachusetts, to Raph and Norma "in consideration of one dollar and other valuable consideration paid by Raphael C. Thomas and Norma W. Thomas." This became their home for the rest of their lives.

Perhaps because his responsibilities had been reduced, the provision of his new home, and the prospects of a different kind of ministry, Raph felt "fit and ready for anything" in February of 1935. Writing to Mrs. Doane from Georgetown, he commented concerning the heavy snow that it had no terrors for him "as I find I stand the cold weather surprisingly well for a Filipino." He added that he rarely had a cold, and that he had plenty of vigor to face his daily tasks. In fact, he added, "My physical condition is excellent. Tipped the scales at 189 the other day, when I read the proper weight for six feet one was 181. That is not so bad. Feel fit for anything."[253]

As late as 1937, Raph expressed to Mrs. Peabody his disappointment that a medical doctor, Dr. Murphy, who had been watching Raph's physical condition had been advising the Executive Committee that Raph and Norma should not return to the Philippines for visits. Raph felt that his own view of his condition was not being considered. This, and other disappointments, he kept to himself.

CHAPTER 26

Later Ministries

For he shall not much remember the days of his life; because God answereth *him* in the joy of his heart. —Ecclesiastes 5:20

STATESMAN

Although Raph did not practice medicine regularly after he returned from the Philippines, he was always a healer. He continually looked for a way to stitch together the wounds that divided Baptists in the United States.

One project that occupied Raph's alert mind during the 1930's was that of finding a way to get the Fundamentalist Baptist Separatists together with the fundamental "really fine men" still in the Northern Baptist Convention. His desire was for peace, fellowship, and cooperation in regard to missions. He was not foolish enough to think that those who had fought to leave the Convention would want to get together on a doctrinal or administrative basis. Rather he suggested forgetting their differences and emphasizing their agreements on one issue to begin the process of reconciliation. He used the phrase "Baptist Money for Baptist Work," as the slogan by which he intended to get these good men together to support Baptist missionary projects. His hope was that through agreement on this one matter, these Baptist leaders would find that they could get together to discuss some other "non-inflammatory topic," and more progress would be made. Raph admitted that it would seem ironic to some that a man with his own record of leaving the ABFMS would be speaking out in favor of reconciliation. His response was simply that no one would better understand the issues at stake, and he was willing to stake his reputation on this effort.[254] Though he was ultimately unsuccessful in the attempt, no one could fault him for having failed to try with enthusiasm. Some examples of his work will increase understanding of both the burden he carried, and the humility with which he approached the problem.

Raph regularly wrote Dr. Curtis Lee Laws with affection. Dr. Laws was a Fundamental Baptist pastor and the founding editor of the Watchman Examiner. He is credited with being the first to use the term "fundamentalist" to describe those who believe and defend the fundamental teachings of the Scriptures. Dr. Laws had been present at the Watch Hill, Rhode Island, meeting called by Mrs. Doane in 1927 to discuss the needs of the Philippines following the resignation of Dr. and Mrs. Thomas. Although he thought it would be best for him to take no official position on the Board of the new mission, he promised his support of the ABEO, and expressed a willingness to publish its news in the Watchman Examiner.[255]

Their relationship appears to have been close. He wrote a thoughtful and revealing letter on February 4, 1938, to Dr. Laws after the death of Mrs. Laws' mother and brother. With affection, Raph wrote:

> I well remember your admonition to cherish my good mother-in-law when we were at Groton last Summer, and I realized what you said was quite true. I have no doubt you felt the same esteem and affection for this dear one who is gone, and how deeply your wife must have loved and even idolized such a mother. To this day my own mother's love abides with me. I can never forget it, even though she was well advanced in years. Advanced age seems to make no difference in such a parting, except, perhaps, to make the ties more binding. This bereavement must have been sad indeed; but to have to suffer a second one, in the loss of beloved brother was almost too much. How we both grieve for your dear wife. May the Lord sustain

> her and you, as we know He will, and turn this bitter experience into a tender memory that will always abide, but in time will lose its "sting." Though I am a medical man and should long ago have become accustomed to death, I confess I have never yet been able to do so, for as a minister I have looked upon it in a different way. But I also have learned in my own bereavements to know that little can be said to lighten the burden of woe that test upon us at such a time, but it does help, in a way, to know that others grieve with us.

One letter, written to Dr. Laws on December 30, 1937, provides both an interesting summary of the challenges Raph was facing in his attempts at reconciliation and a quote that is remarkable in the way it brings together the year 1937 and the first two decades of the twenty-first century.

Starting with the latter, here is Raph quoting columnist Walter Lippmann's article in a Harvard Alumni Bulletin entitled "Dogmatism and Tolerance:"

> People are separating themselves into factions which have almost ceased to communicate intelligibly, one with the other. They become so passionately dogmatic about their own views, so irreconcilably suspicious of the views of others, that it is excessively difficult for their minds to meet . . . what we have not got at the present time is the capacity to differ without denunciation, the capacity to argue without impugning motives, the capacity to consider proposals without regarding them as conspiracies.[256]

Raph's conclusion was that if a columnist is honest enough to write like that, it seems that professed Christians ought to be able "to sit up and take notice."

The connection between this column and Raph's burden is easy to imagine. He confessed that having been "out of the world" for so long [in the Philippines], he had not yet come to tolerating an attitude of inevitability concerning the separation "among the Conservatives in the East and Middle West." He was impatient for change that could easily be brought about if everyone would just see the need and cooperate.

He had attempted to gain a hearing in the East for a new movement for missionary giving promoted by a Dr. Savage as a means of promoting unity and reconciliation among Conservative elements of the Northern Baptist Convention. Apparently, Dr. Savage had been involved in an issue related to the Ntondo mission in the Congo which had not gone well.[257] Raph was hoping that could be set aside, and that the pastors in the East could be encouraged to unite through this movement. As he communicated to Dr. Laws, his dream of this connection was fading as he feared

> that the East will have none of it, as it will have to be given publicity by INVITATION from pastors of the N.B.C. churches, and how many of them will risk disapproval by inviting any representative . . . to tell the plan now that Dr. Savage's embroglio [sic] over Ntondo makes his personal relationship to the new movement a detriment? It is just the same battle I have fought here in New England. Just because I separated under local conditions that few of these men would have tolerated for the ten years or so I did . . . they regard all I say or do as tainted by "separation."[258]

Raph told Dr. Laws that, with that attempt behind him, Raph was beginning to work on a "ministry of reconciliation" using the "mission problem" as a basis, but he knew that somehow, he would have to develop a forum for "chats" between the good men of the "Middle West," and of the East. He added, "Wouldn't such a campaign be worth while? If your Watchman and Strathearn's "Beacon" took up the slogan BAPTISTS GET TOGETHER, what a New Year it would make – or would it be a ROW?"

Another of the pastors with whom he corresponded was Joseph Hakes, at that time pastor of Nepperhan Avenue Baptist Church, in Yonkers, New York. A good portion of the letter is worth quoting since it so clearly reveals Raph's heart concerning peace among Baptist churches and organizations.

> This is my first letter of the New Year, and it concerns the biggest thing we should hope for and that is PEACE. Of course I know full well that many of my friends will laugh in their sleeves when a man with my record attempts anything in that direction. Perhaps that is one of the very

reasons why I am the one to do it. My long missionary experience certainly should qualify me to KNOW the facts at least on that score (and that is the BIG score in establishing any peace among Fundamentalists, as you know). Moreover, being something of a loafer during the past four years here in the U.S.A. I've had time on my hands, that few pastors have. Moreover, I have made a special point of "surveying" the WHOLE situation, both here and in the Middle West, where most of the trouble has been. Few have attended so many conferences and read the literature more carefully than I. The Watchman [Examiner], Baptist Bulletin, Baptist Beacon, Christian Beacon, Fundamentalist, etc. etc. I have read them all. Also have made a really carefu[l] study of the Laymen's Movement, even going to the Library at Union Theol. to read the Fact Finders Report and the literature there on the whole subject. Then went to Chicago and talked with Ewald, the Secy of the Movement for World Christianity. He gave me a digest of Re-Thinking Missions, evidently active still, in spite of the word of certain Fund. Leaders with N.B.C. to me that it is "dead". I "know my onions" on all of this and yet honestly say I have no bitterness in my heart but only am anxious to do what I can to "pour oil on the troubled waters" and, if possible, get the men WHO REALLY HAVE INFLUENCE in the Denom. to make some reasonable attempt to make a start in the direction of reconciliation. Of course I know that many will just smile sweetly and say "It can't be done". Would the Lord really approve of such an inertia if He came right now? What do you think? And if He would not approve, there must be some way out of such a predicament. I know that what I suggest may not be the RIGHT way, but it might be better than nothing, if no one else will suggest one. Just to wait and wait and pretend we are satisfied with the speed the Funds. are making WITHOUT any such unity of the Spirit, is not enough to satisfy me. I think it is just the lethargy of an inertia that has become habitual. No PAST history however discouraging can justify that.[259]

> If one of the leaders here in the East could agree on ANY PLAN OF ACTION at all that would tend to cement a new relationship between the MODERATES (for I am not talking of the EXTREMISTS) that eventually might grow into a reconciliation – not administratively, but just in the matter of giving at the outset – wouldn't it be at least a START? I am sure that it would be folly just now to try to have complete UNITY on a doctrinal basis, and certainly on an administrative basis – but on a missionary basis, the REAL bone of contention at present, I think there is hope.
>
> A little article will appear in our Message, put out by the Assn. of Baptists, and I may add a little to that and have it out soon as a pamphlet. This idea of BAPTIST MONEY FOR BAPTIST WORK I long have been contemplating. It seems only reasonable to me. Also it seems reasonable to a number of men who are leaders in the Denom. It should appeal to Separatists as well. In short, it may be the very EXCUSE I have been hoping might get some of these men from N.B.C. and INDEPENDENT Baptist churches together to TALK IT OVER. That in turn would be just another excuse to get them ACQUAINTED and praying together on a common project, forgetting the PAST and also their DOCTRINAL differences and ALL ADMINISTRATION. In other words, they would "forget their differences" and emphasize their agreements". ONCE THEY WOULD DO THAT they might be on the way to further reconciliation. You see I have been tagging around so faithfully and meeting so many of all camps that I just can't understand the attitude of either party that flouts and discounts men who are really fine. Now to be exact, for example. ...[260]

After the last sentence fragment in the quotation, Raph listed dozens of names of individuals he had in mind of those in the East and the Mid-West, those who were still in the Northern Baptist Convention, and those who had separated from it, who would be likely to be brought together and find common ground. For the sake of this biography, it is unnecessary to include those names, but for the sake of history (and for those who are curious), they will be mentioned in Appendix 5.

The pamphlet Raph mentioned entitled BAPTIST MONEY FOR BAPTIST WORK, was both an exhortation and an encouragement to think of the needs of the work already being done in the Philippines. It read,

> A large amount of Baptist money is going to undenominational and interdenominational work. Two reasons for this are clear. First, denominationalism is becoming unpopular. Secondly, Baptists are divided amongst themselves.
>
> "Denominationalism," if it implies centralized control, is hardly a legitimate term for Baptists, who have always insisted on the complete independence and authority of the local church; but freed of such illegitimate ecclesiastical control, some form of large group consciousness, call if what you will, tends to promote Baptist welfare. Among other fellowship interests thus favored is stewardship. Corporate giving has many advantages. . . The Baptist group, particularly, with its emphasis on liberty of conscience, the independence of the local church, and exact obedience to the Scriptures, has in its soul the longevity of eternal values. **Denominational giving should continue.**
>
> But the second hindrance to united Baptist giving – division within the ranks – is more disrupting, as internal trouble always is. Moreover, it is a struggle between Conservatives, who, above all others, would most deplore Baptist disintegration.
>
> The chief reason for this unfortunate division has come from the confusion of loyalties due to the advent of the Northern Baptist Convention, familiarly known as the "N.B.C." Certain Conservatives disapproved of its leadership and policies and separated from it, hopeless of its reform. Others, believing reform possible and yielding to the insistent declaration that "the N.B.C. IS the Baptist Denomination," refused to separate from it lest they be

disloyal to their Baptist heritage. Agreeing on doctrine, they were widely at variance on administration and policy.

Under such conditions, to expect complete agreement among Baptists in the matter of administration and policy would be oversanguine; but it does seem unfortunate and unnecessary that these conservative groups, already in agreement in so many ways, cannot discover some common ground for **united giving to missionary work.** This is precisely what they so far have failed to do. Both Separatists and Conservative Baptists co-operating with the N.B.C. have, in many cases, preferred to patronize undenominational and interdenominational "Faith Mission" work.

The Separatists long have been committed to such a policy, having begun it at a time when no similar Baptist wok existed. Many now continue to pursue this policy, justifiably enough, as such interdenominational "Faith Mission" work is praiseworthy, but hardly warranting **continued expansion** in this direction at the expense of similar Baptist "Faith Mission" work, which now exists.

The Conservatives co-operating with the N.B.C., on the other hand, fall into three distinct groups. Some of them feel they can give to the N.B.C. "Unified Budget" conscientiously. Others feel they cannot, but designate their gifts to Conservative N.B.C. projects and workers, for which they will receive credit on their apportionment. A third group, apparently a large one, feel they can do neither and give ONLY to undenominational and interdenominational mission work.

Without criticism of any of these four groups, since it may be assumed that all act conscientiously, one might venture to suggest that the two now giving so freely to interdenominational agencies – the Separatists from the N.B.C. and the third group co-operating with the N.B.C., who give neither to its "Unified Budget" nor designated work – could profit by thinking through this slogan:

BAPTIST MONEY FOR BAPTIST WORK. It would lessen criticism for those who still co-operate with the N.B.C. and be more logical for the Separatists.

Both groups appear impressed by the fact that "Faith Missions" (so-called) send not a "fractional dollar" but nearly all their money to the foreign field; that their programs are predominantly evangelistic; and that, without direct financial appeals and campaigns, they nearly all have advanced during the financial depression, while organized denominational boards have failed to do so. Evidently, they attribute these results, at least in part, to the difference in missionary method, and intend to continue their giving to "Faith" work.

As such money seems inevitably lost to the "Unified Budget" of the N.B.C. anyway, co-operating Conservatives would incur no more opprobrium by giving some of it to BAPTIST FAITH WORK instead of patronizing interdenominational "Faith" work alone. This would materially strengthen the whole Baptist mission program. The same policy for giving would prove the Separatists even more consistent, since it was because of Baptist principles they separated. Moreover, when both groups realize that interdenominational missions have access to ALL denominations, while Baptist missions are limited to Baptists for support, the appeal should become doubly urgent.

Three accredited representatives of such Baptist "Faith" work, at least, are the Association of Baptists for Evangelism in the Orient, Schaff Building, Philadelphia, Pennsylvania; Mid-Missions, Mishawaka, Indiana; and the Interstate Evangelistic Association, Temple Building, Rochester, New York, which operates in the home field, to say nothing of several other truly Baptist "Faith" enterprises. Literature of these various organizations, or information about them, may be obtained at headquarters. Those interested may send for it and judge for themselves as to the merits of such Baptist work.

BAPTIST MONEY FOR BAPTIST WORK!
WHAT A SLOGAN FOR BAPTISTS!

As the war approached, in 1939, ABEO started a work in the Amazon River area of the country of Peru. This expansion out of the Philippines resulted in the change of the Association's name to the Association of Baptists for World Evangelism (ABWE). This was the beginning of multiplication of countries in which ABWE chose to work, and the development of field councils – sometimes more than one in a country depending on the area where the missionaries were located. This expansion was explained in a slip of paper added to the pamphlet quoted above. Raph's heart and his dependence on God for victory is found on that same slip of paper in a request for prayer that "ALL Baptists, whatever their administrative affiliation," would cooperate in Great Commission work.

For those who have experienced the struggle of a pastor, or of a church, embroiled in the process of making the painful decision to part company with a fellowship of churches or a larger Christian organization for reasons of conscience, doctrinal differences, or growing ecclesiological incompatibility, Raph's efforts to bring the NBC. and Separatist moderates and fundamentalists together with an eye toward reconciliation may seem either noble or quixotic. Yet his deeply felt desire to find ways to bring God's people together in the unity Jesus emphasized in His High-Priestly prayer in chapter seventeen of John's Gospel is both laudable and compelling.

SPEAKER

In the 1930's, a well-travelled missionary speaker was always liable to be the subject of an article in a local paper. Newspapers would include sections on individual towns in the district where they were read, and in the January 24, 1938, edition of the *Lawrence Daily Eagle* (Lawrence, Massachusetts; 1868 – 1959), a lengthy article described a lecture given on the Philippines by Dr. R. C. Thomas (now a resident of North Street, Georgetown) at the HiY club of the Perley High School. Along with some interesting information on the work of ABEO and the Gospel Ship in the Philippines, he spoke on such issues as the problem of the Moros (Muslims), who never desired to be under the control of the government of the Philippines, and the difficulties in the establishment of the New Republic in the islands. In response to a question about the future of the Philippines politically, Raph gave the following perceptive response:

> he advised his hearers to keep an eye on Japan. As Corregidor is one of the most strongly fortified positions in the Far East and as Japan might covet a naval base in the Philippines, which would make her mistress of the Oriental seas, it is not too much to imagine that she might decide that the Philippines needed "development" and that she was called to be the one to develop them by holding this stronghold. Nobody knows what the outcome will be, but it will do no harm to be on guard.

That, of course, is exactly what happened!

On February 15, another article appeared, describing Raph's ministry at a meeting of the Haverhill Christian Endeavor Union at the Amesbury Baptist church. He highlighted the response of the people to the Gospel Ship, and the ministry of Henry DeVries among the Moro, comparing his amazing, dangerous experiences with those of John G. Paton.

Raph was interested in more than meetings with pastors. He mentioned in his report to the mission for February and March, 1937, that at an Association meeting he had attended, a deacon from a nearby local church approached him about being a speaker at their Mission Meeting, "but the pastor caught him in time to explain that it was not expedient." Raph wrote that this demonstrated the "laymen's viewpoint," and he was hoping that the Movement for Laymen sponsored by the New England Fellowship would develop helpful contacts for the mission. He added, "Laymen long have been my hobby and now even more so."[261]

AUTHOR AND CORRESPONDENT

In addition to representing the mission, keeping up with missionaries and mission business, and looking for ways to get Baptists together for the sake of the gospel, Raph wore out his typewriter in the task of writing. He wrote gospel tracts, articles for the Message and other Christian magazines, columns for newspapers and a flood of letters to editors throughout the country. Anyone living and reading newspapers in the northeastern part of Massachusetts from the late 1930's to the mid-1950's would probably have read Raph's articles on Asia, the War, and politics in the *Lawrence Eagle*, *The Salem Evening News*, and the *Boston Daily Globe*.

Many of his letters before, during, and after World War Two, demonstrated a great deal of thought, study, and God-given insight into the strategic and political aspects of the war. Throughout his life, well into the 1950s, he was a voluminous correspondent, careful always to date and make carbon copies of his letters. He maintained a continual commentary on the War in Asia. Despite the clear-eyed, insightful, and studied quality of what he wrote, his articles also tended to be lengthy. This resulted in 1951 in his receiving a letter from the editor of the *Salem Evening News* who lamented that because of the space requirements of the newspaper, he would have to ask Raph to refrain from sending further articles until "the space situation improves."

His letters to editors ranged from the prosecution of the war in Asia to McCarthy, from war with Red China to the health of President Eisenhower, and from the Korean war to Billy Graham. Here are a few of the headlines for his articles: "Timing All Important in War; MacArthur Urges Speed"; "Fortifying Truk Important"; "Philippine Conquest Gathering Momentum"; "Escape of Prisoners in Luzon should be Occasion of Universal Gratitude"; "Is Our Present Foreign Policy Satisfactory?"; "Should We Invade Japan Now?"; "Could Japan Fall Before Germany?"; and "Post War China".

In 1951, after writing for a while to the *Salem Evening News* and the *Haverhill Gazette*, Raph wrote another editor (of an unnamed publication) to both reintroduce himself and request that his editorials be published by the paper. His self-introduction included both a reason for his writing these editorials, and an interesting summary of his qualifications for writing them. If only he had left a record of a few of the trips he mentioned only here; for example, his journeys on the Trans-Siberian railroad and on the pathways of Palestine! The letter read,

> My excuse now for writing again is that I feel in a measure under obligation to share with others the fruit of long experience with things Oriental. To reintroduce myself,

> as no doubt you have forgotten all about me in the long interim of silence on my part, I will say I went to the P.I. in 1904, and six times after that; visited China and Japan a dozen times or more; came home by Trans-Siberian Railroad; roamed over Europe and Palestine etc. etc. Moreover, our missionaries (for I was a Medical Missionary), are in close touch with us, and their letters are frequent. On this basis I can speak with some authority on the Orient. My constant attention to radio and news items also have kept me up to date. . ..

The depth of his concern for Asia, especially the Philippines, was mentioned as that letter continued:

> Just now I feel we are at a crisis. It is of national importance! I feel Taft's summary of the situation is right! IF we do not change our policy for Korea etc., we are doomed! To lose Formosa means to lose the P.I. and Japan. That means my lifework in the P.I. is to be largely wasted! You may now see why I again pester you as I am doing. Have just had a fine letter from Senator Lodge! His clearsighted estimate of the Orient encourages me to do my best to do what I can, as he is doing, to enlighten my fellow citizens.

Here is a portion of an editorial written in April of 1953:

> [President Eisenhower] is cautious, but he will seize the initiative according to plan, as his famous speech indicates! We may safely leave it to him, but it does involve heartbreaking responsibilities! He has ASKED OUR PRAYERS! The evangelist, Charles Fuller, in his "Revival Hour" on the radio, Sunday, said "There never was so great a need for prayer: "Our President has asked us to pray for him." ... Nor is it the evangelists alone who have pointed out this critical menace in Laos! Commentators, like the Alsops, in the Globe (Apr. 25th), said: Laos provides the ideal jumping-off place for an invasion of Thailand or Burma. – What is happening in the strange little Indo-Chinese state of Laos may well

> have as much meaning for the future as what is happening in the truce tent at Panmunjom." The Globe, in which all this is carried, says in large capitals "LAOS, KEY to ASIA". When both evangelists and commentators warn us, we better take the matter seriously! The President has asked our prayers! LET US PRAY FOR HIM!

In 1955, in another editorial letter to The Globe, Raph wrote the following concerning Dr. Meek, who was returning to the pulpit of the Old South Church after a six-month absence due to a throat problem:

> [Dr. Meek] is quoted as saying . . . "I learned to be freed from the bondage of the unnecessary ---I discovered that many of the things I was doing were no of primary importance." How true this is for all of us who have been shut in for a period of time by illness! Maybe if we listened more carefully to words like these . . .we would begin to realize that tension and other causes of neurosis and psychosis that fill over half our hospital beds is "bondage to the unnecessary." Mental disease, the curse of modern mad hurry and worry, would fade away! Dr. Meek is right!

In May of 1955, Raph commended The Globe for its April 30th report that in Glasgow, formerly notorious for its "Scotch and Soda" on a Saturday night, 50,000 people stood in the rain to hear Billy Graham preach. Raph rejoiced in the news that "among Glasgow's listeners were 16,236 who decided to make their 'Decision for Christ.'

> Such news as this really is "GOOD NEWS", surpassing the murders and other popular headlines that some of our papers exploit! The Globe was smart to make such a scoop! We are certain that many of its readers will commend it.

It is interesting that so many of Raph's comments in the 1940's and '50's seem so appropriate to the present world. Some things stay the same!

Raph wrote a novel, entitled *The Medico* – a Spanish term, spelled *Mediko* in the Philippines, for medical workers – and submitted it to Fleming H. Revell Company. This is the novel that was referred to in

Chapter 10. Publisher Fleming Revell Jr. wrote him on November 27, 1936, that he had written "a splendid story, especially in the delightful character of the nurse," but added that it would be inadvisable for the Revell Company to take on the "entire risk of publication." His suggested basis for publication was that "you would agree to pay for the first thousand copies which would be and remain your property."[262] The cost per volume to Raph would have been 90 cents, and this may be the reason that, to the best of my knowledge, the book was never published.

He wrote several short portions of another book-length manuscript entitled "Paging the Philippines." He intended to write about "smaller town life" in communities like Iloilo. The topics he intended to include were "The Home; Hospital; Lepers; School; Itinerating; Too late (delays in reaching patients); Character; Woman; Hunger; Pagans; Voyages; the Future; and Medical Outlook."

Raph also wrote at least one short story, perhaps for use in a mission publication, called *Pepita's Problem*. Though the copy in the archives is not signed, and Norma was also a writer, there are enough characteristics in common with Raph's writing style that declare the story to be his. Because it is short, filled with local color, and expressive of the heart and imagination of missionary Thomas, it has been included as Appendix 7.

He wrote many published and unpublished articles on biblical subjects, including a scathing review titled "How Will the Revised Standard Version Affect Mission?" His letters to his grandchildren included a lengthy discussion of the relationship between the biblical account of creation and the prevalent view of evolution that the grandchildren faced in school. For missionaries, to encourage them to protect their health, he wrote "A Few Hints on Health."

The autobiographical sketch that the author of this biography has used was submitted to the Atlantic Monthly/Reader's Digest "I Personally" competition that took place in the late 1940's and early 1950's.

RECRUITER

Raph also continued to look for ways in which he could influence college students toward Christ and encourage young men and women toward evangelism and the mission field. He spoke on WHEB, which now is a Rock station (quite a change in direction since his time!) out of Portsmouth, New Hampshire, with a program entitled "Christian SERVICE Volunteers." His purpose was "to arouse young people" to missionary activity, by which he meant "soul winning" (Matthew 28:18-20). Always possessed of a big vision, Raph's hope was that this class of Volunteers would not be stuck in a "movement," or a social organization, but would be the "flame" to reach their contemporaries and to expand the fire of evangelism. He lamented not being able to be in the Philippines, because of the war, but he wanted to make himself available to the young people. He encouraged them to write him, or to call him [at his 4-digit phone number] so that he could bring his motion pictures and describe to the young people the spread of the fire of evangelism in the Philippines.

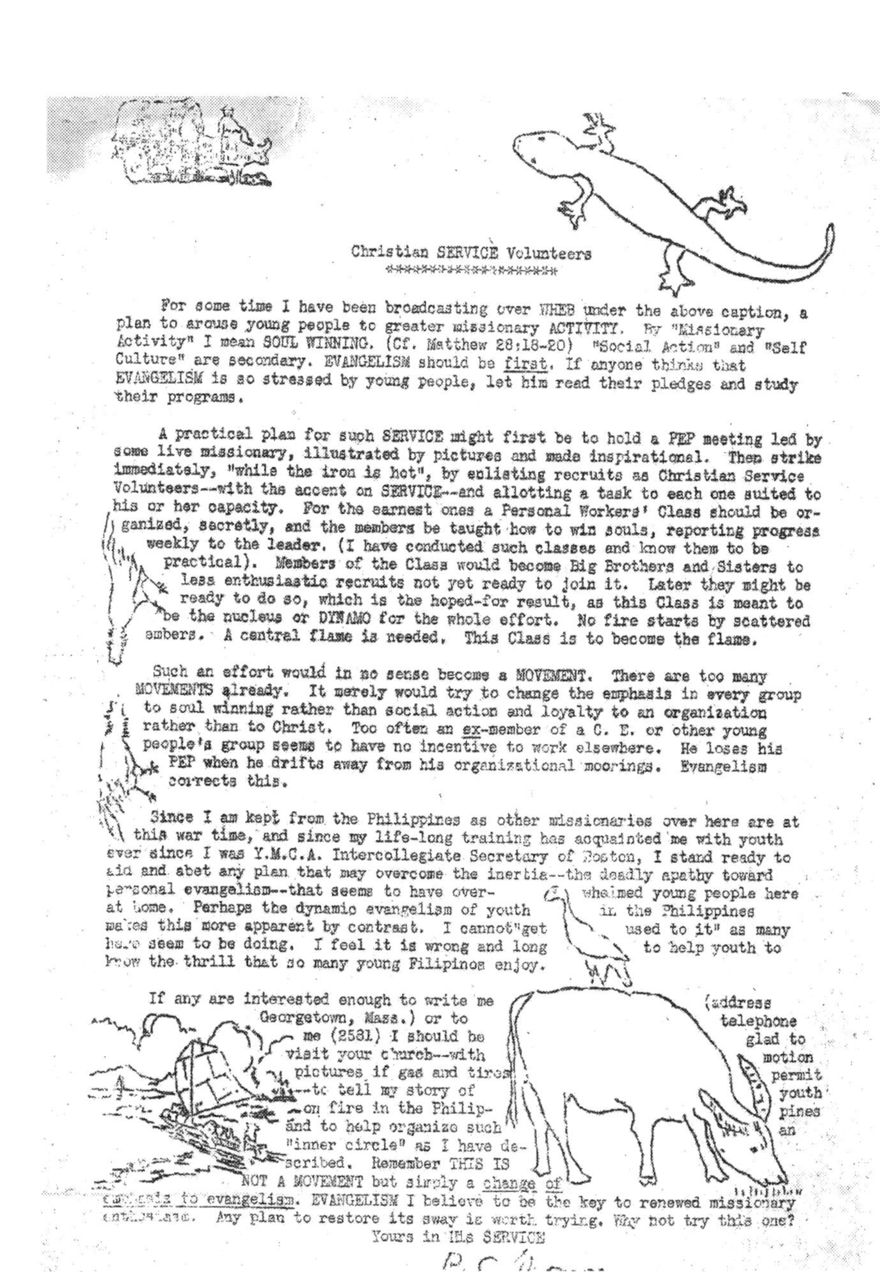

Christian SERVICE Volunteers
****

For some time I have been broadcasting over WHEB under the above caption, a plan to arouse young people to greater missionary ACTIVITY. By "Missionary Activity" I mean SOUL WINNING. (Cf. Matthew 28:18-20) "Social Action" and "Self Culture" are secondary. EVANGELISM should be first. If anyone thinks that EVANGELISM is so stressed by young people, let him read their pledges and study their programs.

A practical plan for such SERVICE might first be to hold a PEP meeting led by some live missionary, illustrated by pictures and made inspirational. Then strike immediately, "while the iron is hot", by enlisting recruits as Christian Service Volunteers--with the accent on SERVICE--and allotting a task to each one suited to his or her capacity. For the earnest ones a Personal Workers' Class should be organized, secretly, and the members be taught how to win souls, reporting progress weekly to the leader. (I have conducted such classes and know them to be practical). Members of the Class would become Big Brothers and Sisters to less enthusiastic recruits not yet ready to join it. Later they might be ready to do so, which is the hoped-for result, as this Class is meant to be the nucleus or DYNAMO for the whole effort. No fire starts by scattered embers. A central flame is needed. This Class is to become the flame.

Such an effort would in no sense become a MOVEMENT. There are too many MOVEMENTS already. It merely would try to change the emphasis in every group to soul winning rather than social action and loyalty to an organization rather than to Christ. Too often an ex-member of a C. E. or other young people's group seems to have no incentive to work elsewhere. He loses his PEP when he drifts away from his organizational moorings. Evangelism corrects this.

Since I am kept from the Philippines as other missionaries over here are at this war time, and since my life-long training has acquainted me with youth ever since I was Y.M.C.A. Intercollegiate Secretary of Boston, I stand ready to aid and abet any plan that may overcome the inertia--the deadly apathy toward personal evangelism--that seems to have overwhelmed young people here at home. Perhaps the dynamic evangelism of youth in the Philippines makes this more apparent by contrast. I cannot "get used to it" as many here seem to be doing. I feel it is wrong and long to help youth to know the thrill that so many young Filipinos enjoy.

If any are interested enough to write me (address Georgetown, Mass.) or to telephone me (2581) I should be glad to visit your church--with motion pictures if gas and tires permit--to tell my story of youth on fire in the Philippines and to help organize such an "inner circle" as I have described. Remember THIS IS NOT A MOVEMENT but simply a change of emphasis to evangelism. EVANGELISM I believe to be the key to renewed missionary enthusiasm. Any plan to restore its sway is worth trying. Why not try this one?

Yours in His SERVICE

Raph's letter to young people to recruit them to evangelism.

CHAPTER 27

Last Years

And even to your old age I am he; and even to hoar hairs will I carry you: I have made, and I will bear; even I will carry, and will deliver you. —Isaiah 46:5

CHERISHED RELATIONSHIPS

Though Raph and Norma experienced personal sorrow in some of the life-choices made by Winifred and Burgess, as is often true of loving parents, they tried to be as faithful to them and their grandchildren as they could be. Friendships were cherished into old age, and a bond of love kept Raph in close correspondence with Mrs. Marguerite Treat "Daisy" Doane, whose generous gifts through the years had blessed the ministries of both the American Baptist Foreign Mission Society and ABWE in the Philippines; and Dr. Commons, ABWE's President. He and Mrs. Thomas always enjoyed a visit from one of their coworkers in the Philippines.

A story about Miss Martien, who quietly and effectively served her Lord in the Philippines for decades – many of them in collaboration with Raph and Norma - would be appropriate here. Ruth Woodworth tells of Ellen's leaving the Philippines in 1940 in the following endearing way:

> About two months later, Ellen Martien, our senior missionary . . . came to Manila to sail to the United States. Because of the war rumors, her brother in Baltimore had called her to come home. She was 72 years old and she said, "I know I will be a hindrance to you all when war comes. I can not run as fast as the rest of you." Ellen had a wonderful sense of humor. "You recall," she said, "the Bible says 'The wicked flee, when no man pursueth' (Proverbs 28:1) and I am that wicked *flea*.""[263]

The May 1958 *Message Magazine* included a memorial for Ellen. In it, mention was made of the fact that after her return to America,

> she kept in constant touch with missionaries and nationals, supporting the work with her gifts, counsel, and effective ministry in prayer, to say nothing of the encouragement of her correspondence. Perhaps there are few missionaries who have had so many national and missionary children named after them, as the great number who bear the name of "Ellen" and even "Ellen Martien." . . . For some time, she had an active part in the work of the Filipino Christian Center in New York City as well as activities for her Lord in Baltimore Sunday Schools, Mother's Clubs, and Shut-in Classes . . . faithful in her church attendance even to the Lord's Day just before her death.

Ellen died where she was born, in Maryland, in 1957.

Of course, Raph never forgot his beloved Filipinos. He maintained a long correspondence with Alberto, who called him "Dad." Although Alberto was subsequently able to have a successful ministry outside of the leprosarium at Santa Barbara, Raph's description of his "son" in relationship to his life and ministry in that facility is moving and full of love:

> There was but one course open, admission and segregation at Santa Barbara. Alberto left wife and home and his dear little girl with another child expected, whom he never might hold in his arms. He faced it manfully, and when in the Treatment Station he became so useful that now he is

> an integral part of it all. In fact, a recent letter tells us that an official reported that the morale of this leper station is the best in the world, and that Franco is responsible for it! What a tribute: Does anyone wonder why I love the Filipino!
>
> Last time I saw him, some years ago, I could not shake hands, as that was not permitted, but his poor leprosy scarred face was shining, and it has been ever since I am sure, for his letters are most cheerful. Friends over here have given him a building in which to teach the illiterate and carry on a church.[264]

After a brief period of residence in a home for the elderly, Mrs. Lucy Waterbury Peabody passed into the presence of her Lord on February 26, 1949. At the time of her funeral, Raph and Norma received a Radiogram from Dr. Commons in which he wrote the following concerning this dynamic woman of faith:

> On behalf of the entire association of Baptists I send you our deepest sympathy and assurance of sustaining prayer in your present sorrow. Mrs. Peabody was a grand soldier of the cross and the memory of her leadership and devotion is a constant inspiration to us. She being dead yet speaketh and we sorrow not as others who have no hope. May the God of all comfort comfort your hearts just now.

In a letter to Dr. Commons, in which Raph expressed his appreciation and that of Norma for the kindnesses shown by ABWE in remembering Mrs. Peabody, he wrote the following tribute to the one he had called "Mother:"

> ... the weather was clear and the whole ceremony was far from being gloomy. Had Mrs. Peabody failed to lead a triumphant life there would have been room, perhaps, for greater sadness, but her devoted service to her Lord and her constant endeavor to glorify His name by her lifelong service, left no room for regret. She "fought a good fight

> and finished her course and had kept the faith" and now she enjoys the well merited crown that always remains for such a life of unselfish devotion.

On March 17, 1949, the *Watchman Examiner* included in its pages a lengthy article by Susan T. Laws about Mrs. Peabody. Her many accomplishments, ministries, and affiliations were described, including her being one of the founders of the Association of Baptists for World Evangelism.

In the 1950's, Raph sent letters and copies of *The Message* to heads of seminaries, like J.O. Buswell, Billy Graham, Carey Thomas, and others, to introduce them to ABWE's work, to encourage them in the Lord's work, and to encourage them to consider sending Baptist teachers to the Philippines to continue to train needed leaders there. As he wrote to the dean of Fuller Theological Seminary:

> If any should be interested in the Seminary work, and fitted for it, and taken on to our faculty there, I honestly believe they would not only be [amply] satisfied but also would be doing a monumental piece of work for the Lord, in that Archipelago where Americans so long have adopted our "Little Brown Brothers". I love them after seven periods of service there. And other fields as well have an appeal, such as Chile, and Japan and elsewhere, where we are now starting mission work.[265]

On December 27, 1953, Raph provided some current information on his family to Mrs. Doane:

> Our family ties hereabouts never have been so very important. My only brother and sister have large families of their own now. My brother Leo, older than I, partially paralyzed, has five children. Three are married and they have brought him nine grandchildren. A number of them were at his home for Christmas. My only daughter also has four children, but they are in Long Beach, California; and my only son is a purser on the American President Line, and at present he is out near Japan. This is Burgess, of whom you have heard. Our little Marguerite, named

> after you, (of which you so beautifully reminded us when you sent us that beautiful miniature) awaits the coming of the Lord in that quiet little cemetery in La Paz,-a spot the Japanese spared I believe when they invaded Panay Island.

The recipient of this letter, Mrs. Doane, was taken home on October 17, 1954, one month shy of her eighty-sixth birthday.

Raph's daughter, Winifred, married Glenn Sadler, and lived, as Raph mentioned, in the Los Angeles area. She died on October 28, 1997.

Raph's son, Jesse Burgess Thomas died on March 27, 1973, in Washington, D. C. of a heart attack (at age 52). According to an April 9, 1973, article in Time magazine, Jesse had been a compulsive collector who frequently suffered from financial troubles. Newspaper accounts from the period told the sad story in greater detail.[266] Jesse had married, but he and his wife were living apart. He had not paid his rent for months, so he was evicted from his Washington apartment. The apartment was full of items he had collected during his travels, and other collected items with which he filled the apartment. When his belongings were removed from the apartment, neighbors proceeded to loot and steal much of what was there. When Jesse returned to the apartment and found his things scattered and destroyed, he had a heart attack. He died a short time later. How heartbroken his folks would have been to see their son die under these sad circumstances. The experience of being an MK (missionary kid) with great cross-cultural experience can lead to exceptional achievement and spiritual victory, but it is no guarantee of stability and success.

NO REGRETS

In his 1954 letter to the Durhams, a couple of "new recruits," Raph described his memories of the prayer and thought processes he had gone through in deciding to serve as a medical missionary in the Philippines; both during his formative years, and then after his later stateside ministries in New York City. He wrote:

> My talents, if we care to call them that, as GIFTS of God for which we are responsible, were as I have related, and

> to fit them in aright surely was God's intention for me. As I look back now in the light of experience I am sure this decision for the P.I. was right. The Filipinos love music, and I could evangelize in ENGLISH, and train others to speak in a way to win (trained some of those who did that). Right here let me say that the Filipios are really orators, some of them; and they appreciate such training. If I had gone to China I would have been overwhelmed with medical work. In P.I. I had plenty of time for evangelism and religious work. I had a hospital where I could emphasize personal evangelism, and had classes of my nurses (some fifty of them) and urged them to do work at the bedside. I also had plenty of time for the starting of Student Church, DEI and later M.E.I. etc. In other words, IF I had not gone to P.I. the work at LaPaz might never have begun, and if I had not labored there the ABFMS [ABEO] (now the ABWE) might never have begun; for it was my resignation that started the ball rolling. You see how God arranged it all, and the entrance into Manila paved the way for our work there, the Seminary and now work from one end of the Islands to the other; all a part of God's plan I firmly believe. My later decision to return, after being called home for father's illness, also was right in line. It really was a <u>second</u> decision, without which all these later developments would have been impossible, unless some one else were called to make them possible, but MY opportunity to have had a hand in it would never have been possible.

At the end of his "harkening back" essay for the *I Personally* Award, Raph wrote a beautiful summary of his ministry as a missionary in the Philippines:

> And so the Philippines and the incidents close packed thru the years 1904 to 1948 fade away into oblivion, with a composite of faces, Antonio, Demetrio, who just before passing away in Los Angeles said with a smile to me: "I am not afraid to die", (the acid test), Winceslao, Alvarez and others; and the background of a perennial green landscape

> and the languor of a tropical clime to soften it all and iron out the wrinkles of hardship and sadness that come to all missionaries, willy nilly, as they do to those here at home. But the game was "worth the candle" and if I had it to do all over again, I'd welcome the chance!

With reference to a phrase appropriate to years gone by when electricity was unavailable, and a decision about a game had to be made as to whether the gains to come would be worth the candle to be used to light it, Dr. Raphael C. Thomas declares that the decisions made, and the life lived in service to the people of the Philippines was most certainly "worth the candle."[267]

GOING HOME

After sitting up all night at the bedside of his dying brother, Raph developed a painful back condition which confined him to bed for weeks during the winter of 1956. On January 4, 1956, Raph described that experience and his physical condition in a letter to Dr. Commons that reveals that he was saddened by the loss of his dear brother, but that he had not lost his sense of humor:

> Dear Hal: Hope the two "glossies" of my ugly mug reached you safely: but felt the hastily composed recital of my checkered career was not best suited for the data desired. If more is desired, please send me a card, or direct your secretary to send a brief word as to what is needed, for just now I have been thru a hard ordeal and might not think straight. A "ghost writer" such as you or someone else, could better formulate the proper wording and data, which would be suitable.
>
> Have just lost my only brother [Leo], Hal, about four years older than I. Was two nights and part of three days at his bedside, with catnaps between times, and it was a hard experience as the bonds of the flesh were hard to loosen. He was buried Friday, and when I got home my

voice practically disappeared, and since then the old back started up its shenanigans again, so now I can't prolong a letter, fortunately for you, as I know how busy you are. Glad to say the knees now are practically well, and back cleared up before, so I'm hoping this will be the last "kick in the gallop" that ran me down so many months ago. Feel fine otherwise: just the myositis or fibrositis, or whatever it may be. Let me wish you and yours a Blessed New Year, Hal! Do be careful to take necessary rest, for to do otherwise would be madness. You have a big job to do, and relaxation is indispensable for its completion. Best to all at the rooms. Hoping to be at the meetings again eventually! So Hallelujah!

Cordially, Raph Thomas[268]

On May 7, he asked Norma to write to Dr. Commons to apologize for his not being able to make the meeting, and to express his hope that he might be at the September meeting. That was not to be. His condition developed into pleurisy, with other complications, and the Lord took him home on June 4, 1956. His work on earth was done; his time of enjoying His Lord and those who had gone on before was just beginning.

In his will, Raph left everything to Norma, having made separate provision for Winifred, and entrusting her with the responsibility of providing for their son Jesse. Norma, having lived to her ninetieth year, died on Saturday, May 11, 1974. Burial was held in the family plot in Harmony Cemetery, Georgetown, Massachusetts, where Raph had been buried 18 years before.

REMEMBERED

If the final pages of this biography were filled with tributes to Dr. Raphael Thomas, Raph would undoubtedly scold us, reminding us that he could have done none of this apart from the gracious work of the Lord in him. He would also remind us that many Filipino/a and American servants of the Lord made the ultimate sacrifice in death, while he was blessed to live a full life.[269]

In the November 1956 issue of *The Message*, a special issue in Raph's memory, Don Mackay, a member of the ABWE Board of Directors, wrote the lead article. The following paragraph is a fitting statement of Raph's impact on the work in the Philippines:

> The name of Dr. Raphael Clark Thomas is still well-known and loved in the Philippine Islands. The fruit of his labors is still evident. Many are the spiritual sons and daughters who have arisen to call his name with blessing. The training schools he founded for the nationals are flourishing in both centers. He insisted that these were necessary for the development of the indigenous policy. The continuance and growth of these schools greatly rejoiced his heart in his later years as he followed with interest every report that came of the Lord's blessing. Members of the Board at home are still affected by the consecration and zeal of this man of God and have been challenged by both his burden and his vision.[270]

At the time of the production of the volume celebrating the 75th Anniversary of ABWE, missionary to the Philippines Elaine Kennedy (who authored a *Baptist Centennial History of the Philippines*) wrote an email containing a suggestion. She was concerned that too often the picture given of the beginning of ABWE is that of a few ladies financing a "separation," missing the values exemplified by "a great man," Dr. Thomas. As an example of Raph's influence, she mentioned Pastor Caspe, who at the time of Elaine's letter was the only living pastor who had personally known Raph. He told Elaine and Craig, her husband, that while he was a small boy, he was neighbor to Dr. and Mrs. Thomas. Raph's life so touched his heart that he attended the basketball training at the Student Center, and he came to know Christ as his Savior. Elaine rightly asked, how often does one's LIFE reach out to draw someone to Christ? So many who died long before this was written could add their own recollections and words of tribute to those of this godly Filipino pastor.

POSTSCRIPT

In conclusion, this account of the life of Dr. Raphael C. Thomas, however incomplete, has hopefully been beneficial in several ways. First, by placing Raph and his writings back in the milieu in which he lived, new life has been breathed into our understanding of him as a man of his age.

Second, through following the progress of Raph through several of the prominent influences in his life, the origins of his convictions and motivations have become clearer. Without this basic information, a mere listing of some principles he held is as sterile as a listing of the major points of the Declaration of Independence without the language and the historical background of the document.

Third, though the limitations of time, space, and purpose of this book prevented a more thorough examination and exposition of the interactions of Raph with the Philippines, her people, other missionaries, and family members; the few examples adduced throughout the book reveal a man with a great heart, as well as a great mind. The domination by Christ and the Word of God of both of those faculties undoubtedly contributed to the fundamentals of his philosophy of ministry. Raph's dedication to reaching the lost, preparing practically educated and disciplined young servants of Christ, building up the church, seeking unity, and submission of talent, experience, and giftedness to the will of the living God exemplify a true man of God.

Both in his life and thought, Raphael Thomas has been seen to be a gentleman of firm conviction, high ideals, great compassion, and unswerving devotion to God and the people to whom God sent him. He has also been seen to be a very human being; and this explains to us his faults and failures. His relentless search for Baptist unity underlines both the breadth of vision, and the God-given humility of this Christian gentleman.

But this is not the end of the story. After physical problems forced my wife and me to leave our beloved Japan and return to the United States, I had the privilege of working in the International Headquarters of ABWE. While Bob Dyer and I were tasked with developing the Training Division, I was asked by the President, Wendell Kempton, to work on a special project. I spent many hours plowing through old documents in the archives of the mission with the primary goal of developing a full report on the "planting" of local churches in the early days of ABEO-ABWE in the Philippines. What a humbling experience it was!

Compiling statistics on the growth of churches even marginally related to the first decades of the work of this mission in the Philippines revealed a story of growth and expansion that was nothing short of incredible. Not just to the Second World War, but through the war, evangelism by missionaries and Filipino/a evangelists, church planters, doctors, teachers, and pastors resulted in the planting of hundreds of churches throughout the islands of the Philippines. The death and destruction rained down on the Philippines during the war did nothing to deter believers from witnessing, gathering, worshipping, and starting churches, many of which exist to this day.

How many of the faithful servants and followers of the Lord Jesus Christ in the Philippines who obeyed the Lord and performed those ministries were initially evangelized, baptized, discipled, and prepared for ministry by Raph, his wives, and early colleagues – serving with the American Baptist Board, the Presbyterian Board, and ABEO/ABWE – only the Lord knows. They lived, they served, and they went home to be with their Lord. Some worked with and were known by the missionaries; some were only known by Filipino and Filipina coworkers and those they led to Christ; and some were known only by the flocks of believers they served during their lifetimes. But they were all well-known to their faithful God, to whom all glory is due.

In a way, this is not their story. Most could not be mentioned here by name and reputation. But if Raph and his missionary colleagues were assembled in heaven and asked what their greatest achievements were, they would look around them at the hundreds of thousands of former citizens of the Philippines and countries around the world who, through their influence and the influence of those they loved to Christ are now their fellow-citizens of heaven, and they would point to them.

APPENDIX 1

Too Many Named Jesse Burgess Thomas?

One of the more difficult genealogical problems related to the life of Raphael Thomas is the number of individuals in his family tree with the name Jesse Burgess Thomas. To display the relationships, the following chart is provided.

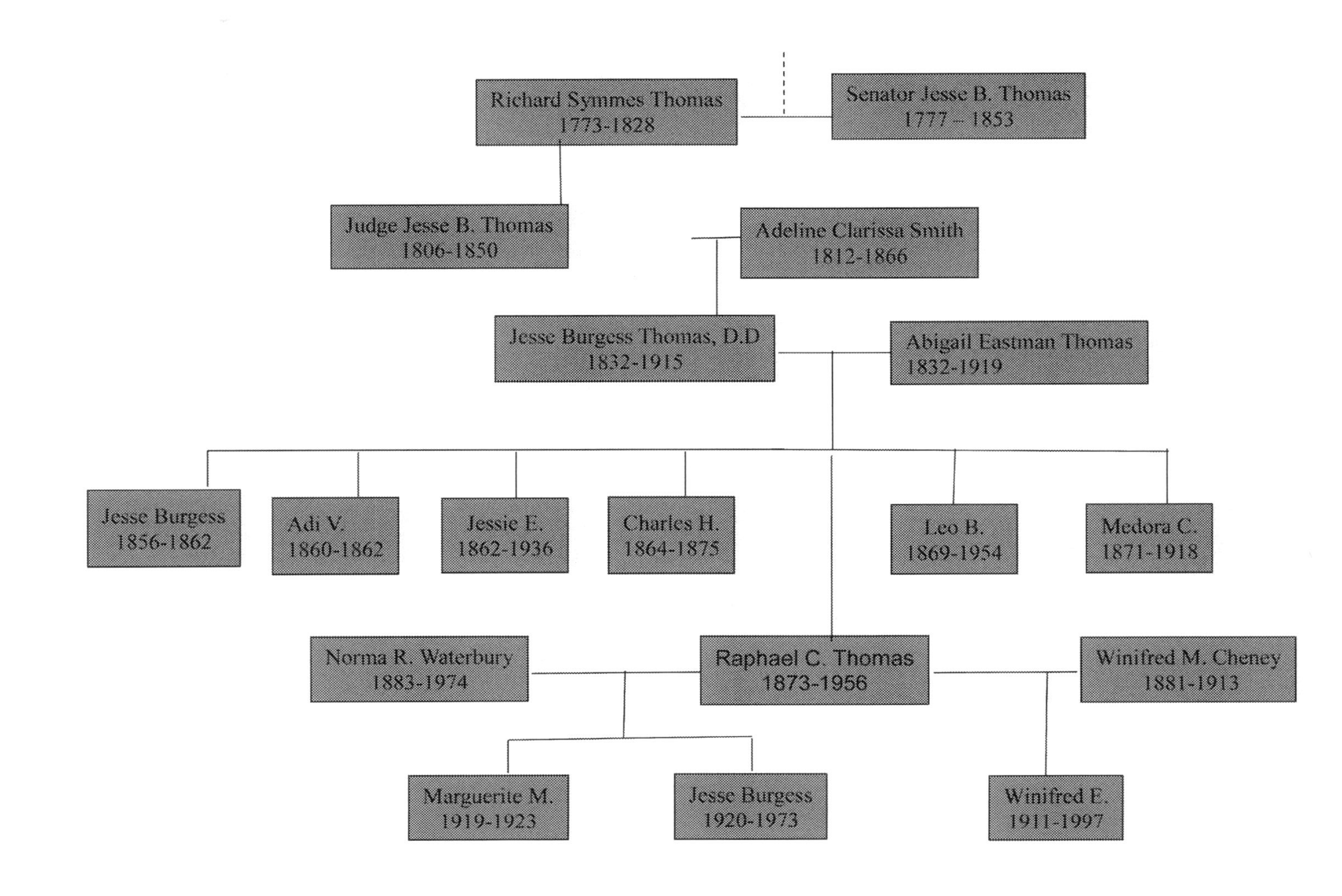

Richard Symmes Thomas
1773-1828
Senator Jesse B. Thomas
1777 – 1853
Judge Jesse B. Thomas
1806-1850
Adeline Clarissa Smith
1812-1866
Jesse Burgess Thomas, D.D
1832-1915
Abigail Eastman Thomas
1832-1919
Jesse Burgess
1856-1862
Adi V.
1860-1862
Jessie E.
1862-1936
Charles H.
1864-1875
Leo B.
1869-1954
Medora C.
1871-1918
Norma R. Waterbury
1883-1974
Raphael C. Thomas
1873-1956
Winifred M. Cheney
1881-1913
Marguerite M.
1919-1923
Jesse Burgess
1920-1973
Winifred E.
1911-1997

APPENDIX 2

Early American Baptist Missions

In 1810, with the encouragement of Adoniram Judson and Luther Rice, a conference was held in Massachusetts to request support for their evangelistic missionary proposals. In response, the American Board of Commissioners for Foreign Missions was organized.

In 1845, the Southern Baptist Convention was formed in Augusta, Georgia. In the same year, the Triennial Convention, or the General Missionary Convention (GMC) of the Baptist Denomination in the U.S.A. (formed in Philadelphia in 1814) was renamed the American Baptist Missionary Union.

In 1871, the Woman's Baptist Foreign Missionary Society (WBFMS), with offices in Boston, and the WBFMS West, with offices in Chicago, were formed. In 1877, the Woman's Baptist Home Missions Societies of the East and West were formed. In 1907, the Northern Baptist Convention (NBC) was formed in Washington, D.C.

The various societies of the NBC were to remain autonomous, but were to act cooperatively in the areas of planning and budget. The agencies, like the ABMU, were to continue their ministries as agencies of the Convention. The ABMU changed its name to the American Baptist Foreign Mission Society in 1910. In 1913, the Woman's Baptist Foreign Missionary Society of the East and that of the West were united into the Woman's Baptist Foreign Missionary Society.

APPENDIX 3

Other Baptist Theologians Who Downplayed Millennial or Pre-Millennial Views

John Broadus (1827–1895) developed a long-lasting *nonchiliastic* (opposed to the concept of a literal millennial reign of Christ on earth) tradition at Southern Seminary, that deemphasized the millennium while focusing on the *parousia* (return of Christ).[271]

E. Y. Mullins (1860–1928) felt that the millennium should be deemphasized because of the many problems inherent in the subject, and because of the injury it brought to fellowship. He suggested that

> We should be so eager for the coming of our Lord, that if he should come to-morrow we would not be taken by surprise. We should so hold ourselves in restraint, that if his return should be delayed a thousand or ten thousand years, we would not be disappointed. And our hearts should be ever filled with joy at the prospect of his coming and the certain triumph of his Kingdom.[272]

Augustus H. Strong (1836–1921). The frequently revised textbook of A. H. Strong was perhaps the most likely candidate to be chosen by Dr. Nathaniel Wood to replace that of Dr. Hovey. Strong's *Systematic Theology* was the work of a Baptist theologian, and its seventh edition was freshly published in 1902. By that edition, evidence of Strong's ethical monism, shifting thoughts on inspiration, and the inroads of a form of evolutionary thinking were apparent, but the bulk of his work was acceptable and useful for the theological student.

Strong's position on the second coming of Christ is described under several headings in the large print of the section on eschatology. As to the nature of His second advent, it is to be "outward and visible."[273] As for the time of Christ's coming,

> we discern a striking parallel between the predictions of Christ's first, and the predictions of his second, advent. In both cases the event was more distant and more grand than those imagined to whom the prophecies first came. Under both dispensations, patient waiting for Christ was intended to discipline the faith, and to enlarge the conceptions, of God's true servants. The fact that every age since Christ ascended has had its Chiliasts and Second Adventists should turn our thoughts away from curious and fruitless prying into the time of Christ's coming, and set us at immediate and constant endeavor to be ready, at whatsoever hour he may appear.[274]

Strong's statement certainly discouraged "fruitless prying" into "the time" of the coming of Christ, and his way of thinking could easily have become a warning to theology students that concern about the "imminent return of Christ" is tantamount to being like "Second Adventists" who had repeatedly prophesied the time of His coming.

Strong's subsequent description of the "precursors" of Christ's coming is postmillennial. He states that the kingdom of Christ's steady increase will reach a point where "Jews and Gentiles alike become possessed of its blessings, and a millennial period is introduced in which Christianity generally prevails throughout the earth."[275] Evil will also continue to grow until the millennial period, when it will be set aside until the end, at which time it will be given free reign again, only to be ultimately destroyed by the returning Christ. At that second coming, the just and the unjust will be raised, and the general judgment will take place. An interesting footnote to Strong's position on the relationship of the coming of Christ to the millennial period is found as a footnote.[276] After rejecting the concept of two physical comings, Strong offers an interpretation that "suggests a possible way of reconciling the premillenarian and postmillenarian theories." He summarized that interpretation in his sermon before the Baptist World Congress in London, July 12, 1905, in which he said

> Let us expect the speedy spiritual coming of the Lord. I believe in an ultimate literal and visible coming of Christ in the clouds of heaven to raise the dead, to summon all men to the judgment, and to wind up the present dispensation. But I believe that this visible and literal coming of Christ must be preceded, and prepared for, by his invisible and spiritual coming and by a resurrection of faith and love in the hearts of his people. . . . Let us hasten the day of God by our faith and prayer. . . . Our faith can certainly secure the coming of the Lord into our hearts. Let us expect that Christ will be revealed in us, as of old he was revealed in the Apostle Paul.[277]

This solution, like that of modernists who suggested that Christ's resurrection was spiritual rather than physical, is unacceptable to so many who are eagerly waiting for the bodily, visible return of Jesus Christ, our living Hope!

APPENDIX 4

Those mentioned in Raph's 1938 Correspondence as Possible Participants in his Attempt toward Reconciliation

The following is from the letter written by Raph to Pastor Joseph Hakes in January of 1938 (quoted in part in Chapter 26). As Raph continued to lay out to Pastor Hakes his plan for reconciling and uniting Convention and non-Convention pastors through the avenue of missionary giving, he included a list of names of men he thought would be of a quality to move in that direction.

> Now to be more exact, for example, I'd like to see men like Rogers, Miller, MacKay, Raymond, Hughey, Ayer, Taylor, Bronson, Laws, Marsh, Mobre (Bloomfield) and yourself from the New York area, not to mention others whom we know to be O.K., such as Dr. Gordon Palmer, Benny Livingston, and others and around Boston a host of them such as Brownville, Rider, Murphy, Littorin, Nathan Wood, Chellis Smith, Doloff, etc. etc. I know a lot of them here.
>
> For the Middle West men like Cole, and Muntz, and Kamm, and Annette, and Kehrl, and Savage, and many others still with N.B.C. but of open mind.
>
> Then for the Separatists I am sure that men like Strathearn (I know him well and believe he is a throughgoing

Christian), and Bob Ketcham and Fulton, and John Muntz (of Forrestville, New York) and Reese, and Bedford, and Griffith, and Keene, and Ralph Carr, and others would make a good group for such a friendly discussion. I realize that the Separatists would not have separated had they not felt the N.B.C. to be impossible for them. It might be they would object more than the N.B.C. men to such a meeting, but I feel that ALL these men are fine fellows, and that much of all this misunderstanding is due to lack of close and intimate fellowship.

If such a meeting, even of a few, would enable ALL to agree on this one matter of saving Baptist money for Baptist work, why would it not dawn on these good fellows that they COULD fellowship more than they have done, even though flying different flags: then maybe they would meet again, and discuss some other non-inflammatory topic, and attend conventions and read more literature etc. etc. In a photo of an Interstate Conference I see the fair faces of Don Marsh, MacKay, yourself and Commons all in a row. That's what I mean. If MORE would get together as a few of you have done, it would be different. But how few attend. Moreover, how few of you Fundamental N.B.C. men attend the State Convention in New York. I was amazed at that. Why? Is it not possible that all the Fund[amentalist] Men (both inside and outside the N.B.C.) could really fellowship better than they do WITH EACH OTHER?

APPENDIX 5

Legacy: Raph's Philosophy of Missions Reviewed

The Foundational Principle of Evangelism

As has been mentioned many times, Raph saw his medical ministry as a vehicle for evangelism. "In 1904 I went as a medical missionary to the Philippines . . . both to practice and to preach."[278] The following summary clarifies the fact that there was an evangelistic thrust to every aspect of his ministry:

> The program from the outset was one that made medicine a means to the end of evangelism. In Capiz it was carried out in district touring. Later, in Iloilo and Jaro, it was maintained by assuming full control of an evangelistic field of about fifty thousand. Later still, when the Union Mission Hospital was established under the joint auspices of the Baptist and Presbyterian Boards, I found an outlet for evangelism in the Hospital itself, in field and student dispensaries, and in student work for the Iloilo High School.[279]

Medical Work

In 1926, before leaving the field as an ABFMS missionary, Raph wrote up a document entitled "Suggestions on Mission Policy (Medical Work)."[280] It is unnecessary to quote the entire document, but a few of the points will be summarized here. Raph was concerned that the working budget should be reduced, and that some of the balance of funds be banked. He felt that the time had come for greater dependence to be placed upon Nationals in the hospital, and that more support should be given to Dr. Porras, his coworker, for the District Dispensary work. He reemphasized his conviction that medical mission work should not center at the hospital, but be spread out through district medicine, student work, and church work. He believed that the policy should include a "more elaborate" program of preaching to the patients. He hoped that better follow-up work for patients discharged from the hospital could be done. Finally, he felt that the townspeople should be involved more in supporting the dispensary work.

Raph reemphasized some of these points in a pair of articles written for the *Watchman Examiner* and published the following year.[281] Realizing that the end of his ministry with ABFMS was near, Raph apparently wanted to leave a legacy of thought for future medical missionaries, regardless of what his future might be.

Student Work

Raph felt himself under an obligation to take up student work on the basis of his training, and as a result of living beside the students at the Provincial High School of Iloilo. He felt he needed to minister to both the physical and spiritual needs of the students. His summary of the impact of this ministry also provides a glimpse into his heart for Christian and church growth:

> From the outset great blessing attended this student work. Over seven hundred and fifty were received by baptism in four years and a half, with baptisms practically every Sunday. All the activities of a live church were maintained. Over two hundred were listed as regular contributors. Over two hundred attended our last communion service before leaving the Islands. Bible classes, Christian Endeavor, prayer meetings, Personal Work Groups, house visitation and evangelism all were provided for. Hundreds were reached for Christ. In every way a stable program was attempted. The slogan for years was "The intensive development of the church membership." And my share in

> all this was supervision and a reasonable amount of time given to preaching and teaching, so far as it could be given without trenching unduly on my medical practice.[282]

Opening Undeveloped Fields

From the earliest days of Raph's ministry in the Philippines, he strongly felt the necessity of pushing out the boundaries of the work through extensive outreach to undeveloped fields. In other words, rather than settling down and working intensively in a few areas, he felt the Pauline compulsion to preach the gospel where no others had preached before.

> The "INTENSIVE POLICY" of the ABFMS stunted its growth. From the time of my arrival in the Philippines, when my first charge was in Capiz, I discovered that a large area was largely neglected. I urged the Board to care for it, without avail; after a six weeks pioneer trip to Northern Mindanao I besought the Board to take over that rich field as the Congregationalists to whom it had been assigned were not doing it justice, and I had good reason to believe it would be granted us . . .[283]

Policies for the Work of the ABEO resulting from experience

A meeting with the new missionaries of the ABEO. sometime after the Association was formed, provided an excellent opportunity for Raph to share a policy statement (mentioned above in Chapter 21) labeled "For our missionaries only." It included the following:

> First- We believe our return to the Visayas wholly justified, because the Doane Evan[gelistic] Inst[itute] was being dropped. We were obliged to continue this great work and in conjunction with it the Doane Hall and district work as an outlet for our student workers. To abandon the Visayas now would be unthinkable.
>
> Second – Our mission policy is in accord with the Assoc[iation] slogan "The apostolic message and method".

> This we understand to be a proclamation of the gospel wherever it is needed, with special attention to unoccupied and neglected districts. We also understand that it advocates evangelism rather than education, medicine, or institutional work.
>
> Third – Our attitude toward other missionaries of our own Board, as well as other Boards, is meant to be friendly. We desire to pursue our own course permitting them to pursue theirs, which should be a constructive program. Our separation from groups that are modernistic in tendencies is wholly due to conscientious scruples, and not to personal antagonism or animosity. The fact that we, perforce – are separatists – is supported by our great objective of a sound gospel message. We seek quietness and unobtrusive service, keeping our own counsel, with prayer and humility.[284]

An analysis of this three-fold summary reveals not only some principles that have already been stated, but also some new principles of attitude and soundness of the message. The first point is the justification for maintaining the Visayan work, and that of the Doane Evangelistic Institute. He could not think of abandoning an area where work was still needed, nor an ideal ministry to prepare students for the work of the Lord. His second point is that in keeping with the apostolic method, 'unreached areas' need to be reached, and evangelism is the way to reach them. This puts the priority, once again, on evangelism.

It is the third policy that breaks new ground, for here he calls for a constructive program with proper attitudes. Separation from modernity does not require personal "antagonism or animosity." Every effort should be made to do the work of the Association with the characteristics demanded of the servant of Christ: quietness, friendliness, prayer and humility; doing their own work, while others are left to do theirs.

A Clear Restatement of His Principles and Policies

The opportunities afforded to Raph to restate some of the earliest principles and practices of the new Board were many. One such opportunity was the twenty-fifth anniversary of the founding of the Association. Dr. Commons invited him to address the Board and other ABWE personnel at the formal celebration, but Raph was unable to attend. He offered to send a greeting and some of his thoughts, and the offer was gladly accepted. The first draft sent to Dr. Commons was considered too lengthy, so a second, shorter message was prepared at last. The version of the document reproduced below includes several of the omitted lines from the first draft. In it, Raph set out to describe some of the earliest "principles and practices" that governed the program of ABEO, but with the omitted lines included, it becomes apparent that Raph was thinking back to even earlier days, when he the other "old timers" were still with the ABFMS. He begins with the primary objective:

> From the outset it has been, as I remember it, and I think that the other "old timers" would agree with me, was to make EVANGELISM the foundation of all our efforts. By this I mean mass evangelism, preceded and followed up by personal, house visitation, and field evangelism; and church membership the objective.
>
> The second most important objective, of course, was the establishment of more SOUND BAPTIST CHURCHES, which eventually were to become INDIGENOUS, self supporting; self governing and self perpetuating.
>
> The next, and exceedingly important objective, was to raise up a WELL EDUCATED MINISTRY. Of course it may be taken for granted that we meant by this a ministry sound in the faith. We also believed that for such a ministry education must be Christ centered, with the Bible as its mainstay, but ALSO education accompanied by PRACTICAL service in "working out" what God "worked in" both to "will" (motivation), and to "do" (action), "of His good pleasure; after the laboratory method. In other words, to offer an illustration, we wished to introduce the practical methods of a school like Moody, and the more advanced instruction of a sound Seminary! [**lined out**: At least I imagine this may have been in the

> back of our minds, although at the outset we had to confine ourselves to a very academic course, as we aimed at that time to develop merely religions workers, not pastors, as Central College started a Theological School. We were not supposed to compete with that, though in a way we were doing so, as our School was strictly Conservative. Their's was not.] This combination of both educational and practical methods was based partly on my firm conviction of the value of a "CLINIC", familiar to doctors, as a method of practical application of what is learned, in contradistinction to a "SEMINAR" when one merely adds to his store of knowledge. Seminar education may become top heavy; clinical, never!
>
> The way in which these fundamental principles have obtained in the years that followed may best be determined by examining the records . . . Among these fundamentals the one I regard as of unique importance in building up our work is the practical application of evangelism for our students while they study. We rejoice that this practical method of developing successful evangelists never has been abandoned.[285]

This statement discloses basic principles already seen, as well as new principles. Evangelism once again takes pride of place, but with church membership as the stated objective. The indigenous principle of planting Baptist churches, though not emphasized as much in what has been written before, is one that is found in a variety of ways in Raph's writings going back to the beginning of his ministry in the Philippines; both as the approach encouraged by his Board, and as his own favored approach to church planting. The indigenous principle was part of his motivation to turn much of the work of the hospital over to the Filipinos.

His third objective reveals that he had a significant philosophy of education. Raph emphasized that education was to be done in a practical way, based upon his "firm conviction" of the value of a "CLINIC." Using Philippians 2:12 to emphasize the practical service component of the educational preparation of the servant of Christ, he compares it with the clinical, or "laboratory method." This method requires of the doctor that he practice while he learns, and it compares favorably with the "modern" concept of interactive, hands-on adult education. He even contrasts it with the seminar approach, which "merely adds to his store of knowledge." How remarkable that such a practical form of education for the ministry was in practical use in the Philippines before it became fashionable for missionary and Bible school student training in America! The part of the text later deleted includes a further elucidation of the limitations of the application of this form of education early on due to the requirement that they not compete with Jaro, though Raph felt that the approach of the two was so different as to constitute no competition.

APPENDIX 6

Certificates and Diplomas

Certificates and Diplomas in the Archive Collection of ABWE, Inc.

1. Appointment and Commissioning as Major in the Newton High School Battalion for the school year 1891 and 1892. June 28th, 1892. Signed by Hibbard (Mayor); Goodwin [headmaster]; and Benyon [military instructor].

2. Newton High School Battalion. Honorable Mention for proficiency in the manual of arms, together with steadiness and general soldierly bearing. Name not inserted, no date. Signed by Major Patrick, and judges.

3. Diploma of Graduation from Newton High School
Description: "Presented to Raphael Clarke Thomas who has honorably completed the Classical Course of study prescribed for the High School. 28th Day of June, 1892. Signed by Herman E. Hibbard, Mayor; Amos E. Laurence, chairman of the High School Committee; and Edward J. Goodwin, Master.

4. Certificate of Admission to the Membership of the Delta Upsilon Fraternity [founded in 1834], on the 16th day of November in the 13th year of the chapter, and the 59th of the Fraternity. Signed by Walter L. Van Kleek, Secretary of the Chapter, Samuel S. Hall, Secretary of the Executive Council, Delta Upsilon; and Edward Kennard Raud, President of the Chapter.

5. Harvard University Diploma of Graduation.
   Description: Granted to Raphaelem Clarke Thomas. Baccalaurei in Artibus, cum laude. Juni XXIV anno Salutis humanae MDCCCXCVI. Signed by Jacobus Mills Peirce, Dacanns; and Carolus Gail Eliot, Praeses.

6. Certificate that by the payment of fifty dollars, Raphael C. Thomas has been constituted a member for life of the American Baptist Home Mission Society. Signed by Porter, Snelling, and Morgan. June 18th, 1896.

7. The Boston City Hospital. November 27, 1901. Mr. Raphael C. Thomas. Dear Sir: At a meeting of the [see above] you were appointed House Officer in the Second Surgical Service for the term of six months, beginning Monday, Jan. 6/02 to July 7/03. Hoping [etc.] Yours very truly, Conrad J. Rueter, Secretary. [Handwritten note: "Kindly report at the Superintendent's Office, Monday, Jan. 6th, 1902. At 9:00 A.M. If at the end of six months, your work and conduct have been satisfactory, you will be promoted."]

8. The Boston City Hospital. July 2, 1902. Mr. Raphael C. Thomas. Dear Sir: At a meeting of the Trustees of the Boston City Hospital this day you were promoted to the position of Junior Interne in the Second Surgical Service for the term beginning Monday, July 7/02 to Jan. 5/03. Hoping to receive your acceptance of the position, I am, Yours very truly, Conrad J. Rueter, Secretary. [Handwritten note: "If at the end of six months, your work and conduct have been satisfactory, you will be promoted."]

9. Commonwealth of Massachusetts. Board of Registration in Medicine. Certificate that Raphael Clarke Thomas of Newton a graduate of Harvard University in 1902, having passed a successful examination before this board has been registered by the laws of the Commonwealth. Boston, July 10, 1902. Signed by Miles, Chairman, and Harvey, Secretary. Certificate # 6595.

10. Certificate of honorable 'dismissal" from Newton Theological Institution. Having finished the regular course . . . Dated: June 9, 1904. Signed by Nathan E. Wood, John M. English, Charles Rufus Brown, Jesse B. Thomas, Frederick L. Anderson, and Winfred Donovan; Professors.

11. Certificate of Satisfactory Performance of all duties by Raphael Clarke Thomas, certified by the Society of the Lying-In Hospital of the City of New York, dated August 31, 1908. He served as house surgeon from May 1, 1908 to August 31, 1908. Signed by Baylies and Polk.

12. Zeugnis. From the Medical Faculty of the University of Vienna. May 1912 to August 1912, for completion of a clinical and operative course at the University. Signed by the faculty.

13. License to Practice Medicine and Surgery in the State of New York. Description: Granted to Raphael C. Thomas, M. D. License No. 12433 under seal of the University of the State of New York, September 25, 1914. Signed by the president of the University and Commissioner of Education, and the Medical Examiners of the State of New York.

14. Certificate, County Clerk's Office, County of New York. On the 19th day of February, 1915, Raphael C. Thomas having first subscribed and verified an affidavit in the form of Schedule C of Chapter 344 and of the Laws of 1907, made an entry in the Register of Physicians and Surgeons kept in the office of the Clerk of New York. Transcript follows: Raphael C. Thomas, Residence: 20 Clinton Street, Brooklyn, New York; Birthplace and Date: Chicago, Illinois, October 3, 1873. The University, State of New York, September 25, 1914. License No. 12433. Signed by Schneider, Clerk of New York County.

APPENDIX 7

Pepita's Problem

It was a bright day in July. On the broad sandy beach close by the town of Oton on the southern shore of Panay Island in Iloilo Province, two Filipino girls were chatting together. One was stretched out on the warm sand sunning herself after a dip in the surf, still clad in the patadion or skirt that Vizayan girls wear in bathing (quite different from the fragmentary affairs worn in our own country), with her long black hair spread out to dry. The other was sitting listlessly gazing out to sea, her forehead puckered in a puzzled frown. She nervously brushed aside a tiny fiddler crab that had popped out of its hole near by and answered her friend curtly as she made some remark to her.

"What's the matter with you, Pepita?" said her friend, hurt by this curtness, as she sat bold upright and looked the nurse in the face – for Pepita was a nurse in training in the Union Hospital in Iloilo. In fact she was nearly ready to graduate though but sixteen, for she was an unusually clever girl and the Hospital had admitted her before the customary age. She looked very natty in her white uniform and this frown on her face was not in keeping with it, as nurses are always supposed to be good natured.

"You aren't your usual self, Pepita", continued her friend. "I've noticed that of late you seemed to be worried over something. Can't you share your troubles with me? Are we not close enough for that? Come on. Tell me about it."

"Perhaps I better", said Pepita with a sigh. "I surely need some one to share this burden with me and you are closer to me than anyone else, except my parientes (relatives) with who I dare not talk on these matters.

They have troubles enough of their own. It would but make matters worse for me to stir them up, especially as I an do nothing about it myself. You see, It is this way. I hate to admit it even to you but our home is heavily mortgaged. We are likely to lose it. Don Arturo Lopez holds the mortgage and threatens even now to foreclose, if my parents do not pay within thirty days. They have nothing to pay now and are not likely to be able to do so within the time allowed. If I were only out and at work as a nurse I might help, but of course I can't nurse yet for pay as I have not taken the Insular Board Examination and to practice now would be against the law."

"But Pepita, Don Arturo surely would not deal hardly with you. He is a fine Caballero and Spaniards are so courteous."

"Narcasis, you do not realize what men will do for money. I know for a fact that Don Arturo is heavily in debt. He gambles freely and my brother Carlos told me that he knew he had lost thousands of pesos in recent months. He must make money now to cover his debts and save his honor, which means everything to a Spaniard, as you know. You see he wishes to have our place because it is near the sea and will make a fine fish corral. That means money for him and Don Arturo must have money and have it soon. No, my dear, it is sad indeed, but Don Arturo will foreclose. I am sure of it. But hush. There he comes now."

Narcisas looked up the beach where Pepita had glanced and there he was, a graceful rider on a spirited horse, cantering along with the nonchalance that a Spaniard always can assume however heavy his burdens. What a contrast he presented to the group of fishermen heaving at their nets down where the waves were rolling up the beach. They were a bright spot in this sandy waste, with their red turbans and their colored breechchclouts [loincloths], for they were clad only in a shirt and little else. Among them Narcasis caught a glimpse of Pepita's father, for he was a fisherman, one of the leaders to be sure, but yet a humble peasant, whom this haughty Spanish haciendero looked down upon as of no importance. To be sure he felt a bit sorry for him, as he planned to take away his little homestead by the sea that he loved so well. But business in business, and Arturo Lopez would lose caste and friends if he did not soon cover his gambling losses, his debts of honor. He must have dinero and have it soon. The homestead must be sacrificed.

As he cantered along the beach showing off the paces of his fine stallion, he was not unaware of the two little figures ahead of him. Such men as he always had a weakness for the fair sex and these two peasant girls were attractive with their smooth brown skin and jet black hair and sparkling brown eyes. He was not averse to a little flirtation even with a tao girl and he glanced away from the seaward view, which was most attractive, made up as it was of blue waters with with white caps here and there, and green islands dotted about toward the horizon, and closer by, of land, the rows of fronded coconut palms skirting the shore, adding to the beauty of the scene. But human nature interested him more than nature just then. He would have a word with the girls. As he passed Pepita's father on the beach, as he strained at the net, he nodded condescendingly, and the fisherman nodded back. He dared not do otherwise. The *gente* (gentry) were not always gently with the *taos* and he knew that to lose his home was not the worst that Don Lopez would do to him if he angered him.

As the Spaniard approached the girls he raised his Panama hat and twirled his waxed moustache and smiled and remarked: "Buenas Dias, Senoritas. It is a fine day, No?"

Narcasis smiled back, showing her white teeth, and replied in the affirmative. She could not persuade herself that Pepita was right in assuming that Don Arturo, Caballero that he was, would be so cruel. She felt sure he would relent and give these good people more time to pay their debt. Pepita however did not reply or even look at this dapper, self satisfied Spaniard. She could not. But she said nothing. Don Arturo noticed this and addressed her directly.

"You do not look happy Senorita", he said. "What troubles you?".

And then Pepita lost control. Tears welled in eyes and she looked the man squarely in the face. "Don Arturo," she said, "You ought to know why I am sad, when you mean to foreclose that mortgage and drive us from our home: the only home I have known since I was a tiny little girl. Oh I love these shores and the palms that border them and the fresh winds off the blue sea. I love it all and the stars at night with the bright moonlight that glimmers on the dark waters. All this I am to lose. Don Arturo, I beg of you to give us time on that mortgage. I shall be nursing soon and I'll save every centavo to pay it off. I promise you I will. Oh, Don Arturo, have pity." She stopped with a sob and the Spaniard bit his lip. This was a predicament, but of course this girl did not realize what it all meant to him. For her, it was home; for him honor. His honor was at stake and what was a tao girl's infatuation for her home compared with loss of a Spaniard's honor? No. He could not satisfy her whim, but he must sooth her. A little guile would do no harm.

"My dear Senorita", he said, "of course I will think it over. Trust me to do the fair thing," and with a slap on the neck of his stallion he dashed away over the beach and soon was but a speck in the distance.

****

Pepita found the house deserted when she reached home from the beach, but in a few moments she saw her [mother] trudging back from market carrying a flat basket with the rice, a little dried fish and some green bananas she had just purchased, which was for the simple meal. Her mother was depressed. Her face had become careworn during the past months. Pepita had noticed it. It hurt her to see her mother growing old under the anxiety that they all were experiencing, as the loss of their home became more and more certain. Her father, too, as he trudged long up the trail from the beach, with his basket full of fresh fish which must be sold in the market, and a drawn, almost a haggard look. Pepita could hardly stand it. They always had been so care free. The home had been a happy one. The brother Juan had gone out to service. He and Pepita were the only children. She too would soon be earning a salary as a nurse, and if Don Arturo would only wait she and her brother could cover the payment on that dreaded mortgage and save their home. But she knew in her heart that Don Arturo's words on the beach were evasive. She read his real intent. Her womanly intuition told her that Don Arture would foreclose.

"Where have you been, Pepita?" said her mother. "Down on the beach with the crabs and seagulls?" She tried to smile but it was a sad failure. She said little about the mortgage, but of course she knew the children were aware of it. Her sad smile hurt Pepita more than it would have done had she not tried t smile at all. It was a brave attempt to cover up a wound and her daughter knew it.

"Mother," she said, "Don't try to cheer me up when you are so sad yourself. Tell me frankly. Is there any change? Do you think there is the slightest hope that Don Artureo will relent and give us time on the mortgage?"

"Wala gid" (not at all): this comment from her father who had heard Pepita's question. "No my daughter. We shall have to take it all bravely, but must not deceive ourselves. I have had direct information recently from friends who know Don Arturo well. They tell me he will surely foreclose."

Pepita cringed. This was facing cruel facts and she was only a girl. Life had not been stern for her so far. To be sure they were not rich and she had known at times what it was to be hungry. But no real want ever had threatened them, for bananas on the trees and fish in the sea and a handful of rice always was available. She found no real hardship there, but not it was different. Losing their home would be bitter, the home they had known and loved so long. She bowed her head and the tears came in spite of her resolution to be brave. It was her first ordeal, and it was bitter.

****

The frugal supper of rice had been cooked in the little clay pot on the wooden table with the metal slab that served as a stove. A few embers of charcoal serve for fuel. Fingers served for forks, for although a trained nurse, herself, Pepita's parents were slow to adopt foreign ways and she humored them in their lifelong customs. Dried fish and a banana and the meal was over. Rice is always the piece de resistance. The rest does not matter.

"It looks stormy tonight", said Pepita's father, as he glanced out the window, just a frame of bamboo with an overhanding life sloping outward. As he spoke the wind began to sough through the palms and there was a low muttering in the distant West. It sounded ominous. Storms are sudden in the Tropics and some of them are terrific. The typhoon is known the world over. The very name is dreaded. On land these storms are bad enough, rooting up great trees, blowing down bamboo houses and stripping iron roofs off upper class dwellings and hurtling them down the streets, a menace to life and limb, and cutting up other fantastic capers, all of them prodigious and destructive.

"Before I left the beach" said Pepita's father, "I saw Don Arturo starting out in a prao (two-sailed dugout with bamboo outriggers). "I warned him that the weather might be nasty, but he only laughed at me."

"You certainly were good to him after all he has done to you", said his wife bitterly. "Wish he might founder out there. It would serve him right."

Pepita caught her breath. This sorrow was embittering her mother. She never was like this before.

"Oh, mother dear," she said softly, "you don't mean that. You know they teach us at the Mission Hospital that we must love our enemies".

"Yes child," her mother answered sadly. "I fear this sorrow has hardened me. I did not really mean that. The sea is a monster when it devours human beings. None of us would side with the sea on that. But forget all this my child," she continued, forcing a smile,. "You must get some sleep for your vacation is over and tomorrow you must return bright and early to the Hospital. God bless you my dear and now Ma-ayong Gabi (Good night)."

****

All was quiet in Pepita's home. They were asleep on their hard pallets. The parents slept on a bamboo bed and Pepita on the split bamboo floor on a grass mat, the customary bed of the Filipino peasant. Suddenly Pepita awoke with a start as a sudden crash of thunder resounded through the night. The wind was blowing a gale and the bamboos were creaking aloud as their waxy barked trunks swayed against each other. The shack shook in the last and the animals herded beneath it, pigs and goats and carabao, were stirring about in agitation. These dumb creatures deserve more attention than human beings give them in times of storm. They seem to sense its severity. Now they were stamping about an jostling one another. Pepita knew their customs and she was disturbed. The storm was increasing in violence. It was a real baguio. She rose on one elbow and looked out. She could see the sea in the distance. Huge waves were dashing up the beach, their white spume shining in the moonlight. The moon is radiant in the Tropics, so clear that one can read by its light. This storm had blanked out the stars but through a rift in the inky clouds the moon had appeared for a moment and then a flash of lightning completed the picture vividly. Pepita cried out. What had she seen? Yes, it was a boat, a *praao*, and it was fighting for its life out there not far from where the breakers were being dashed into foam as they rolled up the beach. No ship could live in that sea. She knew that. The *praao* was doomed.

"Father, Father," she cried, terrified. "Wake up. There is a *praao* near the shore. I am sure it will founder. Wake up Wake up," and she shook her father's arm to bring him to his senses. A filipino sleeps like the dead ordinarily, but this fisherman was more alert. He awoke and almost immediately his instinct as one born and bred to the sea told him the story. One glance through the window, as another flash of lightning framed the laboring *praao* in its square aperture, and he was on his feet and catching up a rope he was off.

"Bring your medicine kit", he called back to Pepita, as he leaped through the door and down the bamboo step ladder at a bound. "There may be some one who will need your aid".

Pepita, trained for emergencies now was at her best. Sorrow was a new experience for her and she had almost broken under its strain: not sorrow for herself primarily, but sorrow for her dear ones. Now she was in her element. She was a nurse, nearly a graduate. She did not know too much of medical treatment, but she knew enough to do her best and glory in it. It thrilled her to feel she might be of use in this emergency. She caught up her leather kit bag and a Nurses' cape, blue and natty on her white uniform, and followed her father on the run.

As she approached the beach she saw him bending over a form lying near the spot where she and Narcasia had been that day, but now how different it was. Bleak winds hurtled the spume all about them as the huge waves were dashed into fragments on the beach, her cape was flying wildly in the wind and all about her it was so gloomy and dark, save for the vivid flashes of lightning that startled her as the thunder rolled almost as they flashed, a sure sign that the center of the storm is near.

"Pepita, Pepita", her father called through the roar of the wind, "Do not be shocked my child. This is awful. If this man dies, and he looks to be near death, you mother will never get over it after what she said. It's Don Arturo."

Pepita gasped, but that was all. She did not faint or even feel like it. She was a nurse, or almost one, and the honor of the profession was at stake. Such honor is more worthy then that of Don Arturo who had felt no qualms in deceiving a peasant girl when his honor was a stake.

He looked ghastly in the dim light of their lantern, but she did not waste a moment in forebodings. A touch on the wrist and then a hand on the heart assured her that life was still there. She opened the medicine case and drew out a syringe and quickly administered a stimulant, and then at once began the familiar method artificial respiration familiar to every Boy and Girl Scout over here, but an unknown method over there, in Philippine land. It was a hard fight for a half hour but she won. Slowly the breath came evenly and the flickering pulse began to respond. She knew Don Arturo would live. It thrilled her. She had saved a life. It might mean the loss of her home, but that did not matter. She had done her duty and saved a life. She covered him with her cape and ran to the house for blankets. Such cases demand warmth.

****

The next morning was a bright one. The Tropical storm was over as quickly as it had begun. Pepita was tired by her labors of the night, but she was ready for the thirty kilometer ride to Iloilo and the Hospital. She was about to leave the house when she heard a pony close by and a muchacho dismounted and handed her a little envelope. With a "Buenas Dias" he was off as he cried: "It is from Senor the Don Arturo Lopez, with his best felicitations".

Pepita opened the envelope. It enclosed the mortgage – <u>cancelled</u>.

LIST OF MAPS AND ILLUSTRATIONS WITH CREDITS

MAPS

1. The Philippines. Borrowed with permission from *Beyond Prison Walls* by Marian D. Bomm, published by The Association of Baptists for World Evangelism, Inc., Cherry Hill, NJ, 1987.
2. Panay and Negros Islands in the Visayans. The Author.
3. City of Manila. Borrowed with permission from *Beyond Prison Walls* by Marian D. Bomm, published by The Association of Baptists for World Evangelism, Inc., Cherry Hill, NJ, 1987.

ILLUSTRATIONS

1. Portrait of Dr. Jesse B. Thomas. Frontispiece from *The Old Bible and the New Science, An Essay and Four Lectures,* delivered before the New York Baptist Ministers' Conference. Second Edition, 1877, published by the American Tract Society, 150 Nassau St., New York. Digitized by Google, November 28, 2007, from the ATLA Monograph Preservation Program copy.
2. Raphael Thomas in 1904. ABWE Archives.
3. Winifred Cheney Thomas, circa 1908. ABWE Archives.
4. Bird's-eye View of the City of Iloilo (early 1900's). ABWE Archives.
5. Union Mission Hospital (1908). ABWE Archives.
6. Norma Thomas (1916). ABWE Archives.
7. Filipino Boy with carabao. Original photograph in the ABWE Archives.

8. Jesse and Marguerite (1921). ABWE Archives.
9. Mrs. Lucy Peabody. ABWE Archives.
10. Marguerite Doane. ABWE Archives.
11. Doane Hall Evangelistic Institute. ABWE Archives.
12. Doane Rest. ABWE Archives.
13. Alberto Franco and Other Ministry Leaders. ABWE Archives.
14. The First ABEO Missionaries. ABWE Archives.
15. Manila "Carnival Stand." ABWE Archives.
16. First Baptist Church, Manila
17. Left to Right: Simon Meeks, Leland Wang, and Harold Commons at the Keswick Camp near Manila (1936) ABWE Archives.
18. Raphael, Jesse, and Norma Thomas (1941). ABWE Archives.
19. Raph and his daughter "Winky." ABWE Archives.
20. Miss Martien, Pastor Caspe, and his daughter. Three generations. ABWE Archives.
21. The Gospel Ship. ABWE Archives.
22. Dr. Thomas in the 1950's. ABWE Archives.
23. Raph's recruiting letter to young people. ABWE Archives.

BIBLIOGRAPHY

Books

Arnold, Sir Edwin. *Seas and Lands.* New York: Longmans, Green, and Co., 1891.

Barile, Alfredo Franco, Jr., ed. *Recollections. A Biographical History of Doane Baptist Seminary.* Iloilo: Doane Baptist Seminary, 2005. Printed by Fortune Printers & Traders, Ledesma Street, Iloilo City, Philippines.

Barrows, John Henry, ed. *The World's Parliament of Religions.* In two volumes: Chicago: The Parliament Publishing Company, 1893.

Bartholow, Roberts. *A Practical Treatise on Materia Medica and Therapeutics.* New York: D. Appleton and Company. 7th Edition, Revised and Enlarged, 1890.

Beaver, Raymond W. *Partners in Mission. American Baptists in Mission Together*, 1900-1985. Iloilo City (Philippines): Published by the Author.1988.

Bergreen, Laurence. *Over the Edge of the World.* New York: William Morrow, 2003.

Bomm, Marian D. *Beyond Prison Walls.* Cherry Hill: Association of Baptists for World Evangelism, Inc., 1987.

Bosworth, C. E., E. Van Donzel, W.P. Heinrichs, and G. Lecomte. *The Encyclopaedia Of Islam*, New Edition. Leiden: EJ. Brill, 1995.

Boyer, Paul. *When Time Shall Be No More. Prophecy Belief in Modern American Culture*. Cambridge: The Belknap Press, 1992.

Bradley, James. *The Imperial Cruise*. New York: Little, Brown and Company, 2009.

Brainard, Cecelia Manguerra and Edmundo F. Litton, eds. *Journey of 100 Years. Reflections on the Centennial of Philippine Independence*. Santa Monica: Philippine American Women Writers and Artists, 1999.

Bunda, Nestor Distor. *A Mission History of the Philippine Baptist Churches, 1898-1998, From a Philippine Perspective*. Aachen: Verl, an der Lottbek im Besitz des Verlags Mainz, 1999.

Burdett, Henry C. *Hospitals and Asylums Of The World: Their Origin, History, Construction, Administration, Management, And Legislation; With Plans Of The Chief Medical Institutions Accurately Drawn To a Uniform Scale, In Addition To Those Of All The Hospitals Of London In The Jubilee Year Of Queen Victoria's Reign*. London: J. and A. Churchill, 1891.

Bush, L. Russ, and Tom J. Nettles. *Baptists and the Bible. The Baptist Doctrines of Biblical Inspiration and Religious Authority in Historical Perspective*. Chicago: Moody Press, 1980.

Cannell, Fenella. *Power and Intimacy in the Christian Philippines*. Cambridge: Cambridge University Press, 1999.

Castellani, Aldo and Albert J. Chalmers. *Manual of Tropical Medicine*. New York: William Wood and Company, 1919.

Cattan, Louise A. *Lamps are for Lighting*. Grand Rapids: William B. Eerdmans Publishing Co., 1972.

Clement, Ernest W. *Christianity in Modern Japan*. New York: Young People's Missionary Movement of the United States and Canada. American Baptist Publication Society, 1905.

Commons, Harold T. *Heritage & Harvest. The History of the Association of Baptists for World Evangelism, Inc.* Cherry Hill, NJ: The Association of Baptists for World Evangelism, 1981.

Coote, Robert T. *Renewal for Mission. A History of the Overseas Ministries Study Center* (1922-2000) *and its Contribution to the World Christian Mission*. New Haven: OMSC, 2000.

Cushing, Harvey. *The Life of Sir William Osler*. 2 vols. Oxford: Clarendon Press, 1925.

Daniels, W. H. *D. L. Moody and His Work*. Hartford: American Publishing Company, 1876.

Dayrit, Conrado S., Perla Dizon Santos Ocampo, Eduardo R. De La Cruz. *History of Philippine Medicine with Landmarks in World Medical History*. Pasig City: Anvil Publishing Company, 2002.

Dean, John Marvin. *The Cross of Christ in Bolo-Land*. Chicago: The Fleming H. Revell Company, 1902.

Dollar, George W. *A History of Fundamentalism in America*. Greenville: Bob Jones University Press, 1973.

Dorman, William R. *Sketches of Pastorates of the Second Half Century at the First Baptist Church in Pierrepont Street, Brooklyn (The Baptist Temple)*. One Hundredth Anniversary, October – November 1923. Brooklyn: First Baptist Church, 1923.

Douglas, Robert K. *Europe and the Far East, 1509 – 1912*. Revised and Corrected. Cambridge Historical Series. New York: G. P. Putnam's Sons, 1924.

Fairbank, John K. *The Missionary Enterprise in China and America.* Cambridge: Harvard University Press, 1974.

Ferngren, Gary B. *Medicine & Health Care in Early Christianity.* Baltimore: Johns Hopkins, 2009.

Flanagan, Lt. Gene E. M., Jr. *The Los Baños Raid.* Novato, Ca.: Presidio Press, 1986.

Gammell, William. *A History of American Baptist Missions in Asia, Africa, Europe and North America.* Boston: Gould, Kendall, and Lincoln, 1849.

Garrison, Fielding H., AB, MD. *An Introduction to the History of Medicine.* 4th ed. Philadelphia and London: W.B. Saunders Company, 1929.

Greene, Daniel Crosby (Chairman of the Editorial Committee). *Proceedings of the General Conference of Protestant Missionaries in Japan Held in Tokyo October 24-31, 1900.* Tokyo: Methodist Publishing House, 1901.

Hall, D. G. E. *A History of South-East Asia.* Third Edition. London, New York: Macmillan; St. Martin's Press, 1968.

Harrington, Charles Kendall. *Captain Bickel Of The Inland Sea.* New York: Fleming H. Revell Co., 1919.

Hartendorp, A. V. H. *The Japanese Occupation of the Philippines.* 2 volumes. Manila: Bookmark, 1967.

Hirth, Friedrich and W. W. Rockhill, translators and editors. *Chau Ju-Kua: His Work on the Chinese and Arab Trade in the Twelfth and Thirteenth Centuries (entitled Chu-fan-ehi).* Taipei: Literature House, Ltd., 1965.

Hoffman, Phillip T. *Why Did Europe Conquer the World?* The Princeton Economic History of the World. Princeton and Oxford: Princeton University Press, 2017.

Hovey, Alvah. *Manual of Systematic Theology, and Christian Ethics.* Philadelphia: American Baptist Publication Society, 1877.

Hovey, Alvah. *Eschatology.* Philadelphia: American Baptist Publication Society, 1888.

Howe, K. R. *The Quest for Origins.* Honolulu: University of Hawaii Press, 2003.

Hymns for the Family of God. Nashville: Paragon Associates, Inc., 1976.

Iriye, Akira. *Across the Pacific: An Inner History of American - East Asian Relations.* New York: Harcourt, Brace, and World, 1967.

Kamen, Henry. *Empire: How Spain Became a World Power, 1492-1763.* New York: HarperCollins Publishers, 2003.

Karnow, Stanley. *In Our Image. America's Empire in the Philippines.* New York: Random House, 1989.

Keener, Craig S. *Miracles. The Credibility of the New Testament Accounts.* Grand Rapids: Baker Academics, 2011.

Kennedy, Elaine J. *Baptist Centennial History of the Philippines.* Makati City: Church Strengthening Ministry of Foreign Mission Board, SBC, Inc., n.d. [With ABWE Imprint]

Kyle, Richard. *The Last Days are Here Again. A History of the End Times.* Grand Rapids: Baker Books, 1998.

Lach, Donald F. *Asia in the Making of Europe.* Volume I, The Century of Discovery. Chicago: Chicago University Press, 1965.

Latourette, Kenneth Scott. *A History of Christian Missions in China.* Taipei: Chi'eng-Wen Publishing Company, 1966.

Mackay, George L. *From Far Formosa*. 3rd Edition. Taipei: SMC Publishing Co., 2002 (1896).

Marsden, George M. *The Soul of the American University.* New York: Oxford University Press, 1994.

Marsden, George M. *Fundamentalism and American Culture.* New Edition. Oxford, New York: Oxford University Press, 2006.

Matthiessen, Sven. *Japanese Pan-Asianism and the Philippines from the Late Nineteenth Century to the End of World War II. Going to the Philippines is Like Coming Home?* Leiden: Brill, 2016.

May, R. J. "Philippines," in C. E. Bosworth, E. Van Donzel, W.P. Heinrichs, and G. Lecomte. *The Encyclopaedia of Islam*, New Edition. Leiden: E. J. Brill, 1995.

Merriam, Edmund F. *A History of American Baptist Missions.* Rev. ed. with Centennial Supplement. Philadelphia: American Baptist Publication Society, 1913.

Moffett, Samuel Hugh. *A History of Christianity in Asia*. Volume II, 1500-1900. Maryknoll: Orbis Books, 2005.

Moody, William R. *The Life of Dwight L. Moody.* The Fleming H. Revell Company, 1900.

Mullins, Edgar Young. *The Christian Religion in its Doctrinal Expression.* Philadelphia: The Judson Press, 1917.

Nelson, Linnea A. and Elma S. Herradura. *Scientia et Fides. The Story of Central Philippine University.* Iloilo: Central Philippine University, 1981.

Peterson, John W., and Norman Johnson (Compilers). *Praise! Our Songs and Hymns.* Grand Rapids: Singspiration Music, 1979.

Rizal, Jose. *The Indolence of the Filipino*. Project Gutenburg edition, Section 4.

Ruffin, Bernard. *Fanny Crosby. The Hymn Writer*, published by Barbour Publishing, Inc. [Pilgrim Press], 1976.

Sandeen, Ernest R. *The Roots of Fundamentalism. British and American Millenarianism, 1800 – 1930.* Grand Rapids: Baker Book House, 1978.

Smith, H. Shelton, Robert T. Handy, and Lefferts A. Loetscher. *American Christianity. An Historical Interpretation with Representative Documents*. Vol. II: 1860-1960. New York: Charles Scribner's Sons, 1963.

Spivey, James, "The Millenium," in *Has our Theology Changed? Southern Baptist Thought Since 1845,* ed. Paul A. Basden. Nashville: Broadman & Holman Publishers, 1994.

Strong, Augustus H. *Systematic Theology. A Compendium. Designed for the Use of Theological Students.* Westwood: Fleming H. Revell Company, 1907.

Students and the Present Missionary Crisis. Addresses Delivered before the Sixth International Convention of the Student Volunteer Movement for Foreign Missions, Rochester, New York, December 29, 1909, to January 2, 1910. New York: Student Volunteer Movement for Foreign Missions, 1910.

Torbet, Robert G. *A History of the Baptists.* 3rd ed. Valley Forge: Judson Press, 1963.

Tulga, Chester E. *The Foreign Missions Controversy in the Northern Baptist Convention. 1919 – 1949.* Chicago: Conservative Baptist Fellowship, 1950.

Vogel, Ezra F. *China and Japan. Facing History*. Cambridge, London: The Belknap Press of Harvard University Press, 2019.

Wacker, Grant. *Augustus H. Strong and the Dilemma of Historical Consciousness*. Macon: Mercer University Press, 1985.

Williams, Frederick Wells. *The Life and Letters of Samuel Wells Williams*. New York: G. P. Putnam's Sons, 1888.

Woodworth, Ruth. *No Greater Joy. The Story of Ruth Woodworth, Missionary*. ABWE Publishing, 1975.

Periodicals and Collections

A Message from the Association of Baptists for Evangelism in the Orient, Inc., n.d. (1930).

Anonymous, "Norman Mather Waterbury." *The Baptist Missionary Magazine,* Published by the American Baptist Missionary Union, Volume LXVII, 1887: 4-6.

Burditt, Rev. J. F., "The Telugu Mission. Tribute to Mr. Waterbury." *The Baptist Missionary Magazine,* Published by the American Baptist Missionary Union, Volume LXVII, 1887:77-78.

Fowler, Henry T. "A Phase of Modern College Life," *Harper's New Monthly Magazine* XCII (December 1895 to May 1896): 688-695.

Fowler, Henry T. "The Strategic Importance of Japan." Senior Address, Newton Theological Institution, 1904. Newton Theological Institution School Archives, Trask Library Special Collections and Archives, Andover-Newton Theological School, Newton Centre.

Gealogo, Francis A. "The Philippines in the World of the Influenza Pandemic of 1918-1919," in *Philippine Studies*, Vol. 57, No. 2, Public Health in History (June 2009).

Gowing, Peter G. "Christianity in the Philippines Yesterday and Today," *Silliman Journal* 12 (1965): 109-151.

Klein, Amanda P., "The Union Mission Hospital at Iloilo, Philippine Islands," *The American Journal of Nursing*, Vol. 16, No. 3 (December 1915): 227-229.

Ludmerer, Kenneth M. "*REFORM AT HARVARD MEDICAL SCHOOL, 1869-1909,*" *Bulletin of the History of Medicine*, Vol. 55, No. 3 (Fall 1981): 368.

Mackay, Donald J., "Raphael Clark Thomas," *The Message*, Vol. 23, No. 3, November, 1956.

Briggs, Charles W. *Missions in the Philippines.* American Baptist Missionary Union, April 1905.

"New England Educational Institutions, XIII. Newton Theological Institution," *The New England Magazine* 6:34 (August 1888): 358-362.

Norton, Charles Eliot. "Harvard University in 1890." *Harper's New Monthly Magazine* 81 (June to November 1890): 581-592.

Peabody, Mrs. Henry W., "Mrs. Peabody's Resignation," *The Message*, Vol. 1, No. 8, May, 1935.

Report of Association of Baptists for Evangelism in the Orient, Inc., 1928-1929.

Report of Association of Baptists for Evangelism in the Orient, Inc., 1932-1933.

Romani, John H., "The Philippine Barrio," in *The Far Eastern Quarterly*, Volume 15, No. 2, February, 1956. 229-237.

Robbins, J. C., "Capiz Spells "Opportunity," The Populous Province a Waving Harvest Field for Doctor and Evangelist," *Baptist Missionary Magazine*, (April 1905): 148.

Shuster, W. Morgan, "Our Philippine Policies and Their Results." An Address Delivered at Clark University, September 14, 1909, during the Conference Upon the Far East: 70-71. [Early Journal Content on JSTOR].

The Newtonian. Published by the Students of The Newton Theological Institute, Newton Centre, Massachusetts. 1, No. 2 (June 1903) 84-87; (December 1903), 58.

The Ninety-fifth Annual Report of the American Baptist Missionary Union, 1909: 135.

Thomas, Norma "Renfroville Reminiscenses," *Pearl of the Orient* XII (Iloilo, Philippine Islands) (October 1925): 7-8. American Baptist Historical Society, Atlanta, Georgia.

Thomas, R. C. "Iloilo Union Mission Hospital," *Pearl of the Orient* XI (Iloilo, Philippine Islands) (October 1924): 6. American Baptist Historical Society, Atlanta, Georgia.

Thomas, R. C. "Doane Evangelistic Institute," *Pearl of the Orient* XI (Iloilo, Philippine Islands) (October 1924): 2. American Baptist Historical Society, Atlanta, Georgia.

Thomas, R. C. "Theory and Practice for D.H.E.I. Students," *Pearl of the Orient* XII (Iloilo, Philippine Islands) (October 1925): 7. American Baptist Historical Society, Atlanta, Georgia.

Thomas, R. C. "Signal Providences," *The Baptist Missionary Magazine*, (June 1906): 217.

__________, "The Union Hospital at Iloilo. Baptists and Presbyterians in Cooperation," *The Baptist Missionary Magazine*, (December 1908), 452.

__________, "The Evangelistic Program of a Medical Missionary," *The Watchman Examiner*, (September 15, 1927): 1173.

Walters, B. W., "Discussion," in *Proceedings of the General Conference of Protestant Missionaries in Japan.* (Tokyo: Methodist Publishing House, 1901): 163-165.

Archives, Unpublished Papers, and Personal Correspondence

Andover-Newton Theological School Theological School Alumni Records (RG 278), Special Collections, Yale Divinity School Library.

Applications for Appointment of R. C. Thomas, and his wives, Winifred M. Cheney, and Norma Rose Waterbury, found in the following: International Ministries, Group Number 1, [Box 163, folder: Thomas, R.C., M.D. 1904-1905; Box 164, folder: Thomas, R.C., M.D. 1908-1909; Box 164, Thomas, R.C, M.D. 1916-1918], American Baptist Historical Society, Atlanta, Georgia.

Archives. Association of Baptists for Evangelism in the Orient, Harrisburg, PA.

ABEO "Minutes of the Annual Meeting," April 25, 1930.

ABEO "Minutes of the Annual Meeting," April 7-8, 1932.

ABEO "Executive Committee Meeting Minutes," September 9, 1933.

ABEO "Executive Committee Meeting Minutes," June 5, 1935.

ABEO "Minutes of the Special Meeting of the Voting Board," April 27, 1937. TDS. Archives, Association of Baptists for World Evangelism, Harrisburg.

ABEO *Report of Association of Baptists for Evangelism in the Orient*, 1928-1929. Beverly, Massachusetts: Headquarters, 1929.

Commons, Harold. Miscellaneous Correspondence. Thomas Papers, Archives, Association of Baptists for World Evangelism, Harrisburg.

Franklin, James H. Miscellaneous Correspondence Between Dr. Franklin and Dr. Thomas.

Martien, Ellen, Iloilo City, Philippines, to Mr. Commons, August 17, 1940.

Papa [R. C. Thomas], Ventnor, to Winky [Winifred Thomas], September 30, 1927.

Peabody, Mrs. Henry W. [Lucy]. "Reply to the Statement of the American Baptist Foreign Mission Society." *Report of Association of Baptists for Evangelism of the Orient, Inc.* (1928-29): 38-47.

Peabody, Mrs. Henry W., Miscellaneous Correspondence with R. C. Thomas.

Peabody, Mrs. Henry W., Beverly, Mass., to Reverend Harold Commons, July 1937.

Revell, Fleming H., Jr., to Dr. R. C. Thomas, November 27, 1936.

Sutherland, A. M., Puerto Princessa, Palawan, Philippine Islands, to Dr. R. C. Thomas, Ventnor, NJ, July 14, 1932.

Sutherland, A. M., to Association of Baptists for Evangelism in the Orient, care of Dr. R. C. Thomas, Manila, Philippine Islands, November 1, 1932. TL. Archives, Association of Baptists for World Evangelism, Harrisburg.

Sutherland to Pastor Harold T. Commons, Association of Baptists, April 10, 1933. TL. Archives, Association of Baptists for World Evangelism, Harrisburg.

Thomas, R. C. "A Review of the Early Beginnings of the ABEO," n.d. (1953?) TMs. Thomas Papers, Archives, Association of Baptists for World Evangelism, Harrisburg.

Thomas, R. C. "Brief History of the Origin and Objectives of the ABEO. For our missionaries only," n.d. TMs. Thomas Papers, Archives, Association of Baptists for World Evangelism, Harrisburg.

_________. "Some Aspects of Oriental Religion." Senior Thesis, Newton Theological Institution, 1904. Newton Theological Institution School Archives, Trask Library Special Collections and Archives, Andover-Newton Theological School, Newton Centre.

_________. "Statement of the Philippine Situation," n.d. TMs. Thomas Papers, Archives, Association of Baptists for World Evangelism, Harrisburg.

_________. "Suggestions on Mission Policy (Medical Work)," January 25, 1926. TMs. Thomas Papers, Archives, Association of Baptists for World Evangelism, Harrisburg.

_________ . "The Evangelistic Program of a Medical Missionary," *TheWatchman Examiner* (1927): 1173-174; 1207-1208; 1238-1239.

"Winky" [Winifred Thomas], At home, to "Father" [R. C. Thomas], September 24, 1927. Thomas Papers, Archives, Association of Baptists for World Evangelism, Harrisburg.

Letters of Inquiry related to the appointment of Dr. R.C. Thomas in 1904, found in International Ministries, Group Number 1, [Box 163, Thomas, R.C., M.D., (), Burr, Everett D., Letter of Inquiry submitted to the Home Department, American Baptist Missionary Union; Creesy, George W., Letter of Inquiry submitted to the Home Department, American Baptist Missionary Union; Joslin, Elliott P., Letter of Inquiry submitted to the Home Department of the American Baptist Missionary Union; Monks, George H., Letter of Inquiry submitted to the Home Department of the American Baptist Missionary Union], American Baptist Historical Society, Atlanta, Georgia.

Peabody, Lucy, "The Philippine Mission. "Pear of the Orient," n.d. (1924?). International Ministries, Group Number 1, [Box 262, Thomas, R.C., M.D. 1923-1924], American Baptist Historical Society, Atlanta, Georgia.

Smalley, Martha Lund, compiler. Guide to the Archives of the Committee on Christian Literature for Women and Children in Mission Fields, Inc. Yale University Library, Divinity Library Special Collections, June, 1992.

Thomas, R. C., M. D., Miscellaneous Correspondence. Thomas Papers, Archives, Association of Baptists for World Evangelism, Harrisburg, Pennsylvania.

Thomas, R. C., M.D., Miscellaneous Correspondence [See notes] found in the following: International Ministries, Group Number 1, Box 163, folder: Thomas, R.C., M.D. 1904-1905; Box 164, folders: Thomas, R.C., M.D. 1906; Thomas, R.C., M.D. 1907; Thomas, R.C., M.D. 1908-1909; Thomas, R.C., M.D. 1910-1911; Thomas, R.C., M.D., 1912-1913; Thomas, R.C., M.D., 1914-1915; Thomas, R.C., M.D., 1916-1918; Thomas, R.C., M.D. 1919. Box 261, folder: Thomas, R.C., M.D. 1921; Box 262, folders: Thomas, R.C., M.D. 1922; Thomas, R.C., M.D. 1923-1924; Thomas, R.C., M.D. 1925; Thomas, R.C., M.D. 1926; Thomas, R.C., M.D. 1927; Thomas, R.C., M.D. 1928-1929. American Baptist Historical Society, Atlanta, Georgia.

Thomas, R.C., M.D., Miscellaneous Correspondence on Microfilm. International Ministries, Group Number 1, [FM 209, R.C. Thomas]. American Baptist Historical Society, Atlanta, Georgia.

INTERNET SITES AND NEWSPAPERS

http://bcciloilo.tripod.com/ Last accessed December 20, 2022.

http://www.nycago.org/Organs/NYC/html/StMarksHospital.html Last accessed December 20, 2022 http://politicalgraveyard.com/bio/thomas5.html Last accessed December 20, 2022

Brooklyn Daily Union-Argus. (Brooklyn, New York), December 30, 1882.

Rasposas, Al, "Philippines and the Great War," Facebook.com, Thursday, January 3, 2013.

JSTOR. https://www.jstor.org/. Early Journal Content.

OTHER UNPUBLISHED MATERIALS

Thomas, Raphael Clarke, "A Philippine Medical Missionary Harks Back," n.d. [Prepared for the "I Personally Award" Essay Contest of The Atlantic and Reader's Digest]. Thomas Papers, Archives, Association of Baptists for World Evangelism, Harrisburg.

Thomas, Raphael C. "Brief History of the Origin and Objectives of the ABEO" Thomas Papers, Archives, Association of Baptists for World Evangelism, Harrisburg.

Thomas, R. C. "The Strategic Importance of Japan in the Evangelization of the World." Senior Thesis, Newton Theological Institution, 1904. Andover-Newton Theological School Theses Collection (RG 300), Special Collections, Yale Divinity School Library.

Bible Quotations

All Bible quotations are from the Authorized (King James) Version, the one most familiar to Raph.

ENDNOTES

When quotations appear that are not otherwise explained in the text or in the End Notes, they are from Raph's autobiographical essay "A Philippine Medical Missionary Hearkens Back."

Chapter 1

1. B. W. Waters, "Discussion," in *Proceedings of the General Conference of Protestant Missionaries in Japan*. Tokyo: Methodist Publishing House, 1901, p. 163.
2. Raphael C. Thomas [Thomas], "A Philippine Medical Missionary Hearkens Back" [APMMHB], Prepared for the "I Personally Award." n.d. 1. Thomas Papers, Archives, ABWE, Harrisburg, PA [TPA, ABWE]
3. Thomas, APMMHB n.d., 2 [TPA, ABWE]. The Missouri Compromise was an attempt to deal with the request of the state of Missouri to join the Union as a slave state, which would have changed the balance of slave versus non-slave states in the Union. Raph's Uncle, Senator Jesse B. Thomas, offered one of the amendments to the proposed bill to allow Missouri to enter. His amendment included a provision that slavery be allowed south of the 36th parallel, thus the Missouri Compromise.
4. http://politicalgraveyard.com/bio/thomas5.html
5. Brooklyn Daily Union-Argus. (Brooklyn, New York), 1882. Emphasis added.
6. At Newton's invitation, Andover moved its operations to the Newton Centre campus in 1931. The two schools officially merged in 1965 under the name Andover Newton Theological School. The school has changed radically since the time of Raph's studies there. The theological education program there now champions civil rights, social justice, psychological studies, and the ordination of women. Andover-Newton has since merged with Yale Divinity School.

[7] William R. Dorman, "Sketches of Pastorates of the Second Half Century at the First Baptist Church in Pierrepont Street, Brooklyn (The Baptist Temple)", One Hundreth Anniversary, October-November 1923, 2-3.

[8] Thomas, Separate letter on Christian experience, attached to "Application for Appointment as a Missionary of the American Baptist Missionary Union," April 28, 1904, Thomas papers, Special Collections, American Baptist Historical Society, Valley Forge [SC, ABHS].

[9] Thomas, APMMHB, 1.

[10] Thomas, Georgetown, Massachusetts, to Mr. and Mrs. Durham, March 13, 1954, 2[TPA, ABWE].

[11] Thomas, APMMHB, 2.

Chapter 2

[12] George M. Marsden. *The Soul of the American University.* (New York: Oxford University Press, 1994), 184.

[13] Marsden, *American University*, 187-189.

[14] Sir Edwin Arnold. *Seas and Lands.* (New York: Longmans, Green, and Co., 1891), 99.

[15] Arnold, *Seas*, 101.

[16] Charles Eliot Norton, "Harvard University in 1890." *Harper's New Monthly Magazine*, LXXXI (June to November 1890): 585.

[17] Thomas letter to Durham, 3.

[18] Thomas, APMMHB, 1

[19] *Students and the Present Missionary Crisis. Addresses Delivered before the Sixth International Convention of the Student Volunteer Movement for Foreign Missions, Rochester, New York, December 29, 1909, to January 2, 1910.* (New York: Student Volunteer Movement for Foreign Missions, 1910), 36.

[20] *Students and the Present Missionary Crisis*, 36.

[21] He felt that the enthusiasm of the leaders would put pressure on young people to volunteer without a clear call from God. William R. Moody. *The Life of Dwight L. Moody.* The Authorized Edition. (Fleming H. Revell Company, 1900), 358.

[22] Moody, *Life*, 349-376.

[23] *Students* (1910), 17

[24] Thomas letter to Durham, 2.

[25] Henry T. Fowler, "A Phase of Modern College Life." *Harpers New Monthly Magazine,* XCII (December 1895 to May 1896), 688-695.

[26] Fowler, "A Phase," 693

[27] Fowler, "A Phase," 695

[28] Thomas to Durham, 2.

[29] "New England Educational Institutions. XIII. Newton Theological Institution." *The New England Magazine* 6:34 (August 1888), 358-362.

[30] Alvah Hovey. *Manual of Systematic Theology, and Christian Ethics.* (Philadelphia: American Baptist Publication Society, 1877), 349.

[31] Hovey, *Manual*, 349-350.

[32] Alvah Hovey. *Eschatology*. (Philadelphia: American Baptist Publication Society, 1888), 77.

[33] See Appendix 3.

Chapter 3

[34] Kenneth Scott Latourette. *A History of Christian Missions in China*. (Taipei: Ch'eng-Wen Publishing Company, 1966), 229.

[35] Thanks to Ken Cole for this information. The spiritual descendants of Rivenburg's ministry are partners with ABWE in Nagaland.

[36] Roberts Bartholow. *A Practical Treatise on Materia Medica and Therapeutics.* (New York: D. Appleton and Company, 7th Edition, Revised and Enlarged, 1890), v.

[37] "REPORT OF THE COMMITTEE OF THE LONDON COUNTY COUNCIL ON A HOSPITAL FOR THE INSANE." The Committee on a Hospital for the Insane was constituted by a resolution of the Council, passed [in] April 1889; and at a subsequent meeting was ordered to be composed of the following members, namely : . . . The Committee was instructed "to inquire into, and to report to the Council upon, the advantages which might be expected from the establishment, as a complement to the existing asylum system, of a hospital with a visiting medical staff, for the study and curative treatment of insanity." The Committee held its first meeting upon the 13th of May, when Mr. Brudenell Carter was elected Chairman. It was then resolved that application should be made to various eminent medical practitioners, asking them to attend and give evidence at subsequent meetings; and a list of names for this purpose was drawn up and agreed upon. These names included not only experts in insanity, and physicians chiefly engaged in the treatment of diseases of the nervous system with which insanity is not necessarily associated, but also physicians and surgeons in more general practice. From the Appendix of Henry C. Burdett, *Hospitals and Asylums Of The World: Their Origin, History, Construction, Administration, Management, And Legislation; With Plans Of The Chief Medical Institutions Accurately*

Drawn To a Uniform Scale,In Addition To Those Of All The Hospitals Of London In The Jubilee Year Of Queen Victoria's Reign. Volume 2 (London: J&A Churchill, 1891), 159ff. A portion of Dr. Ferrier's speech was quoted in Andrew Scull, *Madness In Civilization* (Princeton: Princeton University Press, 2015) p. 261.

38 Fielding H. Garrison, AB, MD. *An Introduction to the History of Medicine. With Medical Chronology, suggestions for study and bibliographic data.* Fourth edition, revised and enlarged. (Philadelphia and London: W.B. Saunders Company, 1929), 761.

39 Harvey Cushing. *The Life of Sir William Osler.* (Oxford: At the Clarendon Press, 1925), 1:153.

40 Cushing, *Life of Osler*, 1:398-399.

41 Cushing, *Life of Osler*, 2:178.

42 Kenneth M. Ludmerer, "REFORM AT HARVARD MEDICAL SCHOOL, 1869-1909," *Bulletin of the History of Medicine*, Vol. 55, No. 3 (FALL 1981), 368.

43 Raphael C. Thomas, [TPA, ABWE]. n.d.

44 *The Newtonian* was an official publication of the Newton Theological Institution. Volume One, Number One, was published in "MidWinter" 1903.

45 Thomas, "Some Aspects of Oriental Religion" (Senior Thesis, Newton Theological Institution, 1904). Andover-Newton Theological School Theses Collection (RG 300), Special Collections, Yale Divinity School Library.

46 Thomas, "The Strategic Importance of Japan in the Evangelization of the World" (Senior Address, Newton Theological Institution, 1904). Andover-Newton Theological School Theological School Alumni Records (RG 278), Special Collections, Yale Divinity School Library.

47 *The Newtonian*, December 1903, p. 58.

Chapter 4

48 George L. Mackay. *From Far Formosa.* 3rd Edition. [Taipei: SMC Publishing Inc., 2002 (1896)], 337.

49 Sven Matthiessen. *Japanese Pan-Asianism and the Philippines from the Late Nineteenth Century to the End of World War II. Going to the Philippines is Like Coming Home?* (Leiden, Boston: Brill, 2016), 62.

50 Thomas, *Senior Thesis.* The reference to "peculiar people" comes from the Bible, Titus 2:14. The idea of the verse is that Christians are supposed to be a "unique" people, not peculiar in the sense of "strange."

[51] For more detailed accounts of this era, see Akira Iriye. *Across the Pacific.* (New York: Harcourt, Brace, and World, Inc., 1967), and Ezra F. Vogel. *China and Japan. Facing History.* (Cambridge, Mass: The Belknap Press of Harvard University, 2019).

[52] Ernest W. Clement. *Christianity in Modern Japan.* (Young People's Missionary Movement of the United States and Canada, 1905), 150.

Chapter 5

[53] International Ministries, Group Number 1, [Box 163, Thomas R. C., M.D. 1904-1905, R. C. Thomas, Application for Appointment as a Missionary in the American Baptist Missionary Union], American Baptist Historical Society, Atlanta, Georgia.

[54] International Ministries, Group Number 1, [Box 163, Thomas R. C., M.D. 1904-1905, George H. Monks, Letter of Inquiry submitted to the Home Department of the American Baptist Missionary Union, May 9, 1904], American Baptist Historical Society, Atlanta, Georgia.

[55] International Ministries, Group Number 1, [Box 163, Thomas R. C., M.D. 1904-1905, Elliott P. Joslin, Letter of Inquiry submitted to Home Department, American Baptist Missionary Union, May 9, 1904], American Baptist Historical Society, Atlanta, Georgia.

[56] International Ministries, Group Number 1, [Box 163, Thomas R. C., M.D. 1904-1905, George W. Creesy, Letter of Inquiry submitted to the Home Department, American Baptist Missionary Union, May 9, 1904], American Baptist Historical Society, Atlanta, Georgia.

[57] Creesy, Letter of Inquiry.

[58] Creesy, Letter of Inquiry.

[59] International Ministries, Group Number 1, [Box 163, Thomas R. C., M.D. 1904-1905, Everett D. Burr, Letter of Inquiry submitted to the Home Department, American Baptist Missionary Union, May 9, 1904], American Baptist Historical Society, Atlanta, Georgia.

[60] Burr, Letter of Inquiry.

[61] International Ministries, Group Number 1, [Box 163, Thomas R. C., M.D. 1904-1905, R.C. Thomas letter to Mr. Dutton, American Baptist Missionary Union, April 30, 1904], American Baptist Historical Society, Atlanta, Georgia.

[62] Thomas, APMMHB, 3.

[63] Thomas letter to Dutton.

[64] International Ministries, Group Number 1, [Box 163, Thomas R. C., M.D. 1904-1905, Grant Edmands to Dr. H. C. Mabie, September 5, 1904], American Baptist Historical Society, Atlanta, Georgia.

[65] International Ministries, Group Number 1, [Box 262, Thomas R. C., M.D. 1927. All sailing dates through 1927 are from the ABMU Missionary Register for Rev. Raphael Clarke Thomas, MD], American Baptist Historical Society, Atlanta, Georgia.

Chapter 6

[66] Ruth Woodworth. *No Greater Joy. The Story of Ruth Woodworth, Missionary.* (Cherry Hill: ABWE Publishing, 1975) 24.

[67] John H. Romani, "The Philippine Barrio," in *The Far Eastern Quarterly,* Volume 15, No. 2, (February, 1956), 229-237.

[68] K. R. Howe. *The Quest for Origins.* (Honolulu: University of Hawaií Press, 2003) 83-91.

[69] Friedrich Hirth and W. W. Rockhill, translators and editors. *CHAU JU-KUA: His Work on the Chinese and Arab Trade in the twelfth and thirteenth Centuries, entitled Chu-fan-ehi.* (Taipei: Literature House, Ltd., 1965).

[70] R. J. May, "Philippines," in C. E. Bosworth, E. Van Donzel, W.P. Heinrichs, and G. Lecomte. *The Encyclopaedia Of Islam, New Edition* (Leiden: EJ. Brill, 1995).

[71] Philip T. Hoffman. *Why Did Europe Conquer the World?* (Princeton: Princeton University Press, 2015), 16.

[72] Laurence Bergreen. *Over the Edge of the World.* (NY: William Morrow, 2003), 32-35.

[73] See here Charles H. Cunningham, "The Ecclesiastical Influence in the Philippines (1565-1850)." *The American Journal of Theology,* Volume XXII, Number 2 (April, 1918), 161-184.

[74] Jose Rizal, "The Indolence of the Filipino," Project Gutenburg edition, Section 4.

[75] W. Morgan Shuster, "Our Philippine Policies and their Results." An Address Delivered at Clark University, September 14, 1909, during the Conference Upon the Far East. Pp. 70-71. [Early Journal Content on JSTOR].

[76] Shuster, "Philippine Policies," 60.

[77] James Bradley. *The Imperial Cruise. A Secret History of Empire and War.* New York: Little, Brown and Company, 2009, 99. The term "black" was the milder of the terms then prominent. "Nigger" and "Negro" were regularly used by Americans from foot soldiers to Presidents McKinley, Taft, and Roosevelt.

[78] Bradley, *Imperial Cruise*, Chapter 4.

[79] John Marvin Dean. *The Cross of Christ in Bolo-Land.* (Chicago: Fleming H. Revell Company, 1902), 54-55.

[80] Peter G. Gowing, "Christianity in the Philippines Yesterday and Today," *Silliman Journal* XII:2 (Second Quarter 1965), 137. Elaine J. Kennedy. *Baptist Centennial History of the Philippines.* (Makati City: Church Strengthening Ministry of Foreign Mission Board, SBC, Inc., n.d.) [With ABWE Imprint]), 17-19.

[81] Nestor Distor Bunda. *A Mission History of the Philippine Baptist Churches 1898 – 1998 From a Philippine Perspective,* Dissertation for the University of Hamburg, 1999, Band 30, Perspektiven der Weltmission (Aachen: Verlag an der Lottbek im Besitz des Verlags Mainz, 1999), 84-85. Gowing "Christianity," 137.

[82] Bunda, *Mission History*, 84.

[83] Gowing. "Christianity,"137.

[84] *The Baptist Missionary Magazine* LXXXVII (May 1907), 202.

[85] Bunda, *Mission History*, 66.

[86] Bunda, *Mission History*, 64-67.

[87] Bunda, *Mission History*, 68-69.

[88] Bunda, *Mission History*, 71-2.

Chapter 7

[89] One difficulty for the biographer in using Raph's autobiography is the fact that as narrative moves along, the snapshots are not tied to chronology, so it is sometimes difficult to determine exactly which period of his ministry is the context for the memory Raph describes.

[90] Raph wrote many of his recollections, articles, and letters during and after the Second World War and for that reason he often used the term of the day (and for years after) for the Japanese people, "Japs." As a Japan missionary, and as one living in an era when there is a proper greater sensitivity to racial epithets, I have changed "Japs" to Japanese in brackets.

[91] APMMHB, 9.

[92] A letter from Charles L. Maxfield to his supporters in America written in July 1905. This letter is part of a collection of Rev. Maxfield's letters held by Tabernacle Baptist Church in Shoreline, Washington. Used by permission.

[93] Frederick Wells Williams. *The Life and Letters of Samuel Wells Williams.* (New York: G. P. Putnam's Sons, 1888), 80.

[94] Williams. *The Life*, 109.

[95] Thomas, APMMHB p.20.

Chapter 8

[96] Hippocrates. *Aphorisms.* From *Hippocratic Writings*, translated by Francis Adams. The Great Books. (Chicago, London, Toronto: The Encyclopaedia Britannica, Inc. and University of Chicago, 1952), 131.

[97] *The Baptist Missionary Magazine,* (April, 1905), 148.

[98] Charles Briggs. *Missions in the Philippines*, (American Baptist Missionary Union, 1906), 37.

[99] International Ministries, Group Number 1, [FM 209, R. C. Thomas letter to Dr. Barbour, March 15, 1905], American Baptist Historical Society, Atlanta, Georgia.

[100] Craig S. Keener. *Miracles* (Grand Rapids: Baker Academic, 2011), Vol. 1, 43-44.

[101] Gary B. Ferngren, *Medicine & Health Care in Early Christianity* (Baltimore: Johns Hopkins, 2009) 124.

[102] Article by R. C. Thomas in *The Baptist Missionary Magazine* (December 1908), 451.

[103] International Ministries, Group Number 1, [FM 209, R. C. Thomas letter to Dr. Barbour, July 31, 1909], American Baptist Historical Society, Atlanta, Georgia.

[104] From the Testimony of Alberto Franco, reprinted from the book *The Hour Before Sunrise* in Alfredo Franco Barile, Jr. *Recollections. A Biographical History of Doane Baptist Seminary.* (Iloilo: Doane Baptist Seminary, 2005), 250-254.

Chapter 9

[105] R. C. Thomas, "The Evangelistic Program of a Medical Missionary," *The Watchman Examiner*, (September 15, 1927).

[106] Thomas, "The Evangelistic Program."

[107] Linnea A. Nelson and Elma S. Herradura. *Scientia et Fides. The Story of Central Philippine University.* (Central Philippine University, Iloilo, 1981), 1.

[108] Briggs. *Missions in the Philippines*, 38-39.

[109] Nelson and Herradura, *Scientia*, 1-2.

[110] Bunda, *Mission History*, 155.

[111] Barile, Jr. *Recollections,* 81.

[112] Nelson and Herradura. *Scientia*, 13-14.

[113] Rev. R. C. Thomas, MD, "Signal Providences," *The Baptist Missionary Magazine*, (June, 1906), 217.

[114] Thomas. "Signal Providences," 218.

[115] The London School of Tropical Medicine was started by Dr. (later "Sir") Patrick Manson in 1898, after he returned to England after 30 years in China and Hong Kong studying and teaching tropical aspects of medicine. He published his Manual of Tropical Medicine in 1898 (Fifth Edition, 1914). Blanchard referred to him as the 'father of tropical medicine." Garrison, *History of Medicine*, 716-17.

[116] Thomas. APMMHB, 21.

Chapter 10

[117] Winifred M. Cheney letter to Rev. J. P. Haggard, (July 23, 1908)77, Thomas papers, [SC, ABHS].

[118] Winifred M. Cheney. Biographical Sketch of Mrs. R. C. Thomas, Jaro, Philippine Islands, Thomas papers, [SC, ABHS].

[119] Barile, *Recollections*, 83. Barile derived his information from Henry Munger's "Chronology of the Philippine Missions, 1900-29," which was available only in mimeographed form.

Chapter 11

[120] The Ninety-fifth Annual Report of the American Baptist Missionary Union, 1909, 135.

[121] Amanda P. Klein, "The Union Mission Hospital at Iloilo, Philippine Islands," *The American Journal of Nursing*, Vol. 16, No. 3 (Dec., 1915), pp. 227-229.

[122] International Ministries, Group Number 1, [FM 209, R.C. Thomas letter to Dr. Barbour, March 26, 1909], American Baptist Historical Society, Atlanta, Georgia.

[123] International Ministries, Group Number 1, [FM 209, R.C. Thomas letter to supporters, December, 1910], American Baptist Historical Society, Atlanta, Georgia.

[124] International Ministries, Group Number 1, [FM 209, R.C. Thomas letter to Dr. Barbour, June, 1911], American Baptist Historical Society, Atlanta, Georgia.

[125] Ninety-fifth Annual Report of ABMU, 133-134.

[126] Thomas. APMMHBP, p. 36.

[127] International Ministries, Group Number 1, [FM 209, R.C. Thomas letter to Dr. Barbour, July, 1911], American Baptist Historical Society, Atlanta, Georgia.

[128] The information in these paragraphs was drawn from International Ministries, Group Number 1, [FM 209, The correspondence of R. C. Thomas and Dr. Barbour of the American Baptist Foreign Mission Society, 1912], American Baptist Historical Society, Atlanta, Georgia.

[129] August 21st letter from Thomas to Dr. Barbour [TPA, ABWE].

[130] Aldo Castellani and Albert J. Chalmers. *Manual of Tropical Medicine.* (New York William Wood and Company, 1919), Chapters 3 and 4.

[131] Castellani and Chalmers. *Manual*, 112.

[132] International Ministries, Group Number 1, [FM 209, R.C. Thomas letter to Supporters, Nov. 1913], American Baptist Historical Society, Atlanta, Georgia.

[133] Thomas letter to Supporters, Nov. 1913.

[134] International Ministries, Group Number 1, [FM 209, R.C. Thomas letter to James H. Franklin, December 26, 1913], American Baptist Historical Society, Atlanta, Georgia.

[135] International Ministries, Group Number 1, [FM 209, G. B. Huntington letter to R. C. Thomas, March 2, 1914], American Baptist Historical Society, Atlanta, Georgia.

[136] Thomas letter to "Mother," May 22, 1927, [TPA, ABWE].

[137] International Ministries, Group Number 1, [FM 209, E. S. Harrington letter to Baptist Foreign Mission Rooms, Massachusetts, February 28, 1914], American Baptist Historical Society, Atlanta, Georgia.

[138] International Ministries, Group Number 1, [FM 209, James H. Franklin letter to E. S. Harrington, February 28], American Baptist Historical Society, Atlanta, Georgia.

Chapter 12

[139] International Ministries, Group Number 1, [FM 209, R.C. Thomas letter to J. H. Franklin, May 25, 1914], American Baptist Historical Society, Atlanta, Georgia.

[140] Howard B. Grose and Fred P. Haggard, eds. *The Judson Centennial 1814-1914*. (Philadelphia, etc., The American Baptist Publication Society, 1914). 124-129.

[141] An article in the December 19, 1896, issue of the New York Times announced the sale of The Tabernacle Baptist Church to the mortgage holder, The New York Baptist Mission Society. The church was described as at one time one of the wealthiest Baptist societies in the United States.

[142] Thomas letter to Durhams, March 13, 1954, [TPA, ABWE], 3-5.

[143] Thomas letter to Durhams, 5.

[144] St. Mark's Hospital was incorporated as a general hospital in March 1890. Located on St. Mark's Place between Second Avenue and 11th Street, the hospital served the indigent public. On December 15, 1926, the cornerstone was laid for a new five-story $600,000 public wards building. By the end of 1930 the hospital was in financial trouble, and in 1931 attempted to sell its buildings to the City of New York as a hospital for tubercular patients. The city rejected the offer, and the hospital declared bankruptcy on May 17, 1931. The building was acquired by the International Committee of the Young Men's Christian Association, who sold it in July 1945 to the Greenwich House Music School. http://www.nycago.org/Organs/NYC/html/StMarksHospital.html

[145] Thomas letter to Durhams, 5.

Chapter 13

[146] *The Baptist Missionary Magazine*, Published by the American Baptist Missionary Union, (Volume LXVII, 1887), 78.

[147] Louise A. Cattan. *Lamps are for Lighting.* (Grand Rapids: William B. Eerdmans Publishing Company, 1972),16-17.

[148] Essay, "Enter Lucy McGill, September, 1875," by an unknown friend of Lucy McGill. Archive, ABWE.

[149] Martha Lund Smalley, Compiler. "Guide to the Archives of the Committee on Christian Literature for Women and Children in Mission Fields, Inc." Yale University Library, Divinity Library Special Collections, June, 1992, 2.

[150] International Ministries, Group Number 1, [Box 164, Thomas, R.C., M.D. 1916-1918., Norma Rose Waterbury (Affianced to Rev. Raphael C. Thomas, M.D.) Application for Appointment as a Missionary submitted to the Foreign Department of the American Baptist Foreign Mission Society, September, 1916], American Baptist Historical Society, Atlanta, Georgia.

[151] Cattan. *Lamps*, 109.

[152] International Ministries, Group Number 1, [Box 164, Thomas, R.C., M.D. 1916-1918., Norma Rose Waterbury (Affianced to Rev. Raphael C. Thomas, M.D.) to Mr. Huntington (As part of her Application for Appointment as a Missionary submitted to the Foreign Department of the American Baptist Foreign Mission Society, September 11, 1916], American Baptist Historical Society, Atlanta, Georgia.

[153] International Ministries, Group Number 1, [Box 164, Thomas, R.C., M.D. 1916-1918., Helen B. Montgomery, Letter of Inquiry submitted to the Home

Department, American Baptist Missionary Union, September 15, 1915], American Baptist Historical Society, Atlanta, Georgia.

[154] International Ministries, Group Number 1, [Box 164, Thomas, R.C., M.D. 1916-1918., R.C. Thomas letter to Huntington, September 1, 1916], American Baptist Historical Society, Atlanta, Georgia.

[155] Thomas, "Demetrie P's Passing. The Acid Test of True Christianity." Thomas Papers, ABWE.

[156] Thomas, "Demetrie."

Chapter 14

[157] Thomas letter to Franklin, Nov. 16, 1917. Thomas Archives, ABWE.

[158] Franklin letter to Thomas, Nov. 1917. Thomas Archives, ABWE.

[159] Thomas letter to Franklin, Nov. 1917. Thomas Archives, ABWE.

[160] Thomas, APMMHB, 19.

[161] http://bcciloilo.tripod.com/ Last accessed December 20, 2019.

[162] Much of the information for this and the previous paragraph was gleaned from Barile, *Recollections,*85ff.

Chapter 15

[163] Francis A. Gealogo, "The Philippines in the World of the Influenza Pandemic of 1918-1919," in *Philippine Studies*, Vol. 57, No. 2, Public Health in History (June 2009), 261-292.

[164] Al Raposas. "Philippines and the Great War," Thursday, January 03, 2013, Facebook.com.

[165] Raposas, "Great War."

[166] Raposas, "Great War."

[167] International Ministries, Group Number 1, [FM 209, R.C. Thomas letter to supporters, August 1919], American Baptist Historical Society, Atlanta, Georgia.

[168] International Ministries, Group Number 1, [Box 261, Thomas, R.C., M.D. 1921., ABMU Missionary Register for Rev. Raphael Clarke Thomas, M.D., 1921], American Baptist Historical Society, Atlanta, Georgia.

[169] Thomas to "Mother" (Mrs. Henry Peabody), May 29, 1923, [TPA, ABWE].

[170] Letter from Mabelle Rae McVeigh to Dr. R.C. Thomas, June 23, 1923. [TPA, ABWE], 1-2.

Chapter 16

[171] Adopted from Bernard Ruffin. *Fanny Crosby. The Hymn Writer.* (Barbour Publishing, Inc./Pilgrim Press, 1976), 89 ff.

[172] Robert T. Coote. *Renewal for Mission. A History of the Overseas Ministries Study Center* (1922-2000) *and its Contribution to the World Christian Mission.* (New Haven: OMSC, 2000), 5.

[173] Coote, *Renewal,* 5-6.

[174] Cattan. *Lamps,* 112.

[175] Coote. *Renewal,* 5ff.

[176] Stanley Karnow. *In Our Image. America's Empire in the Philippines.* (New York: Random House, 1989), 214.

[177] Karnow, *In Our Image,* 215.

[178] International Ministries, Group Number 1, [FM 209, R.C. Thomas letter to supporters, 1926], American Baptist Historical Society, Atlanta, Georgia.

Chapter 17

[179] Lucy Peabody. *The Philippine Mission. "The Pearl of the Orient."* n.d. (1924?) [Apparently Produced for the WBFMS]. American Baptist Historical Society, Atlanta, Georgia.

[180] International Ministries, Group Number 1, [FM 209, R.C. Thomas letter to supporters, January, 1924], American Baptist Historical Society, Atlanta, Georgia.

[181] Thomas letter to supporters.

[182] Nestor Distor Bunda. *A Mission History of the Philippine Baptist Churches, 1898-1998 from a Philippine Perspective.* Aachen: Verlag an der Lottbek im Besitz des Verlags Mainz, 1999. Pp. 145f, 158f.

[183] International Ministries, Group Number 1, [FM 209, J. H. Franklin letter to R.C. Thomas, July 12, 1924], American Baptist Historical Society, Atlanta, Georgia.

[184] R.C. Thomas, "Iloilo Union Mission Hospital," *Pearl of the Orient,* (Iloilo, Philippine Islands), Vol. XI, October 1924, 6. American Baptist Historical Society, Atlanta, Georgia.

[185] R.C. Thomas, "Doane Evangelistic Institute," *Pearl of the Orient,* (Iloilo, Philippine Islands), Vol. XI, October 1924, 2. American Baptist Historical Society, Atlanta, Georgia.

[186] R.C. Thomas, "Theory and Practice For D.H. E. I. Students," *Pearl of the Orient,* (Iloilo, Philippine Islands), Vol. XII, October, 1925, 7-8. American Baptist Historical Society, Atlanta, Georgia.

[187] Norma Thomas, "Renfroville Reminiscenses," *Pearl of the Orient*, (Iloilo, Philippine Islands), Vol. XII, October, 1925, 7-8. American Baptist Historical Society, Atlanta, Georgia.

[188] International Ministries, Group Number 1, [FM 209, R.C. Thomas letter to J. H. Franklin, January, 1924], American Baptist Historical Society, Atlanta, Georgia.

[189] Raphael C. Thomas, "The Genus Nurse" [TPA, ABWE].1925.

[190] Thomas, "The Genus Nurse," 4.

[191] International Ministries, Group Number 1, [FM 209, R.C. Thomas letter to J. H. Franklin, December 1925], American Baptist Historical Society, Atlanta, Georgia.

Chapter 18

[192] Raphael C. Thomas, "Statement of the Philippine Situation," ["Statement"] (unpublished), n.d., [TPA, ABWE], 1-2.

[193] Thomas letter to Valentine, June 1924. [TPA, ABWE].

[194] R. C. Thomas Case Summary, consisting of correspondence to and from R. C. Thomas with the General Board of the ABFMS, Jan. 18th – 19th, 1926, and 1928-1929. Thomas Papers, [TPA, ABWE].

[195] Franklin letter to Thomas, January 1926. [TPA, ABWE].

[196] Copy of Munger to Thomas letter, dated April 13, 1926; Iloilo, Philippines. [TPA, ABWE].

[197] Thomas letter to ABFMS Board, March 24, 1926. [TPA, ABWE].

[198] Communicated Action of the Board of Managers of the ABFMS on May 11, 1926, in response to conditions proposed by Raph in his March 24 letter. [TPA, ABWE].

[199] Thomas, "Statement," 3.

[200] Personal letter of Thomas to "Mother" (Mrs. Peabody) from Doane Rest, dated April 11, 1926. [TPA, ABWE].

[201] Thomas letter to ABFMS Board, July, 1926. [TPA, ABWE]

[202] Thomas letter to "Mother" (Mrs. Peabody) from Doane Rest, dated April 11, 1926. [TPA, ABWE].

[203] Thomas letter to Mrs. Doane, June 1926. [TPA, ABWE].

[204] International Ministries, Group Number 1, [FM 209, R.C. and Norma Thomas letter to Supporters, January 1927], American Baptist Historical Society, Atlanta, Georgia.

Chapter 19

[205] International Ministries, Group Number 1, [FM 209, ABFMS Board letter to R.C. Thomas, June 4, 1927], American Baptist Historical Society, Atlanta, Georgia.

[206] ABFMS Board of Managers Statement Concerning the Resignation of R. C. and Norma Thomas. [TPA, ABWE].

Chapter 20

[207] Winky (Winifred Thomas), At Home, to Father (R.C. Thomas), September 24, 1927, [TPA, ABWE].

[208] Papa (R. C. Thomas), Ventnor, to Winky (Winifred), September 30, 1927, [TPA, ABWE]

Chapter 21

[209] Minutes of the Annual Meeting of ABEO, April 25, 1930, [TPA, ABWE].

[210] Raphael C. Thomas, *Brief History of the Origin and Objectives of the ABEO,* [TPA, ABWE], 9.

[211] Paul G. Culley, "Touring in the Iloilo District," in *A Message from the Association of Baptists for Evangelism in the Orient, Inc.*, 1930, 3-4.

[212] Dr. Harold T. Commons, *Heritage and Harvest.* (Cherry Hill: Association of Baptists for World Evangelism, 1981), 16-18.

[213] Annual report of Miss Edna Hotchkiss, in the Report of Association of Baptists for Evangelism in the Orient Incl, 1930-1931. [TPA, ABWE], 30 and 31.

[214] The information in this paragraph was taken from Garrison, *History of Medicine,* and Leslie T. Morton and Robert J. Moore, *A Chronology of Medicine and Related Sciences* (Aldershot: Ashgate, 1997), 620.

Chapter 22

[215] *A Message from the Association of Baptists for Evangelism in the Orient, Inc., n.d.* (1930), 1.

[216] Charles Kendall Harrington. *Captain Bickel Of The Inland Sea.* (New York: Fleming H. Revell Co., 1919), 74-79.

[217] Harrington, *Captain Bickel*, 50-51.

[218] Report of ABEO 1932-1933, 32.

[219] Sources: Bomm, Marian D. *Beyond Prison Walls.* (Cherry Hill: Association of Baptists for World Evangelism, Inc., 1987); Lt. Gene E. M. Flanagan, Jr. *The Los Baños Raid* (Novato: Presidio Press, 1986); Elaine J. Kennedy. *Baptist Centennial History of the Philippines*; Harold T. Commons. *Heritage and Harvest*; A.V.H. Hartendorp, *The Japanese Occupation of the Philippines.* (Manila: Bookmark, 1967).

Chapter 23

[220] Thomas, Ventnor, NJ, letter to "Mother" [Lucy Peabody], March 24, 1932, [TPA, ABWE].

[221] "Minutes of the Annual Meeting of ABEO," held April 7-8, 1932, in Philadelphia, Pennsylvania, 1.

[222] "Minutes of the Annual Meeting," 2-3.

[223] "Minutes of the Annual Meeting," 3.

[224] Preliminary Doctrinal Statement in Public report of the Association of Baptists for Evangelism in the Orient, for 1928-1929. Archives, ABEO/ ABWE, Harrisburg, PA.

[225] Thomas letter to "Dear Fellow Missionaries," May 28, 1932, [TPA, ABWE], 2-3. Emphasis added.

[226] A. M. Sutherland, Puerto Princessa, Palawan, Philippine Islands, letter to Dr. R. C. Thomas, Ventnor, NJ, July 14, 1932, [TPA, ABWE], 1.

[227] Sutherland letter, care of Dr. R. C. Thomas, Manila, Philippine Islands, November 1, 1932. [TPA, ABWE].

[228] Sutherland letter to Pastor Harold T. Commons, Association of Baptists, April 10, 1933, Archives, ABWE.

[229] On the name and location of Renfroville, see Chapter 14.

[230] Thomas, Ventnor, NJ, letter to Mrs. Marguerite Treat Doane, October 28, 1933, [TPA, ABWE].

[231] George W. Dollar. *A History of Fundamentalism in America.* (Greenville: Bob Jones University Press, 1973), 164.

[232] Minutes of the Annual Meeting of the Association of Baptists for Evangelism in the Orient, Inc., April 7-8 1932, Archives, ABWE, 3.

[233] Thomas letter to the ABEO missionary team, May 28, 1938, [TPA, ABWE].

Chapter 24

[234] Mrs. Henry W. Peabody, "Mrs. Peabody's Resignation," *The Message*, Vol. 1, No. 8, May, 1935, p. 1

[235] Mrs. Henry W. Peabody, Orlando, Florida, letter to Mr. Commons, January 7, 1937, Archives, ABWE, supplemental page entitled, "Suggested Changes."

[236] Peabody letter to Commons, 2.

[237] Peabody letter to Commons, 2.

[238] Minutes of the Special Meeting of the Voting Board, held April 27, 1937, in New York City, Archives, ABWE, 1-2.

[239] Thomas, Beverly, Mass., letter to "Mother," February 3, 1935, [TPA, ABWE], 1.

[240] Thomas, Georgetown, letter to Bro. Commons, Philadelphia, May 31, 1937, [TPA, ABWE].

[241] Harold Commons, Waterloo, Iowa, letter to Dr. R. C. Thomas, Georgetown, Mass., June 27, 1937, [TPA, ABWE], 2-3.

[242] Thomas, Georgetown, letter to "Mother," July 1, 1937, [TPA, ABWE], 1.

[243] Thomas, letter to Mrs. Doane, April 1, 1953, [TPA, ABWE], 1.

[244] Thomas, letter to Dear Brother Commons, April 9, 1954, [TPA, ABWE], 1

[245] Letter to Mr. and Mrs. Durham, March 13, 1954, [TPA, ABWE], 5.

[246] Handwritten note from R. C. Thomas, Georgetown, to Dear Brother Commons, April 17, 1954, [TPA, ABWE], 1. In a brief note at the top, Thomas wrote: "Type writer is old, like me, and in shop to be cleaned up!"

[247] Harold T. Commons letter to Dr. R. C. Thomas, Georgetown, April 15, 1954, [TPA, ABWE], 1.

[248] Commons letter to Thomaas, March 1, 1956, [TPA, ABWE], 1.

Chapter 25

[249] Executive Committee Meeting Minutes, Association of Baptists for Evangelism in the Orient, Inc., September 9, 1933, Archives, ABWE, 1.

[250] Letter from President Commons to Mrs. Peabody, January 15, 1935. Dr. Commons quoted the Minutes of the Executive Committee meeting of April 3, 1934.

[251] Executive Committee Meeting Minutes, Association of Baptists for Evangelism in the Orient, Inc., June 5, 1935, Archives, ABWE, 3.

[252] Executive Committee Meeting Minutes.

[253] Thomas, Beverly, Mass. Letter to Mrs. Doane, February 3, 1935. [TPA, ABWE].

Chapter 26

[254] A good summary of his thinking on this issue is one of dozens of his letters written on the subject, this one from Georgetown to Rev. Joseph Hakes, Yonkers, New York, January 1, 1938, [TPA, ABWE].

[255] Harold T. Commons. *Heritage and Harvest.* (Cherry Hill, NJ: ABWE. ABWE Insight Series, 1981). 8-9.

[256] Walter Lippmann, quoted by Raph in a letter to Dr. Laws, dated December 30, 1937, [TPA, ABWE].

[257] Raph talked with Dr. Savage about that plan in 1936. The plan involved certain churches being responsible for certain stations in Africa.

[258] Thomas letter to Curtis Laws, December, 1937.

[259] Thomas, Georgetown, Mass., letter to Rev. Joseph Hakes, January 1, 1938, [TPA, ABWE], 1.

[260] Thomas letter to Hakes, 2.

[261] Thomas Ministry Report, February 7 to March 22, 1937. [TPA, ABWE].

[262] Fleming H. Revell, Jr. letter to Dr. R. C. Thomas, November 27, 1936, [TPA, ABWE].

Chapter 27

[263] Ruth Woodworth. *No Greater Joy. The Story of Ruth Woodworth, Missionary.* Harrisburg: ABWE Publishing, 1975, 40-41.

[264] Thomas "Philippine" n.d., 46.

[265] Thomas, Georgetown, letter to Dean of Fuller Theological Seminary, Los Angeles, May 4, 1954; [TPA, ABWE].

[266] John Hanrahan, *Courier-Journal*, Louisville, Kentucky, 7.

[267] This expression has wandered through various European languages for years. It is to be found, for example, in Montaigne's essay "Of Presumption," published in the 1580's in France. Since the 1890's, at least four novels were entitled *The Game and the Candle* by Rhoda Broughton (1899), Francis Davidge (1905), Eleanor M. Ingram (1909), and Margaret Kennedy (1928).

[268] Thomas, Georgetown, letter to Dr. H. T. Commons, January 4, 1956. [TPA, ABWE].

[269] For some of these stories, see Elaine J. Kennedy's *Baptist Centennial History of the Philippines.*

[270] Donald J. Mackay, "Raphael Clark Thomas," *The Message*, Vol. 23, No. 3, November, 1956.

Appendix 3

[271] James Spivey, "The Millenium," in Paul A. Basden, ed. *Has our Theology Changed? Southern Baptist Thought Since 1845.* (Nashville: Broadman & Holman Publishers, 1994), 245.

[272] E. Y. Mullins. *The Christian Religion in its Doctrinal Expression.* (Philadelphia: The Judson Press, 1917), 472.

[273] Augustus H. Strong. *Systematic Theology. A Compendium, Designed for the Use of Theological Students.* (Westwood: Fleming H. Revell Company, 1907), 1004.

[274] Strong, *Systematic Theology*, 1007.

[275] Strong, *Systematic Theology*, 1008.

[276] Strong, *Systematic Theology*, 1014.

[277] Strong, *Systematic Theology.*

Appendix 5

[278] Raphael C. Thomas, "Statement of the Philippine Situation," n.d., [TPA, ABWE], 1.

[279] Thomas, "Statement," 1.

[280] Raphael C. Thomas, "Suggestions on Mission Policy (Medical Work)," January 25, 1926, [TPA, ABWE].

[281] R. C. Thomas, MD, "The Evangelistic Program of a Medical Missionary," *The Watchman Examiner* September 15, 1927, 1173-4; September 22, 1927, 1207-8; September 29, 1927, 1238-9.

[282] Thomas, "Statement," 2.

[283] Thomas, "A Review of the Early Beginnings of the ABEO," a draft of a letter to be read at the 25th Anniversary Celebration of the Association, n.d. (April 1953), [TPA, ABWE], 2.

[284] Thomas, "Brief History of the Origin and Objectives of the ABEO For our missionaries only," n.d., [TPA, ABWE], 9.

[285] Thomas, "Review" Draft 1953, 1-2

Printed in the United States
by Baker & Taylor Publisher Services